BIRD LIFE

An Introduction to the World of Birds

An Introduction

BIRD LIFE

to the World of Birds

ILLUSTRATIONS
AD CAMERON

TEXT
DR. CHRISTOPHER PERRINS
EDWARD GREY INSTITUTE OF ORNITHOLOGY
UNIVERSITY OF OXFORD

PEERAGE BOOKS

Advisory Editor
DR. C. J. O. HARRISON
Keeper of Birds, British Museum (Natural History), Tring

Editor
DR. PETER HUTCHINSON

First published in Great Britain by Elsevier Phaidon
(an imprint of Phaidon Press Limited)

This edition published in 1984 by Peerage Books
59 Grosvenor Street
London W1

© 1976 Elsevier Publishing Projects S.A., Lausanne

ISBN 0 907408 68 0

Printed in Hong Kong

CONTENTS

(Overleaf)
Cryptic colouration enables many birds to escape detection by predators. (1) A Pygmy owl *Glaucidium gnoma* viewed from the front and (2) from behind; (3) Common potoo *Nyctibius griseus;* (4) Rock ptarmigan *Lagopus mutus* in winter and (5) summer plumage; (6) Eurasian bittern *Botaurus stellaris;* (7) Ringed plover *Charadrius hiaticula;* and (8) Whip-poor-will *Caprimulgus vociferus.*

PREFACE

In most parts of the world birds are the most conspicuous animals easily seen by people as they go about their daily affairs. Hence in almost all countries men are interested in birds to a greater or lesser degree. Birds are frequent themes in religion, folklore and custom. They are important economically, providing both food and various products made from their feathers and other parts. Shooting them provides recreation in many developed countries. And in the past two hundred years they have been studied scientifically and have provided the basis of important advances in biological knowledge.

Ornithology, as the scientific study of birds is called, has contributed important facets to our knowledge of evolution, zoogeography, ethology and general biology. Slight differences in the appearance, from one island to another, of the rather nondescript looking Darwin's finches of the Galapagos Islands stimulated Charles Darwin to work out his classic theory, which still holds the field 140 years after he visited the islands. More recently, in 1947, they also led the late David Lack to write *Darwin's Finches,* which many people consider to be the best book on evolution since the *Origin of Species.* Study of the world-wide distribution of birds made by P. L. Sclater in 1858 formed the basis of the zoogeographical regions, Palaearctic, Ethiopian, Oriental, and so on, which are still used today. Contributions to the science of animal behaviour or ethology which have been associated with workers on birds such as Konrad Lorenz and Niko Tinbergen have, on the other hand, taken place during the past twenty or thirty years. Approximately 8,580 species of birds are known in the world today; it is unlikely that there will ever be many more than 8,600, although new species continue to be discovered at intervals, the latest known to me being a new species of honeycreeper in the Hawaiian Islands.

Again because birds are so conspicuous and easily seen and studied, there is no group of animals, except perhaps that equally conspicuous insect group the Lepidoptera (butterflies and moths), to the knowledge of which amateurs have made such great contributions. David Lack himself, the greatest ornithologist of his generation, started as an amateur, making many of his seminal observations on the behaviour and ecology of the European robin in his spare time as a schoolmaster in Devon in the 1930s.

It is not necessary to make important scientific observations to be a bird-watcher. The great majority of bird-watchers, quite rightly, watch birds just because they like doing so. Some people specialize in ticking birds off on life lists or annual lists. To others this seems a rather unrewarding occupation, but there is no reason why bird-spotting should not be a sport, and a very good one. Probably by far the largest number of those who enjoy birds just watch them in their gardens and derive incalculable mental refreshment and joy from this simple pastime.

Nowadays, when people are becoming more and more conscious that they cannot live totally independently of their natural environment, birds perform another invaluable function. Just as the miners of old used to take caged canaries down the pit to warn them of firedamp, so birds, by their health and well-being, can warn us of dangers threatening ourselves in the environment. When Peregrine falcons decreased greatly in numbers as a result of pesticide residues in the environment, they warned us that we too were absorbing into our own bodies all kinds of chemicals with unpredictable side effects. And when action that we take to stop DDT and other toxic substances getting into the environment appears to result in a halting of that decline and perhaps even brings a slight recovery, we have the satisfaction of knowing that we are helping our- selves as well as the Peregrine.

Ad Cameron has provided all the illustrations for this volume. He was born in Flushing in 1939 and, at an early age, drew birds that he observed in his native Holland. He attended the Royal Academy of Arts at the Hague and, at the same time, worked as an industrial artist. In 1969 he exhibited his work for the first time - a collection of drawings of birds of prey. Ad Cameron now works freelance, and has travelled throughout western and eastern Europe as well as Ethiopia in order to watch and draw birds in their natural habitats.

Richard Fitter

INTRODUCTION

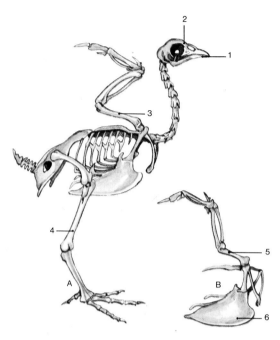

The bird's skeleton (A) displays a large number of modifications that make flight possible. Heavy teeth have been replaced by a light bill (1), the bones of the skull are thin (2) and those of the wings (3) and legs (4) composed of thin-walled tubes. The wing and shoulder girdle (B) are modified to accommodate large flight muscles which run between the forearm or humerus (5) and the keel (6).

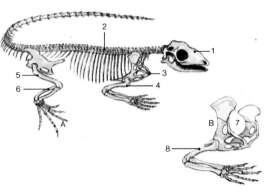

Birds evolved from a group of reptiles closely related to the dinosaurs about 150 million years ago. The skeleton of a reptile such as a lizard (A) is still similar in many respects to that of a bird. The skull (1) articulates with a backbone composed of elements called vertebrae (2). The pectoral or shoulder girdle (3) supports the forelimbs (4), and the pelvic or hip girdle (5) the hindlimbs (6). The pectoral girdle and forelimb are shown in more detail in (B). The girdle is heavily built (7) and articulates with the forelimb (8) which functions to support the front part of the body. This skeleton represents the basic plan seen also in birds, but in the latter, many modifications have taken place.

Man may be rightly accused of having a self centred view of the world. He is pre-occupied both with himself and with the effects he has on this planet. Such preoccupations are understandable and certainly have profound significance, but there is a danger that lessons to be learnt from the study of other animals will be forgotten. This book is designed to stimulate an already considerable interest in birds and to illustrate some of the general principles that are demonstrated by the study of the life of birds.

Birds have always held a fascination for man. They have figured prominently in art and mythology since the Stone Age. More recently, the collecting of birds and their eggs and bird watching became popular especially in Europe and the United States. From these interests grew an enormous popular literature on birds, but most of it suffered from two major limitations. Firstly, books already published on birds concentrated on their external appearance and enabled their readers to do little more than identify bird species and tag on to them their scientific and common names. Secondly, these books were devoted to a description of birds which lived in particular regions such as Britain or the United States. As a result, the fabulous birds that lived in regions such as Antarctica and the Amazon basin remained relatively unknown. Furthermore, the life of birds, as opposed to their appearance, was not appreciated; witness for example the nineteenth century preoccupation with the collecting of birds' eggs which, once identified, simply became specimens for the museum cabinet.

There are about 8,600 different species of birds that are alive today. This diversity is reflected most obviously in the varied and often brilliant plumage patterns seen in birds, not only in temperate parts, but in a most spectacular way in tropical regions of the world. But this variation goes deeper, and one finds considerable diversity of anatomical structure and habit among birds. Many species are unable to fly, yet others are adapted to life on water. Again, birds feed on an incredible diversity of foods such as seeds, fruit, insects, fish and other animals. Certain birds are specialized to feed on certain food items, even limiting themselves, for example, to the fruit or seeds of a particular tree. All these aspects of bird life are described in the early part of this volume. The author follows with a discussion of the habitats of the world that have been colonized by birds.

The second part of the book deals with, among others, two subjects that have stimulated much academic research and an enormous popular interest: social behaviour and breeding, and migration. Birds have evolved, to an extent rarely seen in other animals, intricate behaviour patterns particularly associated with the establishment of territories and breeding groups – sometimes small family units, sometimes enormous colonies. Much has been discovered of the complex ways in which birds relate to one another. Less is known about migration, which remains something of a mystery. Some facts are now well established, but others are the subject of ingenious experiments, the results of which are evaluated by Dr. Perrins.

Almost half the available space in this book is taken up by illustrations of every major type of bird. Special attention has been given to ensure that the birds are depicted in characteristic postures, just as they appear in life. In addition, a large number of smaller drawings illustrate specific points mentioned in the text.

EVOLUTION AND CLASSIFICATION

The Blackheaded gull is classified in the class Aves (1) because it has feathers, in the order Charadrii-formes (2) because of features of its skeleton, and in the family Laridae (3) because it has long wings and webbed feet. It is included with other unspecialized members of the family Laridae in the genus *Larus* (4), and in the species *L. ridibundus* (5) because of its size and colouration. The classification of an animal enables its close relatives to be identified because these are included in the same groups, and provides an animal with two names, the generic and specific names, which are internationally recognized.

Evolution

150 million years ago the air was populated by flying reptiles called pterodactyls, but there were no birds. Birds are relative newcomers and most of their evolution has taken place since then, during a period following the so-called age of reptiles.

Our knowledge of the history of the evolution of birds begins in Germany, where an animal the size of a crow called *Archaeopteryx* lived in a fauna dominated by reptiles. Its fossilized remains have been found preserved in 150 million year old Jurassic limestone rocks quarried at Solnhofen, and they show that *Archaeopteryx* resembled a reptile in having a long, bony tail. But in one respect *Archaeopteryx* was unique, for it possessed feathers. Although this early bird was only able to glide, not fly, the development of feathers was one of the crucial steps in the evolution of birds, and it is from *Archaeopteryx* or a very similar creature that all the birds we know today have evolved.

The task of the paleontologist has been to fill in the details of avian evolution during the period between Jurassic times and today. Unfortunately his task has been a difficult one. The fossil record of birds is incomplete because birds rarely die under conditions favourable for preservation. Only when their carcasses fall into still or slowly moving water is there a chance of them becoming covered with sediment and their delicate bones saved from destruction. As a result, fossil birds have been limited to a few localities and the evolutionary story of birds is one composed of a few pieces in a jig-saw separated by gaps about which only guesses can be made. Even so, new discoveries are being made that help to provide a more complete picture.

The first well-preserved fossils to occur after *Archaeopteryx* are called *Ichthyornis* and *Hesperornis* from the 100 million year old Upper Cretaceous rocks of Niobrara in Kansas. These birds are preserved in chalk deposits, and they lived close to or over the sea, presumably taking a diet of fish. *Ichthyornis* was probably a good flier, but *Hesperornis* had already lost the power of flight and must have used its legs for swimming. Since the Cretaceous, the fossil record is vastly improved. The 60 million year old Eocene beds of the London Clay contain fossils of birds related to herons, vultures and kingfishers, while the somewhat younger beds of the Paris Basin and parts of America contain vultures, flamingoes, geese, rails, partridges and pheasants. By the end of the Miocene, some 11 million years ago, the majority of bird families in existence today and many of the genera are recorded as fossils.

This seemingly rapid increase in the number of different birds preserved in progressively younger sediments is due to two causes. Firstly, it is due to the fact that fossil remains are more readily found in recent rocks than in ancient ones but, more importantly, it reflects a real multiplication in the numbers of different birds during the past 50 million years. By flying, birds have been able to reach habitats everywhere in the world, and they readily colonized islands which could not be reached by amphibians, reptiles or mammals. This great mobility enabled birds to discover new sources of food, and much recent evolutionary change has produced groups with specialized feeding habits, as can be seen, for example, in the variety of bill shapes in birds described in the pages that follow.

Classification

Birds vary in size from the Ostrich which may stand 8 ft (2.4 m) high to the smallest hummingbirds which may measure no more than 2½ in (6.3 cm) in length including a relatively long bill. Between these two extremes, there are over 8,600 different living species which occupy an amazing number of habitats and which display a variety of characteristics that enable them to pursue their different ways of life successfully.

This diversity is the result of rapid evolutionary change during the past 50 million years. For example, when a flock of birds were accidentally swept, perhaps by a freak storm, to the isolated Hawaiian Islands, they found an environment rich in new food sources which they had not before encountered. After many generations, different members of the original immigrant population became modified to take advantage of the variety of available foods. Some evolved short heavy bills with which to feed on nuts and seeds, while others developed long, curved, slender bills that enabled them to feed on nectar. Today there are 22 different species of honey-creeper on the Hawaiian Islands, and all have evolved from a single immigrant species.

The function of a classification is to make sense of the diversity of species by grouping together related forms. The Hawaiian honeycreepers are grouped together in a single family called the Drepanididae, not only because they have features in common, but because there is good evidence that they have all evolved from a common ancestor.

The family is not the only group to be used in bird classifications. In fact, there are five main groupings: classes, orders, families, genera and species. Species are defined as populations, the members of which are able to interbreed and produce fertile offspring. Closely related species are contained in a single genus, members of closely related genera are contained in the same family, and so on.

Representatives of each of the 34 orders of bird.
(1) Dinornithiformes, (2) Struthioniformes,
(3) Aepyornithiformes, (4) Rheiformes,
(5) Diatrymiformes, (6) Casuariiformes,
(7) Archaeopterygiformes, (8) Ciconiiformes,
(9) Sphenisciformes, (10) Apterygiformes,
(11) Ichthyornithiformes, (12) Pelecaniformes,
(13) Anseriformes, (14) Tinamiformes,
(15) Procellariiformes, (16) Gaviiformes,
(17) Podicipitiformes, (18) Hesperornithiformes,
(19) Odontopterygiformes, (20) Psittaciformes,
(21) Gruiformes, (22) Falconiformes,
(23) Strigiformes, (24) Trogoniformes,
(25) Coliiformes, (26) Galliformes,
(27) Charadriiformes, (28) Passeriformes,
(29) Apodiformes, (30) Piciformes,
(31) Coraciiformes, (32) Cuculiformes,
(33) Columbiformes and (34) Caprimulgiformes.

The principles of classification outlined above can best be illustrated by a particular example such as the Blackheaded gull. The Blackheaded gull is classified in the class Aves because, like other birds, it has feathers. This character alone distinguishes birds from all other animals, both living and extinct, and is evidence that they have all evolved from a 'feathered reptile' such as *Archaeopteryx*. The class Aves is subdivided into 34 orders, the Blackheaded gull being included in the order Charandriiformes along with the terns, skimmers and skuas as well as with other gulls. All members of the Charadriiformes are thought to have evolved from a common wader-like ancestor; evidence for this opinion is based on the fact that they all have similar characteristics of the skull and limb bones. The family Laridae is one of 16 in the order and can be defined as that containing gregarious sea birds with long legs, webbed feet and a relatively heavy bill. All members of the Laridae are efficient fliers. Passing down the hierarchy of groups we reach the genus *Larus*. Most gulls are in fact included in this genus, the only exceptions being rather more specialized forms such as the Kittiwake which, unlike most gulls, spends most of its time over the open sea rather than near the coasts, and which is classified in its own genus called *Rissa*. Finally, the species *L. ridibundus* is distinguished from other members of the genus because it is small, about 15 in (38 cm) long, it has a rather slender bill and is decorated with a brown hood during the breeding season and with a black spot behind each eye at other times of the year. The Blackheaded gull is thus classified as follows:

CLASS	Aves	GENUS	*Larus*
ORDER	Charadriiformes	SPECIES	*L. ridibundus*
FAMILY	Laridae		

In practice not all these names are used, and the Blackheaded gull is usually referred to by its generic and specific names, the generic name often being abbreviated to an initial letter.

The bird's skeleton (1) may appear ungainly, but it is made streamlined by the body's covering of feathers. The all important forelimb supports the wing feathers which provide a large flight surface. To achieve strength and lightness (2), solid bone is replaced by structures composed of struts similar to those employed by engineers.

Bats are among the few animals that are able to fly as efficiently as birds. Their wings (1) are composed of a sheet of skin called a patagium which is stretched between four elongated fingers of the hand, and which extends backwards as far as the feet. The bird's wing (2) is almost entirely supported by the forearm, the fingers being reduced and playing a far less important role.

ANATOMY, LOCOMOTION AND BEHAVIOUR

Anatomy

Almost every noteworthy feature of the anatomy of birds has evolved in order to make flight possible. The birds are one of the few groups of animals that have developed true flight, that is, powered flight not simple gliding. Insects, the flying reptiles called pterosaurs and bats share this ability and all these groups are, or have been, tremendously successful. Being warm-blooded has enabled birds to survive and even flourish in a wide range of areas of the world, including mountains and polar regions where some of these other groups have found it difficult to live.

The avian skeleton is based on the same general pattern as is found in the other vertebrate groups. The skull is joined to a backbone composed of bony elements called vertebrae, while the organs of the body are protected by a rib cage. At either end of the body the girdles support the limbs, the pectoral girdle articulating with the forelimbs which are modified as wings, and the pelvic girdle articulating with the legs. The special modifications of this basic plan are designed to reduce weight and to enable the legs to support the body when the bird is on the ground.

Lightness is achieved in several ways. The teeth have been lost and are replaced by a horny bill; many bones are extremely thin, for example those of the skull; and where strength is required, solid bone is replaced by structures that confer lightness with rigidity. Limb bones and the thicker parts of the bony structure are hollow, with thin internal struts for extra strength where necessary.

The bones of the backbone in the region of the pelvis are fused together. To compensate for this rigidity, the neck is flexible and sometimes extremely long. The wings are composed of the humerus or upper arm, the radius and ulna which comprise the forearm, and the wrist and finger bones. The secondary feathers of the wing are supported by the forearm while the wrist and hand bones are fused together to provide firm support for the primary feathers. The first and fifth fingers are absent and the second is modified to support the alula or bastard wing whose function is so important in flight and which will be discussed later. Still greater strength is achieved by the structure of the joints which do not allow movement except in the plane in which the wing is folded.

The wings articulate with the pectoral girdle. The wing sockets are braced apart by the clavicles, or collar bones, which are fused together to form the furcula or wishbone. As a whole, the pectoral girdle is designed to withstand the stresses which are imposed on the front part of the body when the powerful flight muscles contract. These muscles run from the head of the humerus to the keel of the sternum, a flat plate which projects downwards along the midline of the body.

Because the wings cannot support the bird on the ground, there are many profound modifications in the skeleton that enable the bird to walk on its hind legs—a method of locomotion called bipedalism. Firstly, the backbone between the pectoral and pelvic girdles is considerably shortened. This shortening has the effect of bringing the bird's centre of gravity far back enabling it to balance on its hind legs. The hind legs are modified so that their movement is restricted to a forward and backward swing below the body. It is interesting to note that some similar modifications took place in the evolution of bipedal man from his four-footed ancestors.

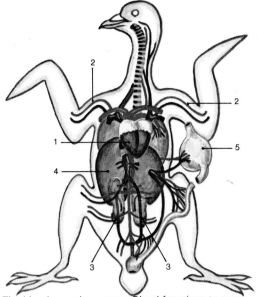

The blood vascular system. Blood functions to carry oxygen and food to the various organs of the body and carbon dioxide from the body to the lungs. Because birds are such active animals, their blood system needs to be extremely efficient. The arteries, depicted in red, are large and carry blood from the heart (1) to the body. Especially prominent are the innominate arteries (2) which supply the wings. Blood is returned to the heart via the veins, blue, from body organs such as the kidneys (3), liver (4) and stomach (5).

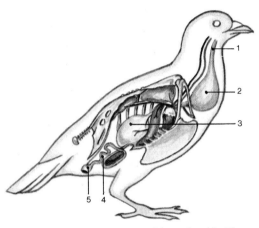

The bird's internal organs viewed from the side. The digestive system is composed of an oesophagus (1) which leads to the crop (2) and a stomach (3) which is divided into two chambers, the proventriculus and gizzard. The intestine (4) runs to the cloaca (5) which serves as the point of exit for the waste products. An important function of the cloaca is to extract water from the waste products.

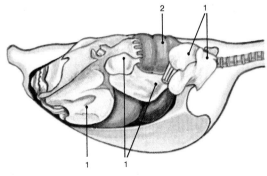

Much of the space inside a bird's body is taken up by air-sacs (1) which form extensions to the lungs (2). They assist the bird to get the large quantities of oxygen needed for flight.

Just as the skeleton is modified for flight, so too is the musculature. The most important muscles are the flight muscles which run between the upper arm and the keel—the 'breast' of poultry and game birds. There are two pairs of flight muscles. The larger pair is called the pectoralis major and provides the powerful downstroke of the wing when it contracts. The upstroke requires far less energy and is achieved by contraction of the second pair of flight muscles, the smaller pectoralis minor. These muscles also run between the humerus and keel, and lie between the pectoralis major and the sternum. They are not attached directly to the humerus. Instead, they terminate in a tendon which runs through a hole between the bones of the pectoral girdle to the upper side of the humerus. Thus the upstroke of the wing results from the pectoralis minor operating a simple mechanical pulley.

Another adaptation for flight is seen in the shape of birds. Their bodies may be elongated or compact but, whatever their shape, they are always streamlined. Streamlining is necessary to reduce friction to a minimum when the bird flies and is achieved, not only because the body itself is streamlined, but because the feathers provide a smooth outer surface. The tail, consisting entirely of feathers, may contribute a great deal to the bird's appearance and there is a great variety in tails, both in shape and length. Similarly with the length of leg: the long legs of, for example, storks are associated with the habit of wading in shallow water or marshy ground, but however long they are, the legs do not affect the bird's streamlining as they are usually tucked in under the body during flight.

When a bird flies, it is able to move in three dimensional space and thus has far more freedom than does an animal which is forced to crawl, walk or run on the earth's surface. However, birds are required to make extremely complex co-ordinated movements. Moreover, a bird such as a swift is capable of flying at 62 mph (100 kph), so these movements must be made extremely quickly. The part of the brain responsible for co-ordination of movement is called the cerebellum and, not surprisingly, this is large and elaborate in birds. Even larger, however, are the cerebral hemispheres, the lobes of the brain that are so well developed in man, which enable birds to perform complex behaviour patterns.

The digestive system is very efficient in birds. This is because, being such active animals, they are forced to assimilate food at an extremely rapid rate. A small bird such as the Goldcrest may eat food weighing one third of its body weight in a single day. Amongst birds there are herbivores, carnivores and omnivores. Herbivores, birds feeding on seeds, fruit and other vegetable matter, have rather more complex digestive systems than do carnivores. From the mouth the oesophagus runs to a storage sac, called the crop, which is particularly well developed in birds that feed on grain, such as the pigeon. Food stored in the crop is macerated before it passes to the two-chambered stomach where it is mixed with digestive juices in the first part, the proventriculus, and ground into a pulp in the second part, the thick-walled muscular gizzard. Herbivorous birds swallow small stones which assist the grinding of food in the gizzard. Carnivores do not usually have a crop or, if they do, it is small. The gizzard is also less muscular and functions as a normal stomach. Some carnivores, notably the owls, do not attempt to digest the bones and fur or skin of their prey. Instead, this material is regurgitated in the form of a hard pellet.

As has been noted above, birds are extremely active animals and, as well as having to assimilate large quantities of food, they must obtain the equally large amounts of oxygen required to transform this food into energy. Oxygen passes from the air into the blood through the thin walls of the lungs. In other vertebrates the lungs consist of blind sacs, but birds have extensions to the lungs called air-sacs. Inhaled air passes through the lungs into these air-sacs and then out again through the lungs. In birds that dive underwater, air may be passed through the lungs several times before it is exhaled, enabling them to stay submerged for long periods.

Oxygen is carried from the lungs to the tissues of the body in a blood vascular system which is basically similar to that of reptiles but which displays one or two

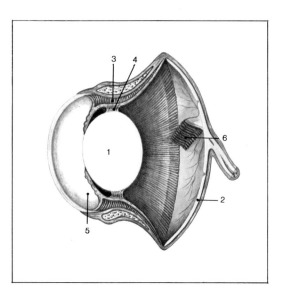

Many birds have more acute eyesight than any other animal. The eye of a hawk is relatively larger than that of man. The lens (1) focusses light onto the light-sensitive cells of the retina (2) and is held in position by a ring of bony plates called the sclerotic plates (3). Focussing is achieved by adjustment of the shape of the lens by the ciliary muscles (4), and the amount of light entering the eye controlled by the iris (5). The function of a group of cells called the pecten (6) is enigmatic. It may be responsible for increasing sensitivity to movement as it is especially well developed in birds of prey.

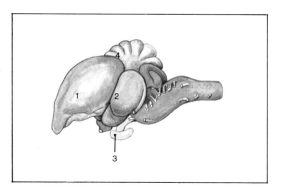

The main parts of the brain seen in side view: (1) cerebral hemisphere, (2) optic lobe, (3) hypophysis, and (4) cerebellum. The cerebral hemisphere and cerebellum are particularly large in birds.

notable modifications. In particular, there is complete separation between oxygenated and deoxygenated blood; that is, oxygenated blood from the lungs is not mixed in the heart with deoxygenated blood returning from the body tissues. The type of blood vascular system that makes this separation possible is found elsewhere only in the mammals, and enables the bird to maintain a high and constant body temperature. This is important, because it means that birds are to a large extent independent of the temperature of their surroundings. Reptiles, which cannot maintain a high body temperature, become torpid when the temperature of their environment drops. For this reason their distribution is limited to the warmer parts of the world and in temperate regions they are forced to hibernate during the winter. Birds do not suffer from these disadvantages, and they are found even in Arctic and Antarctic regions.

The bird's heart retains some reptilian features, but is powerfully built and beats rapidly. In large birds such as the turkey rates of 100 beats a minute have been recorded, but in smaller, more active birds, rates of 500 beats a minute are common.

As well as transporting oxygen, the blood functions to regulate the bird's temperature which is maintained at between 41° and 45°C (106° and 114°F). Heat loss from the body is reduced by the feathers which, as well as being essential aids to flight, provide an insulating layer. In addition, some aquatic birds such as penguins and petrels have a layer of fat which performs the same function. The only parts of the body which are not insulated are the feet and these are used as radiators. When the bird becomes too hot, the blood circulation to the feet and legs is increased with the result that heat is rapidly lost from the feet to the surrounding air or water. Additional heat may be lost through the lungs and air-sacs.

The reproductive organs of birds are not very different from those of mammals. Fertilization occurs inside the female's body and the male has an evertible cloaca to enable introduction of the sperm into the female. Some birds such as the ratite birds, swans, ducks and geese, have a penis. Patterns of behaviour involving courtship and breeding are well developed and will be discussed at length later in this book.

The bird's egg, like those of all other animals, is composed of a single cell. Only after it has been fertilized does this cell begin to divide to produce the chick, a process called embryonic development. Embryonic development is complex and in fact involves two processes, firstly, cell division and, secondly, cell differentiation. To begin with, the cells produced by division of the egg cell are similar to one another, but later they develop different characteristics so that it is possible to identify which parts of the chick's anatomy they are destined to become.

There are three essential components of the egg: the yolk, the egg white or albumen and the shell. The yolk contains fat and protein which nourishes the embryo during its later stages of development, while the albumen serves to protect the yolk by acting as a cushion which absorbs jolts and jars when the egg is moved. The shell also has a protective function and is often coloured so that it blends with its natural background —this is especially true of the eggs of birds which nest on the ground.

The yolk is suspended in the albumen on two strands called the chalazae which enable the yolk to rotate and remain in one position when the egg is turned. This is important because the cells that are destined to produce the chick are formed as a small disc on the upper surface of the yolk. By allowing the yolk to rotate, the chalazae enable this disc to remain always in the same position. The disc, or blastodisc as it is properly called, is at first composed of a single layer of cells but, within the first few days of incubation or even before incubation, these cells divide to produce a double layer called a gastrula. Later, a third layer is produced by which time not only cell division, but cell differentiation is taking place. If an egg which has just begun to develop is examined, a dark line is visible running across the blastodisc at right angles to the long axis of the egg. This line is called the primitive streak and represents the first obvious stage in the life of the embryo. At one end of the primitive streak, cells destined to become the head are visible, while along the streak there are blocks of cells which later grow into the bird's muscles.

The musculature of the wing is dominated by the pectoralis major (1), seen in side view in (A) and from below in (B). The triceps (2) and biceps (3) serve to extend and fold the wing, while a series of tendons (4) hold the feathers in their correct position.

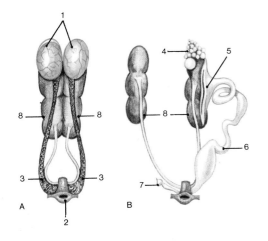

The male (A) and female (B) reproductive organs. Sperm are produced in the testis (1) which is joined to the cloaca (2) by a tube called the vas deferens (3). Eggs are produced in the ovary (4) and collected by a funnel (5) which leads to the oviduct (6) where the shell is formed. Normally, only the left ovary develops, the right one being present only in a rudimentary state (7). In both sexes, the reproductive organs are positioned close to the kidneys (8).

A hen's egg after $3\frac{1}{2}$ days (A) showing the embryo (1) and its network of blood vessels (2), after 10 days (B), 15 days (C) and 20 days (D).

One of the first organs to develop is the heart which pumps blood from the embryo through a network of blood vessels that run into the yolk. Food stored in the yolk is carried along the network to the embryo. Growth is rapid and, after a week of development in the case of the chicken *Gallus*, rudiments of the adult bill, eye, limbs and even feathers are clearly seen. The bill is formed at an early stage and in almost all birds bears on its upper part a structure called an egg tooth. It is with this horny 'tooth' that the chick breaks its shell immediately prior to hatching.

An important organ that grows with the developing chick is a sac of extremely thin tissue called the allantois. This sac begins as an outgrowth of the chick's gut and eventually completely surrounds the embryo and presses against the inner walls of the shell. Without the allantois the chick would never survive because, as the chick grows, it produces waste products in the form of uric acid and carbon dioxide. These products would poison the chick if they were not removed, so the allantois functions as the chick's waste disposal unit and stores uric acid safely away and allows carbon dioxide to pass through its walls and through the egg shell to the outside.

After a month, again in the case of the chicken, the chick is ready to break out of its confining egg shell. Before hatching takes place, however, a number of important events occur. These are necessary because the environment into which the chick emerges on hatching is completely different from that inside the egg. Firstly, the chick swallows the liquid in which it has been 'swimming' and stores the water thus acquired in its body tissues. Secondly, the yolk sac with the unused remains of yolk are pulled into the chick's body. Thus the chick is provided with a food store on which it can depend during its first few days of life outside the egg. Lastly, changes occur that enable the chick to breathe air. During most of its development, the chick obtains oxygen from the gases which diffuse into its blood via the thin membrane of the allantois. But when it hatches, the chick, cut off from this supply, must use its lungs. To make the transition easier, the chick begins to breathe while it is still enclosed in its shell. As a result of evaporation, an air space forms at the blunt end of the egg and, just before hatching, the chick pierces the membranes that enclose it, and breathes in the air from this space. For a while the chick derives oxygen from both the air inside the egg, and from the blood which is pumped from the allantois, but by the time the chick hatches, its lungs are fully operational. To make it easier for the chick to hatch, the shell enclosing it is weakened by the removal of minerals. This is a neat arrangement because these very same minerals are required to make the chick's skeleton hard and able to function when the bird finally emerges.

The time taken for a chick to grow from a single cell to an individual which is able, in almost all species, to break out of its shell is called the incubation period, and it is during this period that one or both of the parent birds is obliged to sit on the nest and prevent the eggs from cooling below the so-called incubation temperature, below which development ceases allowing the chick to die. Incubation periods vary considerably from bird to bird, and depend on the rate at which the chick embryo grows. In general, large birds have long incubation periods and small birds short periods. The Royal albatross, for example, has an incubation period of about 80 days, while many small passerine birds have a period of about 12–13 days.

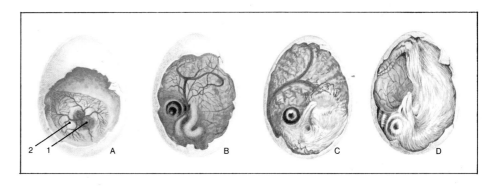

Beaks

The beaks of birds are extremely varied in shape, the individual design being related to the diet of the species concerned. Although some birds have large, well-built beaks designed for undertaking strong tasks, in general they are light compared with the toothed mouthparts of mammals, a factor necessitated by the need to reduce weight wherever possible so as to be able to fly. As a result, birds do not normally grind their food up in their mouths; this function is performed in the gizzard which is nearer to the centre of gravity of the bird. The two mandibles are basically bony structures covered with a layer of keratin—chemically very similar to feathers and to human finger nails. As with the feathers, these horny sheaths wear out and have to be replaced. Often worn sections peel away, but in some species whole sections may be shed at one time. The cutting-edge wears most and is replaced almost all the time.

The mouth is opened by the lower mandible being moved away from the upper mandible—in a way similar to that in humans. The upper mandible is not always rigidly fixed to the skull; usually there is a certain amount of movement, there being a hinged articulation between the skull and the mandible. At times the movement may be very considerable. The bill is not always a rigid bony structure; in some birds there is a considerable amount of movement in the bill. The long bill of the Snipe, for example, is very flexible. On the other hand, the bills of woodpeckers are extremely rigid and powerful in order to chip away at wood.

In many of the wading birds and some other species there are touch receptors in the tips of the mandibles. These organs, called Herbst's corpuscles, enable the birds to feel prey which they cannot see. They are particularly useful in species such as the godwits and curlews where the birds probe deep into soft ground in search of worms. Herbst's corpuscles are also present in the tips of the tongue of woodpeckers for the same reason. Other touch-sensitive cells, Grandry's corpuscles, occur in the palate and also in the tongue enabling a bird to feel the food that it has in the mouth. The tongue is often used, in association with the bill, to help a bird to hold and manipulate its food.

The upper mandible is pierced by the nostrils. Usually the nostrils are near the base of the bill. In some birds such as the Gannet, which dives into the sea from a considerable height, horny coverings lie over the nasal openings preventing water from being forced into them as it dives. Relatively few birds are known to use the sense of smell in their search for food; indeed in most species the sense of smell seems to be poorly developed. However, in the Kiwi it seems to be well developed and is presumably useful in the birds search for food. The nostrils are placed near to the bill tip and probably enable the bird to smell food underground when it is probing for food.

The bill is much used in the displays of birds. Often it is brightly coloured or ornamented. The horny sheath is shed from time to time and some species have different patterns on the sheath at different times of year. Many of the auks, especially the Puffin, have large sheaths over the bill during the breeding season. These brightly-coloured shields are shed after the breeding season and replaced with much smaller, duller sheaths for the winter. These in their turn are replaced prior to the next breeding season. Some pelicans also develop horny protuberances on the bill for the breeding season and shed them afterwards.

The tongue is frequently used in association with the mandibles in feeding. In the finches the tongue is used to position the seeds between the mandibles for cracking. In the Puffin the tongue holds small fish against the upper mandible, enabling the bird to open its beak and catch another fish. Each new fish caught is stacked between the tongue and the upper mandible and in this way the bird can gather a large number of prey before returning to its nest. The back of the tongue and the throat also house taste buds. Although less numerous than those in mammals, birds can distinguish the same tastes as mammals and the use of these is important in feeding.

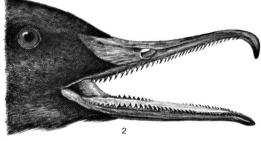

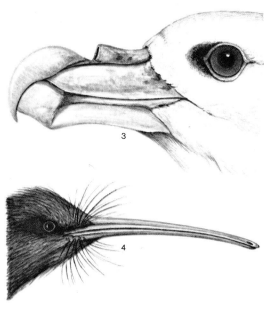

The Flamingo *Phoenicopterus ruber* (1) feeds with its head upside down. In this manner it is able to draw in large quantities of water from which it sieves out small organisms by means of the hair-like processes on the sides of its bill. The diving Goosander *Mergus meganser* (2) holds fish that it catches firmly with the tooth-like projections along its mandibles. The Fulmar *Fulmarus glacialis* (3) catches fish with its sharp beak-tip. It also feeds on offal, especially fish-waste dumped from fishing boats. The Kiwi *Apteryx australis* (4) probes in soft soil for worms and other small animals. Its nostril is close to the tip of the bill and the bird is apparently able to find its food by scent.

Variety of shape in beaks. (1) Scarlet ibis *Endocimus ruber*, (2) Red crossbill *Loxia curvirostra*, (3) Anhinga *Anhinga anhinga*, (4) Toco toucan *Ramphastos toco*, (5) Laughing kookaburra *Dacelo gigas*, (6) Formosan kinglet *Regulus goodfellowi*, (7) Avocet *Recurvirostra avosetta*, (8) White-tipped sicklebill *Eutoxeres aquila*, (9) Swordbilled hummingbird *Ensifera ensifera*, (10) Crimson-backed woodpecker *Chrysocolaptes lucidus*, (11) Great hornbill *Buceros bicornis*, (12) Hawfinch *Coccothraustes coccothraustes*, (13) Sparrowhawk *Accipter nisus*, (14) Pennant-winged nightjar *Semeiophorus vexillarius*, (15) Great crested grebe *Podiceps cristatus*, (16) Shoebill stork *Balaeniceps rex*, (17) Mute swan *Cygnus olor*, (18) Eurasian spoonbill *Platalea leucorodia*, (19) White pelican *Pelecanus onocrotalus*, (20) Indian skimmer *Rynchops albicollis* and (21) Masked lovebird *Agapornis personata*.

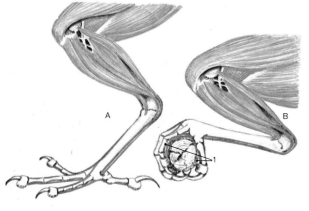

The muscles of the lower leg in birds are reduced for greater flying efficiency (A). In order to perch securely on a small branch or thin wire a bird must be able to grip hard with its toes. This grip is applied when the leg is bent and the flexor tendons (1) tightened (B).

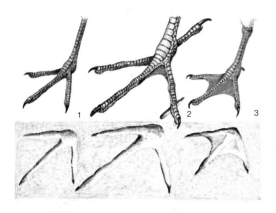

The hind claw is an extremely variable feature in different groups of birds. In the stilts (1) it is absent, while in the herons (2) it is present but at a higher level than the other claws. In the terns the hind claw is much reduced, and does not appear in the foot-print (3).

Legs

For reasons connected with flying, birds have evolved legs which have few large muscles except those at the top of the leg near to the centre of gravity. Unlike our legs, those of birds have three main sections. The femur is relatively short and buried in muscle. Forming a joint with the femur is the section equivalent to our tarsus, but this section, strictly called the tibio-tarsus, is not wholly comparable with our lower leg. The third and lowest section, usually called the tarsus, is basically a bone formed out of the upper bones of the foot. Since this bone is the one most easily seen in birds it is often the one called the leg, but really it is equivalent to parts of the ankle in man. The visible, backward-bending joint is not, anatomically speaking, the knee; which is higher up the leg and hidden by the feathers.

The femur tends to be shorter than the other two bones. The tibio-tarsus and the tarsus vary markedly in length, being very short in some birds such as swifts and penguins and very long in running and wading birds. In any species the two bones are closely similar in length. If they were not, the bird would have great difficulty getting up and sitting down since the centre of gravity would shift in relation to the foot.

Because lower parts of the legs have little musculature, they have to be controlled by a pulley system from the muscles at the top of the leg. A series of tendons run from the muscles at the top of the leg, operating the leg with a series of ropes and pulleys. One of the most important of these tendons runs round the back of the 'ankle' joint and into the toes. When the bird sits down onto its foot the tendon is tightened over the end of the joint so pulling in the toes. This action is particularly important in perching birds where the action of sitting down over the foot causes the toes to curl around the perch and lock the bird into position. By doing this, the bird can hold onto a branch tightly even when it is asleep. Indeed it cannot easily let go of the branch in a sitting position, but must raise itself up off its feet in order to release the toes.

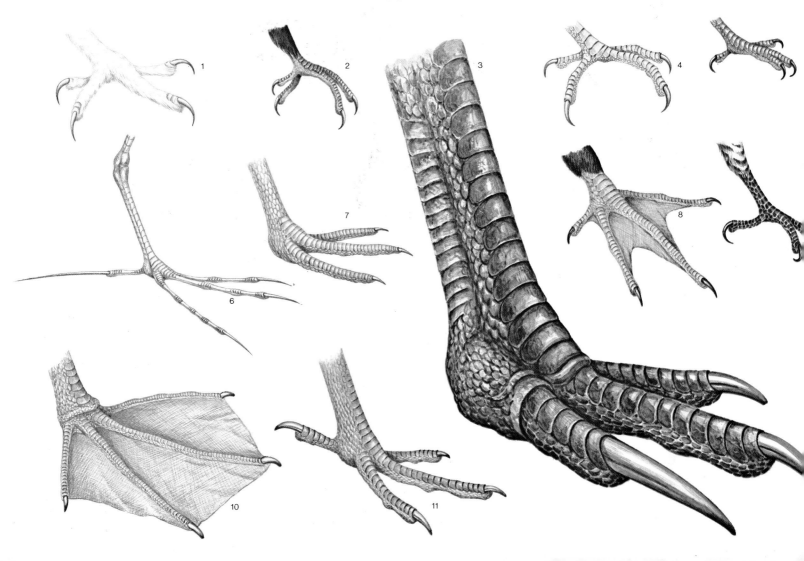

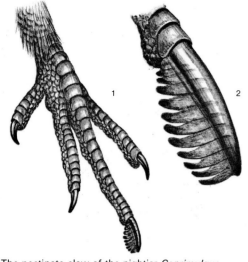

The pectinate claw of the nightjar *Caprimulgus europaeus* (1), shown in detail in (2). Similar claws are found in some herons and in most pratincoles. Their function is not fully understood but they may be used in preening.

Variety of shape in feet. (1) Screech owl *Otus asio,* (2) Cuban trogon *Priotelus temnurus*, (3) Cassowary *Casuarius casuarius*, (4) Oriental cuckoo *Cuculus saturatus*, (5) Kingfisher *Alcedo atthis*, (6) American jacana *Jacana spinosa*, (7) Oystercatcher *Haematopus ostralegus*, (8) Great frigate-bird *Fregata minor*, (9) Three-toed woodpecker *Picoides tridactylus*, (10) Blue-footed booby *Sula nebouxii*, (11) Turkey vulture *Cathartes aura*, (12) Ruffed grouse *Bonasa umbellus*, (13) Night heron *Nycticorax nycticorax*, (14) Slavonian grebe *Podiceps auritus*. (15) Ostrich *Struthio camelus*, (16) Meadow pipit *Anthus pratensis*, (17) Osprey *Pandion haliaetus*, (18) Mallard *Anas platyrhynchos*, (19) Pileated woodpecker *Dryocopus pileatus*, (20) Swift *Apus apus*, (21) Red necked or Northern phalarope *Phalaropus lobatus*, (22) Double-banded courser *Rhinoptilus africanus*, and (23) Common cormorant *Phalacrocorax carbo*.

This movement, together with ones made by the femur can, when done swiftly, cause the bird to be raised up very sharply and be almost thrown into the air. Advantage is taken of this action to launch the bird at the moment that it decides to take off.

Birds may either hop or run along the ground. In order to run really swiftly birds have had to develop very long and powerful legs. To be very fast, the bird has to be fairly large. Hence the development of high running speed has been one of the factors in the development of flightlessness. In some of theese species, fast running has been made possible by a reduction of the size of the foot and by a reduction in the number of toes. This has been taken to the extreme in the Ostrich which has only two toes, one much smaller than the other.

Although bird legs have relatively little tissue in them and do not need much energy to keep them warm, birds that live in very cold climates have developed a further way of preventing heat loss through the legs. The arteries carrying blood to the legs divide into small vessels which intertwine with the returning veins, which are also greatly sub-divided. As a result, on leaving the body, the arterial blood passes much of its warmth to the returning, cooled venous blood. In this way the minimum of heat is wasted and the birds do not get chilled blood entering the body. The legs 'live' at a perpetually low temperature.

The foot has only four toes, the fifth having been lost early in the course of evolution —*Archaeopteryx*, which is known to have existed 150 million years ago, had only four toes. The toes show many adaptations to the birds way of life, often being modified for swimming. Perching birds may have two toes pointing forwards and two backwards, or three pointing forwards and only one backwards. The horny scutes of the legs and feet are, like those of the beak, formed of keratinous material. They are moulted regularly. In the Ptarmigan in winter the scutes of the toes have hair-like processes projecting from the sides enabling the bird to walk in the soft snow as if on snow-shoes. These scutes are moulted in the spring and replaced by normal ones.

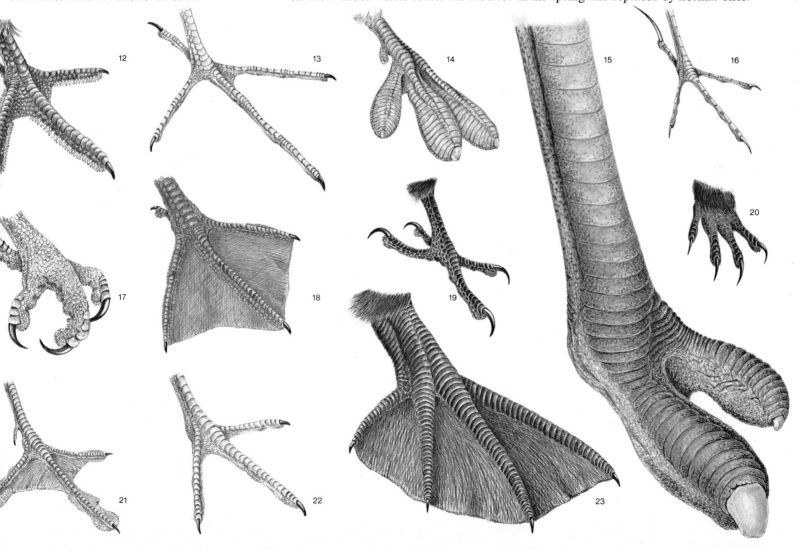

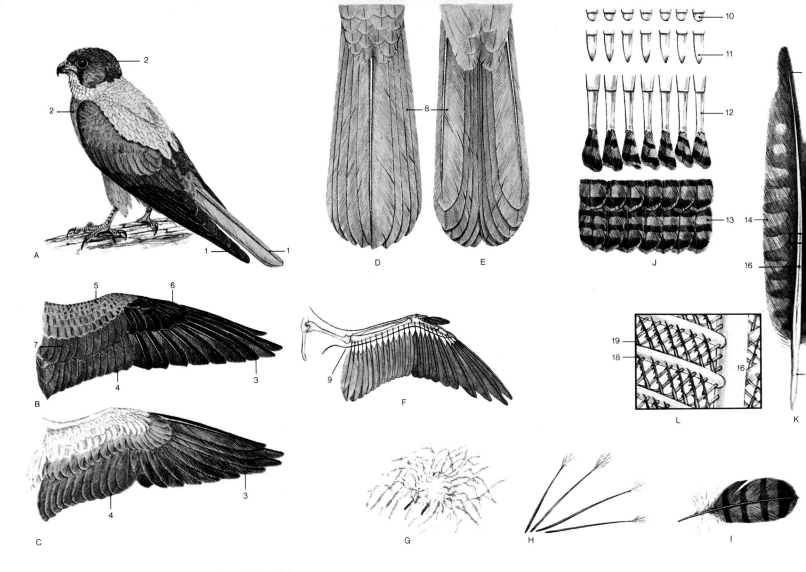

(A) Outer feathers or pennae are of two kinds, flight feathers (1) and contour feathers (2). The flight feathers of the upper (B) and lower (C) wing surfaces are called primaries (3) and secondaries (4). Smaller contour feathers, lesser coverts (5), greater coverts (6) and secondary coverts (7), give the wing its aerodynamic shape. The tail, seen from above (D) and below (E), is composed of flight feathers called rectrices (8). The primaries and secondaries are held in position on the wing (F) by an elastic tendon (9). Other feathers are permanent down feathers (G), filoplumes (H) and contour feathers (I). Growth of a feather (J) begins with the development of a group of cells (10) into a feather germ (11) which breaks through the skin (12) before the vanes develop (13). Flight feathers (K) are composed of inner (14) and outer (15) vanes inserted on a rachis (16) which extends from the basal calamus (17). The vanes are composed (L) of barbs (18) and interlocking barbules (19).

Some feathers have aftershafts which branch from the underside of the base of the rachis. In this example a contour feather (1) has a downy aftershaft (2).

Feathers

The feathers of birds perform four important functions: they form an insulating layer around the body; they create wing and tail surfaces that are essential for flight; they keep the body waterproofed; and finally, their colouration can provide a bird with camouflage by enabling it to blend with its surroundings or make it conspicuous by providing colours and patterns that are used in displays particularly associated with breeding behaviour and courtship ceremonies.

There are two principal types of feather: the pennae, which are the outer feathers, divided into contour feathers and flight feathers; and the plumulae, or down feathers. Other types of feather are either intermediate between pennae and plumulae, or are derived from them. The pennae are shaped like the traditional quill pen, having a flattened vane composed of many interlocking units growing out in one plane from a supporting central mid-rib or rachis. The latter is a continuation of the basal calamus which is hollow allowing passage of nutrient materials from the skin during the growth of the feather. The structure of the feather vane is complex. Along each side of the rachis project several hundred parallel filaments, or barbs, each of which has along its length several hundred pairs of barbules which interlock, zipping the barbs together. In most birds the feathers grow in special tracts with featherless areas in between, an arrangement which is clearly seen in a plucked chicken. The feathers grow from special papillae, 'goose pimples', which produce one, two, or even three sets of feathers each year.

The down feathers are simpler and less varied than the pennae. The rachis is very short and there are no barbules so that the barbs are not attached to each other. This results in the fluffiness of down feathers.

A very important function of feathers is to help control the temperature of the bird's body. Heat is retained by an insulating layer of air which is trapped close to the skin by the feathers. When the bird becomes too cold, the outer feathers are fluffed up to increase this insulating layer. The second function is to give the body a streamlined

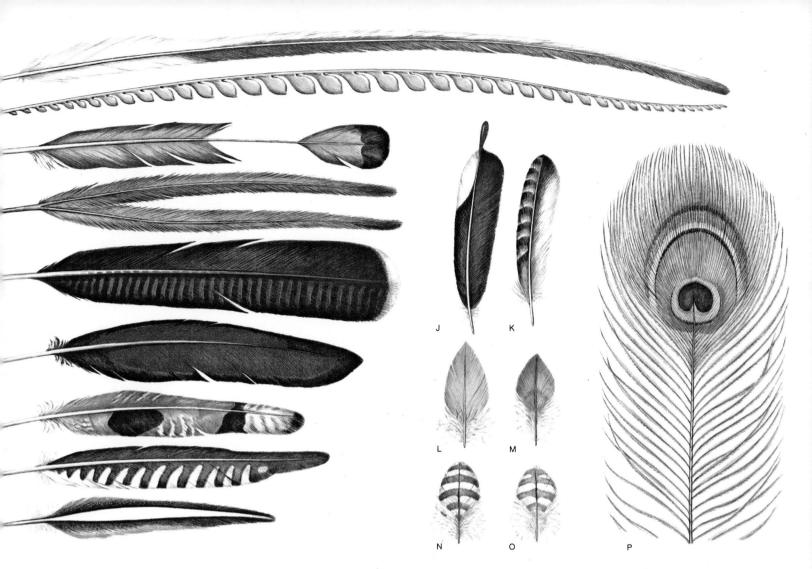

A variety of feather types. Trailing wing plume, Pennant-wing nightjar *Semeiophorus vexillarius* (A); head plume, King of Saxony bird of paradise *Pteridophora alberti* (B); racket tail feather, Turquoise-browed motmot *Eumomota superciliosa* (C); a feather with aftershaft, Emu *Dromiceius novaehollandiae* (D); flight feathers, anhinga *Anhinga anhinga* (E), Blue crested plantain eater *Turaco hartlaubi* (F), sunbittern *Eurypyga helias* (G), and the hobby *Falco subbuteo* (H); neck hackle, Vulturine guinea fowl *Acryllium vulturinum* (I); secondary flight feather, Bohemian waxwing *Bombycilla garrulus* (J); wing covert, jay *Garrulus glandarius* (K); contour feathers, Green woodpecker *Picus viridis* (L), kingfisher *Alcedo atthis* (M), the female (N) and male (O) Sparrow-hawk *Accipiter nisus*; and the brilliant upper tail coverts of the male peacock, *Pavo cristatus* (P).

The edge of an owl's wing feather has unconnected barbs which form a soft fringe. It is believed that this enables the owl to fly more silently.

shape and to provide flight surfaces, and is no less important. The streamlining of the bird is effected by the contour feathers, the main covering of the body. Measurements of flying efficiency suggest that the bird may be able to alter the shape of its body surface under different conditions, by altering the position of its contour feathers, in order to maximize the streamlining. The flight feathers of the wing, the remiges, and of the tail, the retrices, can be spread to provide large, strong, light surfaces which can be varied to give the bird an efficiency of flight second to none in the animal kingdom. There are three groups of feathers on the wing: the primary feathers which are attached to the hand, the secondaries attached to the forearm, and the tertiaries attached to the humerus. The small group of feathers on the alula or bastard wing is also important during flight.

Another function of the feather covering is camouflage. Most birds are counter-shaded, being lighter beneath in order to counteract the effect of their shadow. The plumage of many species also blends well with the background of their normal environment, particularly in the case of hen birds which are therefore rendered inconspicuous when sitting on the nest. Plumage patterns also play important roles in keeping together members of a flock. The flashing of special wing or tail patches act as signals allowing birds to follow one another in flight.

Finally, feather patterns are important in species recognition. A major function of plumes, crests and feather patches on male birds which are shown during courtship displays is to enable the female to recognize the 'right' potential mate.

The number of feathers on a bird varies according to the species and the time of year. The larger the bird the greater the number of feathers in the plumage. For example, a Ruby-throated hummingbird has been recorded with a total of 940 feathers, while a Whistling swan had 25,216. The colder the climate the more feathers a bird has in the winter. It is a surprising fact that the total weight of a bird's plumage may be more than twice that of its skeleton. A Bald eagle weighing 144 oz (4,080 gm) with a skeleton of $9\frac{1}{2}$ oz (272 gm) carried 7,182 pennae weighing $20\frac{1}{2}$ oz (586 gm) and $3\frac{1}{4}$ oz (91 gm) of down.

Change of plumage colour in the Black-headed gull *Larus ridibundus*. (1) Juvenile plumage. (2) plumage of juvenile bird during its first winter, (3) immature bird during its first full summer, (4) adult plumage during winter and (5) adult plumage during summer.

Colour

Birds are amongst the most brilliantly coloured members of the animal kingdom, and to this they owe, to a large extent, their undoubted popularity. As far as the bird is concerned, colour has evolved, not to satisfy the aesthetic needs of man but to perform several important biological functions. These are discussed below, but it is first necessary to examine how colour is produced by birds.

There are two reasons why feathers appear coloured: they can have built into them structural elements that reflect light in different ways, as does a film of oil on the surface of water—these are called structural colours; or they can contain pigment or dyes—pigmentary colours. Structural colours are of two kinds, iridescent and non-iridescent. Iridescent colours change according to the angle at which light hits the feather's surface, and have a metallic appearance. They are produced either by the presence of a thin layer of a substance called keratin which occurs on the surface of the barbules, or by minute granules of a material called melanin which occur in a thin layer just below the surface of the barbules. In both cases, light hitting the feather is split into its component colours before being reflected back to the observer. Iridescent colours are most vivid in such birds as the hummingbirds.

Non-iridescent colours are produced by the scattering of light when it passes through minute air-filled cavities in the keratin of the barbs, and do not change according to the angle at which the light hits the feather's surface.

Pigmentary colours are less metallic in appearance than structural colours, and are not limited to the plumage of the bird. The bill, legs, feet and sometimes head and neck of birds are often pigmented. The most common pigment is a chemical called melanin which, when concentrated, shows black as in crows and the Blackbird. Other chemicals are the carotenoids, responsible for the red in the wattles of the pheasant and possibly also for the pink plumage of the flamingo. It is of interest to note that the flamingo is unable to manufacture its own pigment and must obtain it from its food. Red is also produced by the chemical turacin which is found in the turacos of Africa.

Some birds combine the effects of structural and pigmentary colours. For example the Blossom-headed parakeet has brilliantly purple plumage which is the result of the combination of blue produced by the physical scattering of light, and red pigment.

Colour functions in almost every aspect of life of birds and can be considered under two categories: colours that render a bird inconspicuous—cryptic colours; and colours that make a bird extremely conspicuous. Cryptic colours provide camouflage by enabling birds to merge with their backgrounds. A good example is seen in different species of larks which inhabit desert regions. Each species lives over ground which has a characteristic colour determined by the nature of the local rocks and soils, and each is appropriately coloured. Ptarmigan which live in northern climates are commonly white during the winter and assume a darker plumage in summer. Chicks of ground-nesting birds almost always have cryptic colouration, even though they may assume different colouration when adult. Cryptic colouration is often made more effective by the adoption of certain postures when predators threaten. For example, when a bittern is alarmed, it stretches its head to the sky revealing dark markings on its neck which merge with the pattern of the reeds in which it lives.

Colours that make birds conspicuous serve a number of different functions. Brilliant colours aid the recognition of species and sex by particular birds. Such colours are often used in conjunction with certain displays and with varying degrees of feather erection, and have enabled birds to evolve codes of signals indicating the mood and intentions of an individual. Examples of such signals are seen in threat and courtship.

Finally, some colours are used by colonial birds to keep together the flock. Sea birds are commonly white since white objects are able to approach fish more closely than black ones before they are seen.

22

Structural and pigmentary colours. (1) Quetzal
Pharomachrus mocino, (2) Cuban tody *Todus
multicolor*, (3) Iiwi *Vestiaria coccinea*, (4) Rainbow-
billed toucan *Ramphastos sulfuratus*, (5) Cock-of-
the-rock *Rupicola rupicola*, (6) Impeyan pheasant
Lophophorus impejanus and (7) African pitta *Pitta
angolensis*.

The Scops owl *Otus leucotis* can conceal itself well beside a tree trunk. But if danger threatens it will open its eyes wide and simultaneously switch from a sleek camouflaged posture to one in which the feathers are all fluffed up, thus making itself look as threatening as possible.

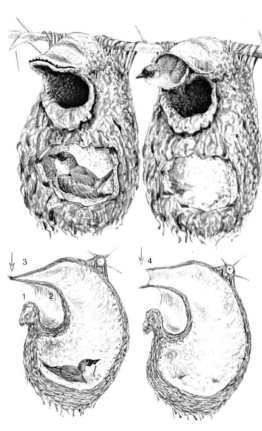

The Cape penduline tit *Anthoscopus minutus* builds a strong pliable nest of felt-like texture. It has a false entrance (1) to mislead predators which is seen to be a blind sac when viewed in section (2). The true entrance is narrower and lies above the false entrance (red arrow). It closes after the bird has forced its way in or out of the nest (3) and (4).

Camouflage

Any animal that is in danger from attack by predators will be at an advantage if the predator cannot find it easily. Many birds resort to camouflage in order to increase their chances of survival; not only the birds themselves but their nests and eggs may be exceedingly well camouflaged.

Some examples of camouflage are obvious: the white of the winter plumage of the Ptarmigan, for example, obviously matches the background of snow very closely. However, the situation is not as simple as that since, in the summer, the snows melt and a white bird would be very striking at this time. Hence as spring arrives the birds moult progressively into a browner and greyer plumage which matches at first the broken patches of snow and open ground and later still the open ground. In autumn the bird moults slowly back into the white plumage.

Some of the most strikingly camouflaged birds are those that nest or live on the ground such as the Woodcock and the nightjars. These birds are so difficult to see that they are usually only found by the observer when he nearly treads on them and so causes them to fly away. Such patterns are called disruptive colouration, since they break up the outline of the bird. In some species such as the pheasants where the female alone incubates, the sexes may be of quite different colour. The female pheasants are almost as well camouflaged as the nightjars, though the males are very brightly coloured. Even in species with nests which are hidden in bushes the males tend to be less gaudily coloured if they help to incubate the eggs than if they do not. Not all birds that incubate eggs on the ground are well camouflaged. Many of the waders that nest in open country are quite brightly coloured. In these places, where it is relatively difficult for the birds to hide, the bird has a wide view and as soon as danger threatens, the bird leaves the nest and flies away, usually quite conspicuously. The predator has little chance of locating the nest of well-camouflaged eggs from this distance. In contrast, some of the well-camouflaged birds that nest in cover, such as the pheasants and the ducks, lay eggs that are quite conspicuous, often white or nearly so. The bird sits tight on the eggs and only leaves when almost trodden on; at that distance even cryptic eggs would be discovered.

An important aspect of animal camouflage involves the elimination of shadows. The undersides of animals are often more palely marked than the upperside. This is known as countershading since it serves to remove, or at least reduce, the darker colour that would result from the bird's own shadow on its underside. In the guinea-fowls, the pale spots are much smaller on the back than on the underside and this serves to reduce the amount of shadow showing on the underside. However, birds

Like many ground-dwelling species, the Little bustard *Otis tetrax* will crouch low when a predator passes overhead. The bird is not only well-camouflaged, but by stretching out in this manner it eliminates all tell-tale shadows.

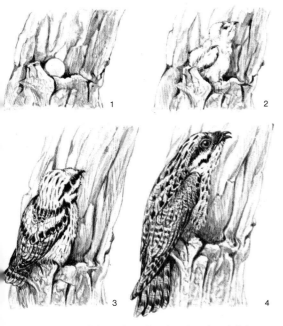

The Potoo *Nyctibius griseus* is related to the nightjars. Instead of laying its eggs on the ground as nightjars normally do, it lays a single egg on a tree notch (1). When incubating, the Potoo sits upright against the tree and in this position so resembles a dead branch that it is extremely difficult to see (4). The developing chick (2–3) also adopts this upright well-camouflaged posture.

Young Siberian jays *Perisoreus infaustus*, birds of the cold taiga forests, huddling together to keep warm.

The Snowy owl *Nyctea scandiaca* lives on the open ▷ tundra where, since there is usually snow on the ground, it is capable of perfect concealment. The female Snowy owl is larger than the male and has light brown barring in her plumage.

stand above the ground on thin legs and if the light is bright, they tend to cast a conspicuous shadow on the ground which may give away their position. For this reason many birds crouch down on the ground when danger threatens so as to eliminate this tell-tale shadow. The head is drawn in or stretched out along the ground in front of the crouching bird.

In all aspects of camouflage the behaviour of the animal is crucial if the effects of the camouflage are not to be ruined. For example many young waders are beautifully camouflaged, but only if they crouch. If they stand up then their shadow gives them away at once. Hence they must immediately obey their parents' warning calls by crouching if they are to avoid the predator. Similarly, the bittern only achieves its best camouflage by drawing itself upright until it matches the vertical lines of the reed-bed in which it lives. Even the most beautifully camouflaged birds still have large eyes which might give their position away; they solve this problem by almost completely closing their eyes and watching the approach of the predator through very narrow slits. In a few species the nest site must be chosen with great care; the eggs of some sand-grouse match the colour of fallen leaves and the near-black eggs of Temminck's courser are said to match the droppings of antelopes. In both these cases the eggs would be conspicuous if laid in the wrong places.

A number of species of larks in Africa and Asia have local races whose colour matches the predominant soil colour of the area in which they live; some of these birds have been reported to be unwilling to leave the correct background when people have pursued them. Camouflage can only be considered in the correct ecological context. Even some birds that look conspicuous in a museum drawer are probably well-camouflaged in nature. The bright green parrots disappear when the birds enter a large tree; one can watch large numbers enter a tree and wonder wherever they have gone. Similarly birds such as the trogons with their bright red or yellow underparts can be exceedingly difficult to see in the tops of the trees in rain forest. Their colours blend with the patterns in the tree tops, where there are almost always dead and young leaves providing a wealth of different shades of colour.

A few species of predatory birds make use of camouflage in order to get close to their prey. The Snowy owl is cryptic against the background when perched; even sometimes when flying it can be extremely difficult to see. The white underparts of many seabirds are almost certainly camouflage in that a fish looking upwards can see a dark object approaching it from a greater distance than a white one and so have a greater opportunity to escape.

Pigeons have been observed to hold one or both wings in a vertical position to expose their feathers to the rain, presumably to wash them.

A White-billed diver *Gavia adamsii* (1) and Tufted duck *Aythya fuligula* (2) rolling onto their backs in order to preen their undersides.

Care of the feathers in the Frilled coquette *Lophornis magnifica*. Hummingbirds practise head and neck scratching with the feet. Sometimes this is even attempted while the bird is airborne.

A Jay *Garrulus glandarius* engaged in anting. Having found a suitable ant-nest, the Jay fluffs out to allow the ants easy access to its feathers. It is believed that formic acid from the ants serves to kill parasites in the plumage.

Preening and Hygiene

All animals need to keep themselves clean and this is particularly true of birds which rely on the delicate and intricate structure of the feathers for so many of their activities. Dirty feathers stick together and reduce insulation and also would make good hiding places for a wide variety of parasites. The large flight feathers are in many ways a great improvement on the wings of bats, pterodactyls and insects; if pierced or hit while in flight the barbs separate, but sustain relatively little lasting damage; the bird just has to repair the feathers at a later stage by preening.

By far the greatest part of a bird's 'cleaning-up' time is spent on feather maintenance. The bird may bathe in water or, as is the case with the domestic hen, in dry dusty earth. This vigorous action helps to shake out foreign objects from the feathers. In preening the bird rubs its bill in the preen gland and distributes the preen oil over the surface of the feathers; particular attention is paid to the flight feathers. The action is very rapid and the preen oil dries extremely quickly. The full purpose of the spreading of this oil is not clear. One presumes that it must help to improve the condition of the feathers in some way, but it is not clear that, as was once supposed, it serves to water-proof the feathers; indeed many birds seem to wet the feathers before they spread the oil. The oil also has another function: on exposure to ultra-violet light it forms vitamin D; it is thought that this might be ingested by the bird in a later bout of preening or possibly absorbed through the skin. Whatever the real function of the oil, it is important to remember that a few birds, such as the frogmouths and some of the pigeons, parrots and woodpeckers, do not possess a preen gland and yet they too keep their feathers in perfect condition.

The bird uses its feet as well as its beak to preen the feathers. Some species of birds comb their feathers with their feet; in some, such as certain of the herons and nightjars, there is a serrated edge to the third claw; it is thought that this might help in preening. The claws are used most on the feathers, such as those of the head, which the bird cannot reach with its bill. In some species pairs of birds may preen one another, again concentrating on the head where the bird cannot easily preen itself. The bill, however, remains the most important structure for preening. There are two main actions. Either the feathers are drawn swiftly through the beak or the bird runs it more slowly along the barbs with a nibbling action. The latter action seems to function to repair small separations of the barbs and in addition the bird will stop and concentrate on a particular spot if it finds a break or a foreign body.

Anting is another aspect of feather maintenance which is imperfectly understood. A bird may settle among a group of ants and let them run around in its feathers or it may even pick up individual ants and pass them quickly across its plumage. Birds seem to prefer to use the acid-ejecting ants and the most obvious substance produced by these ants is formic acid. Assuming that it is this substance which the birds are trying to obtain, the most reasonable supposition is that the bird is spreading it over its feathers in order to kill parasites. Fleas and feather lice may live in numbers in the feathers and would almost certainly be killed by the formic acid. Although anting has been widely recorded in birds, all detailed records seem to relate to passerine birds.

Little is known about the maintenance of other structures. The beak receives frequent doses of preen oil during the action of preening the feathers and some birds also apply the oil to the horny scutes of the legs. The bill is kept clean by the feet or by being rubbed vigorously along a branch or other hard object.

Birds undertake a number of other hygenic activities; those that live in holes must be careful not to foul the site with their droppings, especially in the nesting season. This hygiene is carried to extremes in nestling birds which produce their droppings in small gelatinous bags—faecal sacs—which can be disposed of easily by the parents. When the young are very small the parents eat the sacs, but as the young and the sacs get larger the parents carry them away and drop them some distance from the nest in order not to reveal its site to predators.

Care of the feathers. (1) Anting by the American Blue jay *Cyanocitta cristata*, (2) preening in the Curlew sandpiper *Calidris ferruginea*, (3) scratching in the Ruby-crowned kinglet *Regulus calendula*, (4) care of the tail in the Blackbird *Turdus merula* and of the wing (5) in the Carmine bee-eater *Merops nubicoides*, (6) scratching in the Ruby-crowned kinglet, (7) bathing in the House sparrow *Passer domesticus*, (8) bathing in dust by the House sparrow, (9) preening in the Tufted duck *Aythya fuligula* and (10) oiling the feathers by the Great crested grebe *Podiceps cristatus*.

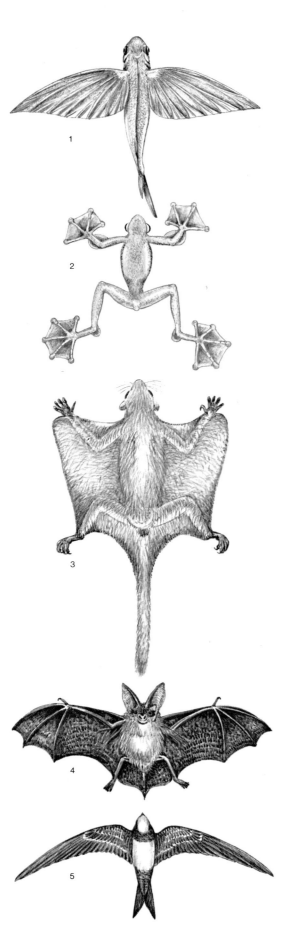

Flying and gliding animals. The pectoral fins and lower lobe of the tail are greatly enlarged in the flying fish, seen here from above (1) which, after leaping from the sea, can glide considerable distances. The flying frog (2) and squirrel (3) glide, usually from tree to tree, supported by 'wings'. In the bats (4), which are capable of true flight, the wing membrane is stretched between the body and several of the fingers. Birds' wings (5) are more resistant to damage than are wings of the membranous type.

Flight and Flying

Although not all birds fly, flight is one of the most striking features of birds. In order to fly a bird must obtain an upward force; we call this force lift. A bird's wing is shaped to enable the birds to obtain this lift; we call a wing of such a shape an aerofoil. The leading edge of an aerofoil is thicker than the trailing edge and the upper surface is more convex than the lower surface. It is easiest to understand the forces on the wing by imagining a stationary wing with the air passing over it—this is the way that aeronautical engineers study the characteristics of a wing in a wind tunnel. The air strikes the leading edge of the wing and divides, some passing under the wing and some across the upper surface. It is here that the shape of the wing becomes important; the upper surface of the wing, because of its greater curvature, has a longer surface than the underside of the wing. In order to travel to the rear of the wing at more or less the same time as the air on the underside, the air on the upper surface must travel faster than the air underneath the wing. The faster air travels across a surface the lower the pressure it exerts on that surface; as a result, the wing's upper surface experiences a lower pressure than the under surface and so lift is produced. In practice, some 80 % or more of the lift results from this, and much less from the increased pressure on the underside.

Lift is only obtained by the wing when the flow of air is smooth over its surface. If the flow of air is turbulent, then lift is lost; we say that the wing is stalled. Stalling occurs when the wing is held at too high an angle to the flow of air so that the air cannot easily flow round the upper surface. Lift is also lost if the flow of air is too slow. Some of the lift is inevitably lost by air spilling round the wing tip; this is known as induced drag and is a more important factor in the flight of short-winged birds than in those with long wings.

Lift is not the only force which the passage of air exerts on the wing. As it passes over the wing the air tends to blow the wing backwards. This force is called drag and is roughly equivalent to the amount of wing exposed to the wind; the flatter the wing the less drag there is, the steeper the angle at which the wing is held—we say the higher the angle of attack—the greater the drag. Three factors affect the amount of lift: the surface area of the wing, the wind-speed and the angle of attack at which the wing is held. The same factors affect the amount of drag, so that the position of a bird in the air is determined by a large number of forces.

It is easiest to consider next a gliding bird in still air. Basically there are two ways in which a bird can glide in still air. Firstly, it can launch itself from a perch and open its wings. If it were to do this its path would be downward and, eventually, it would come to land. Such a glider is acting, effectively, like a toboggan on a hill. It is using the energy provided by gravity so that by losing height it can travel forwards. We have been looking so far at a stationary wing in moving air, though it is clear that the same forces apply if the air is still and the wing is moving.

The second method of gliding involves not the loss of height, but the loss of speed. A bird moving forward in flight may stop beating its wings and glide. As soon as it does this it starts to slow down because of the backwards force of drag. As it slows down it loses lift (because lift is related to the speed of air over the wings). The only way that it can increase lift without losing height or beating its wings is to raise the angle of attack (since lift increases with increased angle of attack). Hence our glider can remain in level flight only by steadily increasing the angle of attack, slowing down all the while. This method of gliding may seem short-sighted since in a relatively short period the bird will be flying so slowly that the wing will stall. Nevertheless the birds use this method of gliding frequently—it is the way they land. In order to land as softly as possible the bird needs to be at the point of stalling when it is just above the landing place. To do this it must judge the landing position from afar and glide into it in this manner, using up all its forward motion and so greatly reducing the shock to the body that a harder landing would entail.

Early flying animals. A small pterodactyl, *Rhamphorhynchus* (1), and the earliest known bird, *Archaeopteryx* (2). In *Rhamphorhynchus* flight was by means of large wings of membrane attached along the body to the top of the hind legs and out along a greatly enlarged little finger. Unlike modern birds, the pterodactyls had relatively heavy heads and also teeth. *Archaeopteryx* had many features of modern birds while retaining a number of reptilian characteristics. It bore teeth and had an elongated tail which, however, was feathered throughout its length. Although the wing and feather attachments were similar to those in modern birds, the sternum (to which flight muscles are attached) was poorly developed. Hence it is almost certain that *Archaeopteryx* did not have muscles large enough for powered flight.

The shape of the wing in birds is determined by the contrasting needs of speed and manoeuvrability. Wings built for speed tend to be long and pointed, while short broad wings make sudden changes of direction possible. (1) Giant albatross *Diomedea exulans*, (2) White-tailed buzzard *Buteo albicaudatus*, (3) Willow grouse *Lagopus lagopus*, (4) Sooty falcon *Falco concolor*, (5) European common swift *Apus apus*, (6) Rufous hummingbird *Selasphorus rufus*, (7) Wallcreeper *Tichodroma muraria*.

In itself, the first method of gliding will not enable the bird to travel very far, but in our example the bird was gliding in still air; in nature the air is often moving. In an efficient glider, such as a vulture, the speed at which height is lost—we say the rate of sink—is low. If the air were rising upwards at the same speed as the vulture loses height in still air, then the bird would stay at the same altitude; it is as if the toboggan in our example were racing down a hillside which was steadily rising into the sky—the toboggan would never reach the bottom of the hill. Rising air is found in a number of situations where birds can make use of it for hours, often hardly moving their wings at all. The vulture normally uses upcurrents or thermals that arise when the surface of the land is heated by the sun. Other species such as the gulls make use of the upcurrents caused when a wind strikes a cliff or hillside. The air is deflected upwards enabling the birds to ride in the updraught.

One group of birds glide in a different way. The albatrosses and related birds make use of the wind across the surface of the open sea. In many areas such as the Roaring Forties a strong wind blows more or less all the time. The albatrosses use this wind and, in particular, they make use of the fact that friction with the sea slows the wind down so that just above the surface of the sea the wind moves relatively slowly, blowing progressively faster as one climbs above the sea until at about 50 ft (15 m) above the surface it is more or less at full speed. The albatross glides very swiftly downwind, starting at about 50 feet above the surface and losing its height as it moves rapidly down-wind. When it has descended nearly to sea-level, it swings sharply into the wind and moves upwards until it is about 50 feet above the sea and once again in the fastest winds; it then turns downwind and the cycle is repeated. This type of flight can only be done at high speed; the albatross must have sufficient 'penetration' when it turns to enable it to move against the wind. The surprising aspect of this flight is that, without having to beat its wings, the albatross can progress against the wind. Where the winds are strong and steady the albatross can make a steady 5 mph (8 kph) upwind gliding downwind about 128 yd (118 m) and upwind about 180 yd (166 m) in each cycle, a net upwind movement of some 52 yd (48 m) on each gliding cycle.

Details of flight revealed by high-speed cine photography. Take off (1) is usually achieved by first jumping into the air. During landing (2) the wings tilt the body into an almost vertical position and act as brakes. A few birds such as the hummingbird (3) can hover. This is achieved by extremely rapid wing beats which may be as fast as 80 per second. In more normal flight (4) power for forward movement is derived from the down-beat of the wing.

Powered flight requires much more energy than gliding. When using their wings for powered flight many birds use the inner parts of the wings as gliding wings (they are held roughly steady) while the end of the wing acts as the oar. Forward propulsion is obtained when the great pectoral muscles drive the wing downwards. In order to fly forwards the downbeat must provide both upward and forward movement of the bird, so that it both stays airborne and moves forwards against the resistance provided by drag. The forwards propulsion comes about in two ways, the proportions contributing to the forwards movement from the two ways differing in different species. The wing bones are in the leading edge of the wing, the trailing edge being feathers. As the wing is flapped the feathers tend to bend so that the backward edge of the wing is above the bones. As a result, although the wing beats downwards, because of its shape it pushes the air not only downwards but also backwards and, of course, pushes itself in the opposite direction. The wing tips push the air in the same direction, but in a slightly different manner. Looked at from the side of the bird, the wing tip is composed solely of feathers pointing end on at the observer. These large flight feathers have their quills near to the leading edge. As the wing moves on the downstroke, the feathers meet considerable resistance from the air. Because the rear vane of the feather is far larger than the leading one, the feather twists along the quill, with the trailing edge above the leading edge. The result of this is that the feather, like the wing, imparts a backwards and downwards pressure. The swivelling of the feathers is particularly important in short, rounded-winged birds where the feathers separate for much of the length when the wing is opened; the Common partridge is a good example. The bending and twisting forces on the wing feathers are considerable and it is not surprising that they have to be replaced by moulting at regular intervals.

Once in flight, birds need to be able to steer themselves. They do this by a variety

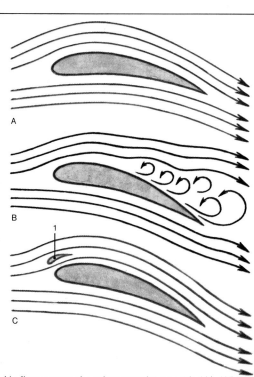

Air-flow across the wing must be smooth (A). When it breaks up and becomes turbulent (B), lift is lost; we say that the wing has stalled. This is likely to happen as the angle of the wing to the horizontal increases. Birds prevent stalling by raising the bastard wing (1) at the front of the wing proper and so smoothing the air flow (C).

of methods. They can turn solely by the use of the wings, as one can occasionally observe by watching a tail-less swallow or martin; their flight seems to be remarkably unimpaired. The bird has only to alter the angle or shape of one wing to throw itself off-balance. By slightly folding one wing, the bird can reduce the drag on that side and start to bank, or by turning any part of itself against the direction of motion the bird will be moved to one side and so turning will have been effected.

Taking off requires more energy than level flight since the bird must accelerate and climb. A small bird takes off in much the same way that it normally flies; merely by tilting the angle of the body at 45° to the ground, the backward and downward forces from the wings then become more nearly upward. In practice, the bird has to beat its wings more vigorously to obtain the extra lift needed. The larger the bird the greater this problem and large birds may have considerable trouble taking off; they have difficulty doing so because they cannot attain the air speed needed to prevent stalling. Most very large birds use additional aids to enable them to take off, they may run into the wind for example; by so doing they get an extra boost in that the air is already passing swiftly over their wings even before they start to fly. Another much favoured way of obtaining sufficient air speed is for the bird to launch itself from a cliff or tree and gain speed quickly by flying 'downhill'. Such a method is used not only by very large birds but also by those which have high stalling speeds such as auks and swifts. These species not only have difficulty gaining sufficient speed to fly, but they also have trouble losing this speed when they come in to land. Commonly they overcome this by aiming at a spot below their nesting site and at the last moment rising sharply, almost vertically upwards and using the force of gravity to slow them down. Such a technique requires considerable practice but may still be difficult, even for experienced birds, if the wind is unfavourable.

The smallest living bird, the Cuban Bee hummingbird *Mellisuga helenae* is here compared in size with the eye of the largest living bird, the Ostrich *Struthio camelus*. The hummingbird is only about 2in (5cm) long and weighs less than 1/10oz (2.5g).

Wingspans compared. (1) The extinct pterodactyl *Pteranodon ingens* (not a bird) 26ft (8m); (2) the extinct albatross-like *Gigantoris eaglesomei* 20ft (6m); (3) *Teratornis incredibilis* an extinct bird resembling the condors, estimated at about 16ft (5m); (4) the extinct relative of the storks and pelicans, *Osteodontornis orri* 16ft (5m); (5) Wandering albatross *Diomedea exulans* 11½ ft (3.5m); (6) White pelican *Pelecanus onocrotalus* 9½ ft (2.9m); (7) Andean condor *Vultur gryphus* 9½ ft (2.9m); (8) Lammergeier *Gypaetus barbatus* 9 ft (2.7m); (9) Rough-legged buzzard *Buteo lagopus* 5 ft (1.5m). All are compared with the artist (10) who has an arm-span of 5½ ft (1.7m).

Size

Birds vary in size from the Bee hummingbird from Cuba which weighs around 1/10 oz (2.5 gm) or less, to the Ostrich. A large male Ostrich may weigh about 300 lb (135 kg). However, the extinct Elephant-bird *Aepyornis* of Malagasy was larger; this huge flightless bird stood over 10 ft (3 m) tall and is estimated to have weighed 1,000 lb (450 kg); its eggs contained around 2 gallons (9 litres) of liquid.

Two main factors impose limitations on the size of flying birds. Birds are very active and need to be warm-blooded. However, small bodies have relatively larger surface areas for their size than is the case with larger ones. Hence in small birds the heat of the body is lost more rapidly from the core through the exterior than occurs with large birds. As a result a very small bird such as a hummingbird uses up a great deal of energy merely trying to stay warm. Hummingbirds survive because for the most part they live in the warmer parts of the world (or in the USA only in the summer months) and in addition because they tend to go torpid at night. By reducing their high diurnal body temperature overnight they can economise on the amount of energy required to stay warm.

The limits imposed on the size of the largest flying birds are very different and are concerned with the energy required for flight. If one doubles the linear dimensions of a body the volume (or weight) increases by the cube, but the surface area increases only by the square. Hence if we compare two birds of the same relative proportions, but one twice as long as the other, the latter will have a wing area four times as large as the smaller bird but a weight eight times as great. Thus the wing loading (weight divided by wing area) of the larger bird will be twice that of the smaller. Flying for the larger bird is thus more difficult. In order to provide the same power, the larger bird must beat its wings more powerfully. Hence in practice our hypothetical pair of birds are not possible; the larger bird must have more powerful and therefore larger wing muscles than the smaller one. This in turn causes problems since the larger muscles weigh more.

The largest flying birds are likely to be as large as is practicable. It is probably no coincidence that birds of several different orders reach similar weights, in the region of 30–35 lb (13.6–15.8 kg). It is also no coincidence that we find that the large majority of such birds 'cheat' in that they find ways of getting extra help when taking off and often do not use powered flight to any great extent. Vultures, eagles, cranes, storks and albatrosses all fly under conditions when upcurrents help them to spend a great part of their time aloft soaring rather than flying, and all migrate by routes which minimise the distances over water where flapping flight would be necessary. Pelicans also use thermals to some extent and frequently flap for a few seconds and then glide for some distance.

In order to be able to fly, large birds have evolved more severe modifications to the skeleton than have smaller birds. Birds have hollow bones in order to reduce their weight, but larger birds have taken this to greater lengths than smaller ones. The larger eagles and albatrosses have more hollow bones than are found in smaller species; and in the larger storks, such as, for example, in the Marabou, even the toe bones are hollow.

Pelicans, swans and geese economise on the effort required for flight by flying in formation. When a bird flaps its wings it produces a slightly increased pressure on the underside in addition to the slightly reduced pressure that occurs on the upperside. As a result air spills round the tip of the wing in an upward direction in order to reduce this difference; this phenomenon is known as induced drag. The resultant air flow produces a little upward eddy of air at the tip of the bird's wing. By flying just above and behind another bird an individual can make use of the lift provided by this upward air current and so save itself effort. This is just what birds flying in V-formation are doing; by changing the leader from time to time, each bird saves itself a considerable amount of energy.

The world's largest birds, past and present, are found among the flightless species. Some of these fairly dwarf the human form. The man in the picture – the artist himself – stands at about 6ft (1.8m). The birds measure as follows: (1) The extinct penguin *Anthropornis* 5ft (1.5m); (2) Emperor penguin *Aptenodytes forsteri* 4ft (1.2m); (3) Cassowary *Casuarius casuarius* 5ft (1.5m); (4) the extinct *Diatryma* 7ft (2.1m); (5) Emu *Dromiceius novaehollandiae* 6ft (1.8m); (6) the largest member of the extinct family of moas, *Dinornis maximus* 10ft (3.1m); (7) Ostrich *Struthio camelus* 8ft (2.4m); and (8) *Aepyornis maximus*, largest member of the extinct family of elephant-birds 10ft (3.1m).

Flightless Birds

While flight may be the most striking form of locomotion used by birds, all birds also use other methods of progression, using the legs either for running or for swimming. A number of species of birds have become flightless during the course of evolution and so rely solely on one of these other means of locomotion. The penguins are one well-known group and the ratities, which include the moas, Elephant-bird, Emu, Ostrich, rhea, cassowary and Kiwi, are another. The rails have produced a number of flightless species usually on islands, the New Zealand Takahe being an example; other relatives of the rails, the Madagascan mesites and the Kagu from New Caledonia are also apparently flightless.

Other flightless species include the Dodo and the Solitaire of the Mascarene islands (probably related to the pigeons), the Kakapo (a New Zealand parrot), some steamer ducks, the Galapagos cormorant, a grebe from the lakes in the High Andes and, of course, the Great auk. Only one species of passerine is known—or believed—to have been flightless. This is the Stephen Island wren of New Zealand which is now extinct. Some other island passerines fly only very rarely.

We can say that these species have become flightless during the course of their evolution with some certainty, for it is most unlikely that any of these birds developed from lines of birds that never flew. Although all species have reduced wings and flight muscles that cannot support flight, all show many characteristics of flying birds. They have the hollow bones and the air sac-systems of flying birds together with the reduction in weight of the extremities, the shortening of the tail and so forth which are believed to be adaptations for flight. Almost all the species have wings and even when these are rudimentary they still show the same basic plan as the wings of flying birds; one can barely escape the conclusion that the wings of flightless birds were, in their ancestors, larger and more effective. Secondary flightlessness must have been developed at a relatively early stage in the history of birds. *Hesperornis*, a relatively early fossil bird, had a body rather like a diver, but very tiny wings; thus, already in the cretaceous, some 70 million years ago, there was a bird whose ancestors had clearly flown.

Why should birds become flightless? There are probably several reasons. Flying is an immensely expensive activity in terms of energy. In order to fly the bird must obtain much greater amounts of food than if it remains on the ground. This alone is an inadequate explanation; why should a bird not merely retain the wings but fly only when the need arises? The answer is that the maintenance of the flying apparatus, especially of the huge flight muscles, is expensive. These muscles may weigh up to about one sixth of the total weight of the bird and must be supplied with oxygen and food. It is an oversimplification to say that one sixth of a bird's food requirements go towards maintaining the flight muscles, but a bird with smaller muscles would need less food than the one with larger flight muscles. Hence at times of food shortage the former would have a greater chance of survival than the latter and so, under conditions where flying was not essential, evolution would favour reduction of the wings and their muscles. There could be other reasons for their reduction; birds the size of Ostriches could not fly anyway, they are too large, and so, in the course of evolution they have evolved large legs for running but have lost the power of flight. Birds such as auks which use their wings for 'flying' under water need small wings for this purpose and they do not fly well; the logical extension of such an adaptation is to become still more aquatic and lose the power of flight, as the Great auk and the penguins have done. There are grave dangers in this course since if a new enemy arrives and flight becomes necessary, these birds are relatively defenceless; even marine birds must come ashore to breed. Such dangers are all too obvious where man has arrived on the scene, and island forms such as Moas, Elephant-birds, the Great auk, the Dodo, the Solitaire, some of the rails and the Stephen Island wren have all been exterminated by man or by animals that he has introduced.

Some birds are efficient runners even though they retain the ability to fly. (1) Cream-coloured courser *Cursorius cursor*, (2) Greater roadrunner *Geococcyx californianus*, (3) Gallito *Rhinocrypta lanceolata* and (4) Steere's pitta *Pitta steerii*.

Running birds. (1) Emu *Dromiceius novaehollandiae,* (2) Kiwi *Apteryx australis,* (3) Ostrich *Struthio camelus,* (4) Rhea *Rhea americana* and (5) Crested tinamou *Eudromia elegans.*

Some ducks such as the Teal *Anas crecca* (1) can take off from the water almost vertically. Other water birds such as the Moorhen *Gallinula chloropus* (2) must run on the surface of the water before take-off.

Cormorants *Phalacrocorax carbo* swim low in the water and can gently submerge by pressing their feathers to their bodies, thus decreasing their buoyancy.

The Scaup *Aythya marila* (1) is able to dive for food, while the Whooper swan *Cygnus cygnus* (2) is able to tilt its body in the water to forage.

Most swimming birds have webbed feet, but some such as the Black rail *Limnocorax flavirostra* have long toes that enable them to walk on floating vegetation.

Swimming birds. (1) The Shoveler *Anas clypeata*, a dabbling duck found throughout most north temperate areas, (2) Peter's finfoot *Podica senegalensis* from central and south Africa, (3) the Grey phalarope *Phalaropus fulicarius* which nests in the high Arctic in this red plumage and is hence sometimes called the Red phalarope. It spends the winter, in grey plumage, at sea, (4) The Pochard *Aythya ferina* a diving duck from the Old World, (5) the Black-necked grebe *Podiceps nigricollis* which occurs in many north temperate areas and also in Africa and (6) the Smew *Mergus albellus* a small saw-billed duck from temperate areas of the Old World. ⇨

Swimming

Fresh and salt water cover great areas of the globe and birds would miss great opportunities if they were unable to make use of these habitats and their rich food supplies. Many species use them widely, their main limitation being that no bird nests on water, all must come ashore to breed. Birds from no fewer than 21 different families in nine orders swim often and well—penguins, divers, grebes, petrels, pelicans and their relatives, ducks, rails including finfeet, and waders (jacanas, phalaropes, gulls, terns and auks). All of these are groups that taxonomists consider to be ancient; none of the supposedly more modern groups have swimming representatives. No passerines swim with the exception of the Dipper and although this species both walks and 'flies' under water and obtains most of its food there, it can hardly be said to be well adapted to aquatic life in comparison with members of the other groups.

Many of these groups swim in very different ways from one another, some using their wings and others primarily their legs. The feet are adapted for swimming and here again this has been achieved in many different ways; the obvious way is development of webbed feet, but even here there are differences in that different groups have different amounts of webbing. By no means all swimming birds have webs; some groups have modified the feet in other ways. The grebes, coots, finfeet and phalaropes have lobed edges to the toes and these provide the birds' swimming power. The rails and jacanas have long toes with broadened and flattened undersides which provide their propulsion. Many of the most specialized swimming birds have extremely flattened legs which offer a minimum of resistance to the water. This adaptation reaches its height in the grebes and divers where, in cross-section, the leg is three to four times as long as it is wide.

Birds belonging to three orders swim mainly with their wings. These are the penguins, auks, some of the diving ducks and some of the petrels, especially the diving petrels. Water is a much more resistant medium than air and a bird could not 'fly' through water with a large wing as easily as it could do through air. Accordingly, both the auks and penguins have very small wings and while these act as good oars in the water, the auks find flying relatively difficult. Some of the diving ducks have solved the problem in a slightly different way in that they 'fly' under water with the wing folded, effectively using only the folded wing, and this perhaps only to a slight extent; the main propulsion coming from the feet. However, the wing may perform another function in these species in that the wing, or just the bastard wing, may be slightly spread so as to form a stabilizer in the same way that the forearms of dolphins act to stabilize during swimming. The wings of penguins are highly adapted for use in swimming. Although the bones are of the pattern and number found in flying birds, they are very flattened and expanded and take up most of the area within the wing; in addition, unlike other birds, the elbow and wrist joints are fused to give greater strength. The wing is covered with small, almost scale-like, feathers which provide a smooth surface to the oar. During the course of evolution birds have faced several problems which they have had to overcome in order to be able to swim efficiently, since the demands for swimming conflict with those for flying and walking. If a swimming bird is too buoyant it will never be able to submerge. Hence diving birds need to be heavier than they should be for flight alone; size for size, diving species have fewer hollow bones than have other birds and relatively smaller air-sacs. Most swimming birds have particularly dense layers of body feathers in order to insulate them from the cold water. The feathers of some aquatic species are specially adapted with very long barbules, many rather erratically arranged so as to form a dense matt. By trapping large quantities of air, these feathers aid the birds buoyancy. Swimming birds spend a considerable amount of time preening ther feathers with waxy substances from their preen gland. If these are removed by washing the bird in detergent, the bird cannot float. This is one of the problems associated with cleaning oiled seabirds, unless the detergents are extremely carefully removed afterwards the bird cannot be

released to sea with safety. However, in order to dive, the birds must reduce their bouyancy and this they do by sleeking their feathers and squeezing out some of the air. Cormorants reduce their buoyancy by having less waterproof feathers than many other species; hence the reason why they are to be seen standing on rocks with their wings held out to dry. Other species such as grebes may carry stones in their stomachs; it has been said that these not only aid digestion by acting as grit, but also serve to help the bird submerge.

A diving bird such as a Gannet, which may drop into water from a height of 30 ft (9 m) or so, suffers a considerable impact on entering the water. Such diving species have fewer hollows in the bones of the skull, presumably in order not to damage themselves on impact with the water. Gannets have a dense mass of subcutaneous air-sacs over the front of the skull and these may help reduce damage from impact when diving.

Most diving birds do not descend to great depths nor do they stay underwater for long periods, two or three minutes being the normal maximum. However, some divers and the Long-tailed duck have been recorded as descending to about 200 ft (60 m) and certain birds, when forced to do so, can remain submerged for 15 minutes without breathing. In order to be able to do this, they possess certain adaptations such as being able to draw oxygen from the oxyhaemoglobin which is stored in the muscles. In addition, they have a high tolerance to carbon dioxide so that they are not forced to breathe until it reaches much higher concentrations in the lungs than would be the case in humans.

The feet of swimming birds are positioned towards the back of the body; as with the propellers of a ship, the most efficient propulsion comes from this position. However, such a position creates some difficulty for the bird when it comes ashore. It is not easy to walk with the legs placed so far back since the centre of gravity is far forward of the hips. Many of the shearwaters, the divers, the grebes and some of the diving ducks are extremely poor at walking. The penguins, and to a lesser extent the auks, have solved the problem in the same way that man has; they stand upright. However, they cannot move with any speed in this position and for their safety the auks are dependent on living near a cliff off which they can easily launch themselves if danger threatens. The penguins may lie down and 'toboggan' if they are in a hurry when on land.

The body of swimming birds is shaped more like a bullet than the more spherical body of most other birds; such a shape allows faster progress through the water. When diving to any depth the body is subject to great pressure from the surrounding water. Here again the more solid skeleton helps to withstand the pressures. To further aid the strengthening, the ribs are stronger than those of other birds and the uncinate processes, which in most birds occur on each rib and overlap the rib behind, in some seabirds overlap two other ribs and give much greater strength to the skeleton.

All birds have to cope with the problems of staying waterproof and keeping warm, but because of the contact with water these problems are more serious for swimming birds. If water penetrates the feathers the amount of heat lost by the body increases greatly; even if this does not happen, the cooling effect of water in close proximity to the bird is sufficient to cause the bird to use up a considerable amount of heat. Water birds have particularly densely packed plumage, often with an unusually thick layer of under-feathers. As already mentioned, water birds spend a considerable amount of time preening their feathers with waxy substances from their preen glands. During the moult, when the birds' feathering is temporarily reduced, they may have to stay out of the water for longer periods; some of the ducks and, in particular, the penguins spend almost the whole period of the moult on land; the penguins build up thick layers of fat on which they can draw during the fast that accompanies the moult. In spite of the good insulation, water birds still lose heat through the extremities, especially the beak and the legs which are not feathered. The legs of many swimming birds are adapted to save as much heat as possible.

Phalaropes such as this Grey phalarope *Phalaropus fulicarius* disturb small organisms in the water on which they feed, by swimming in small circles, usually spinning on their own axes. This illustration shows a single bird in several positions.

When danger threatens, the Moorhen *Gallinula chloropus* submerges and retains its position in the water by holding onto underwater vegetation.

Instinct and Intelligence

Birds show a remarkable range of behaviour. Many of their habits are exceedingly intricate; for example nest-building in some species involves a wide range of activities including the choice of a good site, selection of the right materials—often different at different stages in the building operations—and a number of weaving and turning movements. Nevertheless, a pair of young birds breeding for the first time may successfully undertake these activities and go on to raise a family. Earlier observers tended to put all these activities down to 'instinct' and leave it at that.

Though much still remains a mystery, we now know a great deal more about the behaviour of birds. Careful study has shown that many of a bird's activities are learned and perfected during its life. However, a number of behaviour patterns are still innate in that the bird is born with the ability to do them. This can be tested by raising a young bird in isolation from all others and observing that it behaves in a way characteristic of its species even though there has never been the slightest possibility of learning the behaviour from others. Certain aspects of the songs of many birds are inherited. However, like so many inherited abilities, these are not perfect and the bird has to use them time and again in order to master them. Contact with others of its own species will certainly help the bird to perfect them, especially in the case of song. Again, a species may have a 'sensitive period' in which a certain ability is most likely to become fixed. For example young geese become 'imprinted', in that they learn to follow moving objects soon after hatching. In nature this is, of course, normally their parents, though in captivity it may well be a

Intelligent behaviour in (A) the Cedar waxwing *Bombycilla cedrorum* in which a bird close to a food source will pass fruit to a less well placed individual; (B) the Goldfinch *Carduelis carduelis* which can lift food to its beak using its feet.

Intelligent behaviour in the Hooded crow *Corvus cornix* which behaves in a similar way as the Goldfinch to lift fish caught on lines set by eskimos.

The Black-throated honeyguide *Indicator indicator*, renowned for its ability to guide other animals, especially ratels and more recently man, to the nests of honey bees.

The habit of storing food is well developed in some members of the Corvidae, particularly the Nutcracker *Nucifraga caryocatactes* which is seen here recovering nuts during the winter.

One of the best-known examples of learning in birds is the speed with which the Blue tit's habit of opening milk bottles spread once the birds had learnt that they contained an easily exploited food source.

man. In some species this tendency is very marked within the first 24 hours and then much less so; it is also difficult to reverse. In the case of song, the bird is most likely to modify its song in relation to its neighbours during the period prior to its first breeding season, many months after it was hatched. Hence many activities may include innate aspects as well as those perfected by practice and copied from other individuals.

Watching others of its own species and copying their behaviour is an obvious way in which young birds can learn to cope with their environment. In particular it is very important that young birds learn as quickly as possible which objects are dangerous and which impose no threat. For many species the early days after leaving the nest must be very important and the parents' guidance extremely valuable. Nevertheless, it must be stressed that in other species such as some of the megapodes, shearwaters, swifts and cuckoos, the young birds get no help at all from their parents after leaving the nest. Indeed in the case of the megapodes and cuckoos they may well never see their parents. Nonetheless the young birds survive sufficiently well for the species to prosper.

Learning by trial and error and continued practice may also be very important. New objects must be examined and efforts made to see if they will yield food. Several species can learn to pull up long pieces of thread so as to reach food attached to the end; a combination of feet and bill may be used to do this. Once a bird finds a new source of food, others may swiftly copy it and the new habit will spread rapidly through the population. The habit of opening milk bottles is a good example. In Britain it seems that this habit originated in Southampton in about 1929 and then spread rapidly outwards to different areas.

One must be very wary of discussing how intelligent birds may or may not be. For example parrots and members of the crow family are often thought of as being particularly intelligent. However, the criteria on which such an assumption is based are that the birds can learn to do things that man wants them to do. Birds have evolved their complex range of habits in relation to what has proved best for them in their natural surroundings. Under these circumstances they probably never need to be able to count (though in tests, crows show a simple 'numbers sense') or to do the tricks that man requires of them.

Similarly, actions that seem stupid to us are probably merely those that birds have not needed to adapt to in the wild. For example many species react to certain stimuli with a fairly stereotyped response. The red breast of a European robin acts as such a 'releaser' for other robins, the reaction depending on whether the other bird is a male or a female. However, a robin will show an almost identical response to a bunch of red breast feathers as it will to a live bird. Other species such as some of the waders prefer to incubate eggs larger than their own; these create a 'super-normal stimulus' and the bird may ignore its own eggs in its efforts to incubate giant dummy eggs. Both these activities seem stupid to us, but would never occur in the wild.

Similarly because different species may differ widely in their behaviour it does not follow that one is more less intelligent than another. For example, guillemots and penguins can learn to recognise their own young from a very early stage; in the former species at least, this happens before the young bird hatches since it calls from the pipping egg and the parent learns to recognise these calls. By way of contrast, parent tits cannot recognise their own young nestlings at all. In the guillemots the young birds may get muddled up with one another and the parents need to know which are theirs if they are to feed them. In the tits which nest in holes in trees their young could virtually never get mixed up with those of another brood and so there has been no need to evolve this habit of learning to recognise their own young.

Song

Humans tend to notice birds because they use the same sense organs as we do. The most important one is perhaps colour vision, but hearing lies a close second. Birds tend to have ears that detect the same kinds of sounds as man. They hear, and of course communicate, over a similar range of wavelengths as man. Possibly they are less good at hearing at either end of their scale than a human with good hearing. At any rate the outcome is that they make their calls within the range that is perceptible to humans and we thus appreciate their songs.

The ear of birds is in many ways similar to that of man; in addition, the voice of birds, although produced from a slightly different structure to that of man, bears some resemblances. The ability of some species of birds, such as mynahs and parrots, to mimic man's voice shows that they can produce sounds closely similar to those that we make. One distinctive feature of the voice of birds is that some can produce as many as three or four complex sounds that overlap one another in time; in other words the voice-producing organ can produce different sounds that are not just harmonics of one another simultaneously.

The other important feature of the voice, and hearing, of birds is the speed with which a message can be transmitted and received. Some complex songs may include as many as 80 notes per second. Such sounds seem like a single continuous note to the human ear and can only be seen not to be so by examination of sound spectrograph recordings of the song. Not surprisingly, if the bird can give such calls it can also receive them. The speed of the auditory response of birds may be of the order of ten times as fast as that of man.

The animal kingdom has developed many ways of transmitting messages, but sound is a particularly useful form of communication. Sound travels well in most of the habitats in which birds live and is a much better method of communication in habitats such as woodland than any other type. Thus it is not surprising that birds use sound as one of their most important forms of language.

Bird songs are the most elaborate series of message in the language of birds. Song

A Winter wren *Troglodytes troglodytes* in song. Wrens have well-developed songs which are often relatively loud. Several species maintain their territories for most of the year, and may be heard regularly throughout this period. Song is not only used in territorial defence, but also in a wide variety of other circumstances connected with courtship and nest-building.

Coots *Fulica atra* defending their nest against a marauding polecat. Birds have many methods for defending their nest against predators including the giving of alarm calls so that the other member of the pair, or sometimes other birds, may come to their assistance.

Blackbird *Turdus merula* feeding young. Young birds stimulate their parents to feed them by giving begging calls; the more intensely they call the harder the parents work to feed them. Only when the young are fully satiated do they stop calling for food.

During the breeding season the Snipe *Capella gallinago* has an aerial display which it accompanies with a drumming noise, produced by the passage of air over the outermost pair of tail feathers. The noise can be reproduced by fitting a Snipe's tail to a weight and whirling it overhead on a string.

has tended to be connected with the 'song-birds' (Passeriformes), but this is a very misleading view for two reasons. Firstly some non-passerine birds have complex and beautiful calls—the trilling song of Redshank or Greenshank and the laugh of the Kookaburra to take but two examples. Secondly, other birds with, to us, simpler calls use them apparently in the same way as do the more complex singers and therefore, at least to the other members of the same species, these calls also qualify as song.

Song is not usually produced equally at all times of the year, but is mainly concentrated during periods prior to breeding when territories are being set up and courtship undertaken. The tendency to sing appears to be closely correlated with the presence of sex hormones in the blood and these, of course, reach a peak around the time of breeding. In many temperate species, there is a brief resurgence of territonal behaviour and also of singing in the autumn just after moult has been completed. Song also varies within the day in relation to the bird's other activities, being commonest in early morning or in fine weather and less frequent at other times.

As has been mentioned, songs may be relatively complex. They are, however, highly characteristic, each species usually having a very distinct song. A complex song usually includes a series of notes that are formed into a recognisable pattern; also, the song is often of a fairly characteristic length though it may be repeated again and again.

There are probably three main functions of the song and the importance of each may vary between different species. By recognising their own type of singing, birds achieve reproductive isolation from other species. By singing, a male bird announces his claim to a territory and also endeavours to attract a mate.

Although the song of each species is characteristic of that species, each individual male bird usually develops a song that is slightly different from that of his neighbours.

Song is an ideal means of communication between birds especially in such habitats as woodland, where it is difficult to maintain contact between individuals by any means other than sound. The Three-wattled bellbird *Procnias tricarunculata* (1) lives in thick forest but its calls can be heard at a considerable distance. The passerines generally have the most complex songs, a good example being the Blackbird *Turdus merula* (2). However, such birds as the Oriental hawk-owl *Ninox punctulata* (3) which have simpler calls, do not necessarily have simpler vocal organs, and there are many passerines, for example, the Jackdaw *Corvus monedula* (4) that also have relatively simple calls. Most birds sing with the bill wide open, but the doves make their cooing notes in the throat, usually with the bill closed, as in the Collared dove *Streptopelia decaocto* (5). The parrots, such as the Eclectus parrot *Eclectus roratus* (6) are well known for their harsh screaming calls but many of them are extremely good mimics and can be taught to talk.

Although they may sound similar to us, there are subtle small differences. By recording the songs of individuals and playing them back to the birds it has been established that the birds themselves can easily distinguish between the songs of their neighbours and those of strangers. A territory holder does not respond vigorously to the song of a well-known and established neighbour, but reacts sharply to the song of a stranger. The known neighbour with whom the territory owner has already established some form of 'working agreement' does not pose the same threat to a territory holder as does the sudden appearance of a strange bird that might be trying to usurp his place. Hence the difference in the response. Curiously perhaps, the bird does not seem to recognise his own song, as some species may react to this as they would to that of a stranger.

Other variations within a species have been established. In many species not only does the individual have a recognisable song, but the individuals may have a variety of different songs; repertoires of up to six or eight different song types have been described within individuals. It is not known whether each of these variants carries a different message to others of the species. Attempts to find correlations between the

1

2

3

4

5

6

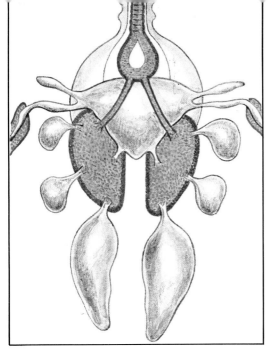

Birds are unusual in that they have air-sacs, thin bags through which air can flow after passing through the lungs. They are thought to aid respiration when the birds are in flight. The air sacs extend into the hollow bones.

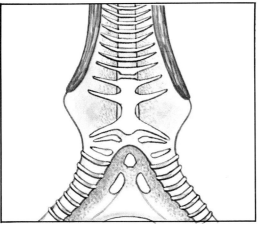

The syrinx is the bird's sound producing organ. The resonating chamber or tympanum is at the bifurcation of the windpipe and contains vibrating membranes formed from the connective tissue between the cartilages. Special muscles control the tensions and positions of the membranes, allowing different sounds to be made.

The trachea through which the air is passed from the nostrils to the lungs is a strong tube strengthened with cartilaginous rings which prevent it from collapsing.

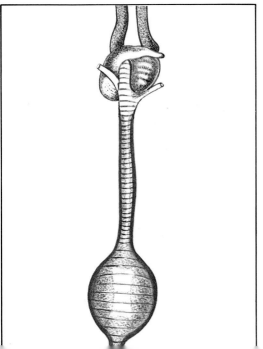

different songs in a repertoire and the circumstances under which they are given have so far proved unsuccessful. Birds appear to switch from one song to another after they have been singing one for a period of time; it is as if they get bored. However, when two birds are actively engaged in a border dispute, they may tend to use the same song type as each other. If one bird switches from one song type to another, the other bird will often follow suit.

One also commonly finds local variations in the songs of different species. These 'dialects' may occur over quite large areas or they may be local in extent. Simply by crossing over from one valley to the next one may find that the song of a given species has changed quite markedly. The European Chaffinch is a species with many different local dialects. Needless to say, on a wider geographical range the language of a species may differ much more than on the local scale.

In recent years some observations have helped to establish how some of these variations come about. Birds raised in captivity in sound-proof cages still develop a song which, although poor and rather muddled, is recognisably that of their own species. Such a song starts particularly poorly and slowly improves although it never reaches a very high standard of performance. It is clear therefore that such birds inherit some ability to produce a song of the basic pattern of their species. When these birds are allowed to hear the songs of others of their own species they rapidly incorporate details of the other songs into their own and so improve their song. Thus their songs could be said to comprise both inherited and learned components. If the birds that are raised in isolation are played songs of other species, even others with fairly similar songs, they do not copy these. Thus, to recognise the song of another species is an inherited ability.

There seems to be a period when the young bird is particularly sensitive to hearing the songs of others of its kind and is most likely to copy songs from other individuals. This sensitive period is often when the bird is approaching one year old—coming up to its first breeding season. Nevertheless, birds may go on adopting phrases from others and improving or modifying their own song throughout their life.

By and large, song is produced by the males and not by the females of a species. However, there are exceptions, some of which suggest that the females of many species may be capable of singing, but just do not do so very often. A female Great tit has been observed in full song defending the territory when her mate was sick for a few days. When he recovered she stopped singing. Female European robins sing regularly in autumn when they maintain their own independent territories. In the phalaropes (where the female takes the dominant role in courtship) the female sings and the male does not. Female Canaries, given doses of male hormones, have developed songs as good as those of males.

There are a number of species in which the female regularly sings. These include species where members of a pair sing to one another, a habit known as duetting. A particularly complex form of duetting is found in some of the African shrikes of the genus *Laniarius*. This type of singing is called antiphonal singing. One bird sings a short snatch of song and the other sings the next. Often the song may be composed of just the two parts, but in other species such as some of the Asian Laughing thrushes, the song may be much more complex with alternate snatches of the song given by each partner. Indeed the whole song is so well synchronized and given so rapidly that even a human observer watching closely cannot be certain which parts of the song are given by which bird. This can only be established by filming in conjunction with sophisticated tape-recording equipment. Such equipment can also produce sound spectrograms which can be analyzed in detail. Such analyses have shown that the speed of response of the second bird to the first bird is extremely fast, at least three times as fast as is possible for humans. This confirms a point made earlier, namely that although the auditory equipment of birds shows many similarities to that of humans, the ability to separate sounds that are close together in time is far superior in birds.

Hole nesting species such as the Great tit *Parus major* may defend themselves by making a loud hissing when a predator such as a squirrel tries to enter. This sound is said to resemble the hiss of a snake.

Displays and calls of Little ringed plover *Charadrius dubius*. When threatening another of its own species (1), the plover exposes the black facial and breast bands fully to its opponent. When the parent bird warns the young of approaching danger (2), they scatter and crouch until the 'all-clear' is given. When a predator is close to the eggs or young (3), the parent may try to lure it away by dragging a wing and pretending to be unable to fly. Once the predator is a safe distance from the nest the bird flies off.

Warning and Fear

As with behaviour in general, one has to be extremely cautious in interpreting the behaviour of other animals in terms of love, hate and fear; it is all too easy to become uncritically anthropomorphic about such activities, to the extent that we think that we have explained them in terms of how we ourselves would feel, when in reality the reason for the animal's behaviour may be quite different. We can, however, see a number of circumstances where birds give calls that have the effect of drawing another bird's attention towards, say, an approaching predator and so enable it to take evasive action. Also birds plainly show avoidance of a number of objects that could be harmful to them; while the behaviour may not necessarily be fear in human terms, it is certainly adaptive for them to take such evasive action quickly.

For the vast majority of birds, there is almost always the threat of danger lurking somewhere and so caution pays off; discretion is the better part of valour. In practice birds soon learn to recognize the inoffensive from the enemy; in the first instance this is done by the young bird observing the reactions of its parents. Later, as knowledge accumulates, the bird only reacts to strange or unknown objects, being wary of these until it has had a chance to gauge the possible threat. Many birds can remember dangerous objects for long periods.

Once an enemy is identified, the bird can take appropriate action. If the marauder is a mammal, the bird can easily avoid it by staying clear of the ground. If, however, the threat comes from another bird then it must be avoided in another way. This might entail diving into thick bushes, onto or under water or trying to outpace it, depending on the species of bird threatened and the area in which it is. Often such flight is accompanied by alarm calls, warning the neighbouring birds of the threat. There have been a number of arguments about the dangers to the individual bird of giving an alarm call and so perhaps attracting the predator to itself. However, these

1

2   3

Woodpeckers may respond to seeing a predator or hearing an alarm call by hiding. Here a Great-spotted woodpecker *Dendrocopus major* ducks under a branch as a Sparrowhawk *Accipiter nisus* passes over.

In some conflict situations, such as when a bird is uncertain whether to attack or flee from another, it may indulge in some quite different behaviour. Here (1) an Oystercatcher *Haematopus ostralegus* hides its beak under its feathers in a sleeping posture. On other occasions, birds will mob a predator vigorously and often succeed in driving it away before it can find the eggs or young. In (2), Lapwings *Vanellus vanellus* mob a Carrion crow *Corvus corone*.

dangers may be outweighed by a number of other factors. Firstly parent birds have to give such calls in order to protect their offspring and secondly there are occasions when there is safety in numbers; by grouping tightly together the birds may be able to make it difficult for the attacking predator to single out and catch any one individual. Faced with a number of rapidly moving prey the predator becomes confused and is unable to make a decision. Thus European coots may pack in a tight group and splash up water when threatened by an attacking White-tailed eagle.

The alarm calls given under these conditions are very characteristic; they are thin, high notes which are particularly difficult to locate; hence they are unlikely to pose a great threat to the bird that gives them. Most species have a variety of warning calls that they give under different circumstances, enabling the other birds to gauge how frightened the calling bird is and of what it is frightened. Many species can 'understand' the notes of other species. For example the warning call described above is given by a number of small passerines, and the mobbing calls of Blackbirds when they have discovered a Tawny owl are also understood by many species. The mobbing probably helps each bird to learn where the potential danger lies and also, perhaps, to drive off the owl. The loud shrieking cries of captured birds may well be 'fear', but they also function to attract other birds to mob the predator and so, hopefully, distract his attention from the prey so that it may escape.

Young birds quickly learn to recognize many of their enemies from the reactions of their parents; they also learn to recognize and give the calls. Small birds, still in the nest, will crouch and remain silent when they hear their parents warn of an approaching predator; they learn to do this before they are a week old. Young nidifugous birds may learn to crouch when warning calls are given at still younger ages, sometimes when they are only a few hours old.

1

2

Bobwhite quail *Colinus virginianus* roosting in a circle. These birds haunt large open areas and by using this formation can guard against predators approaching from any point of the compass.

Masked wood-swallows *Artamus personatus* huddled together for roosting. By choosing a secluded site and keeping close together, they reduce the amount of energy needed for overnight survival.

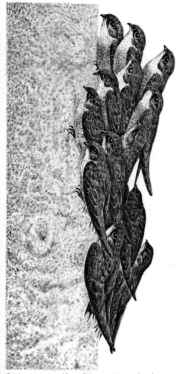

Chimney swifts *Chaetura pelagica* roosting in a huddle. Several other species of aerial insectivore have been recorded clumping together in bad weather.

Sleep

Birds tend to sleep at those times of the day when they cannot feed. Thus not only do day-feeding birds sleep at night and nocturnal birds during the day, but birds such as waders and wildfowl sleep when the tide is high and they cannot feed. Typically, many sleeping birds insert their bill under their feathers and many of the smaller birds sit down on their legs, covering these with their fluffed-up feathers. By doing this, the birds cover the parts of the body from which heat can be most easily lost and so help to conserve energy. When perched in this way the birds are able to lock their feet to the branch securely. The tendon that curls the toes around the branch tightens as the joints bend and loosens as they straighten. Hence, as a bird sinks down onto its feet and relaxes its leg muscles, its feet become firmly locked around the branch.

Birds may roost singly or in huge numbers. Quelea roosts in Africa often contain many millions of birds and starlings may roost in small areas of woodland in numbers reaching into the millions; at times they may roost in such numbers that their droppings kill the trees. Some small birds, and some penguins, roost together in clusters in order to obtain warmth from one another. Long-tailed and bush-tits roost huddled together more closely in cold weather than in mild weather. Migrating swallows, confronted with cold weather, may occasionally clump together in large groups for the same reason. Some small birds that roost in holes or in their domed nests may also roost together. In Europe many Winter wrens are sometimes found roosting together in a single hole. Others, such as some of the sparrows, may build themselves a winter nest in which the pair shelters from the cold.

Some other birds conserve energy by becoming torpid at night. By doing this, the difference between the body temperature and that of the air is reduced and so the rate of heat loss is reduced. The best known example of this type of torpidity occurs in the hummingbirds. These very tiny birds would lose relatively large quantities of heat overnight unless they were able to go torpid. Some of the small birds such as the tits may lower their body temperature at night in very cold regions.

In order to minimize heat loss, roosting sites are normally chosen in sheltered positions where the wind and rain and most intense cold will not penetrate. A few Arctic species such as the Redpoll and some of the game birds roost in burrows in the snow. Such a position enables them to get some protection from the severest night temperature though presumably a few must perish by being buried in a very heavy snowfall and being unable to dig their way out in the morning.

Finding a position that is relatively sheltered from the weather is only one of the main prerequisites of birds. They must also find one where they are relatively safe from predators. This need undoubtedly dictates the use of a well-sheltered place in thick foliage where the bird will not be visible to owls. Some ground-dwelling birds, for example the Common pheasant, fly up into trees to roost where they are safe from predators such as foxes. Others may roost in the middle of open ground where they have ample warning of approaching enemies. Quail are reported to sleep in a small circle, facing outwards, so that they have a good opportunity to see any predator. Almost certainly one of the functions of the very large roosts is protection from predators. If one bird sees, or is attacked by, a predator it gives the alarm to all the others.

Many water birds roost either on islands where they are relatively safe from predators or in the middle of a large expanse of water. The flights of gull towards reservoirs at dusk are now a familiar sight in many areas of the world. Under such conditions, deep sleep is impossible because the birds need to swim from time to time to avoid drifting to the bank.

A few species have odd roosting habits. Woodpeckers roost on the vertical trunks of trees in much the same position that they are seen to cling during the day. European treecreepers also roost in this position, but in crevices in the soft bark of trees. At

The Poorwill *Phalaenoptilus nuttallii*, a nightjar, is the only bird known to hibernate. Whether it spends the whole winter in a state of torpidity, or merely a few days at a time is not, however, known. Several other groups of birds become torpid for short periods, often only overnight. These include the swifts, humming-birds and colies, all species closely related to the nightjars. In the Colorado Desert in California, a Poorwill has been recorded hibernating in the same rock crevice during four successive winters.

Dunlin *Calidris alpina* roosting on tidal flats. Many waders have to feed at low tide and so sleep at high tide regardless of whether it is night or day. Much of their feeding is done by touch.

times they may hollow out the bark for this purpose and several birds may roost in adjacent hollows. The bat-parrots, *Loriculus*, hang by their feet, upside down, from the branches where they roost; hence their name.

Among the most extraordinary roosting habits known is that of the Common swift of Europe. Very many of these birds spend the whole of the night on the wing. These birds do not find it easy to land or take off from the ground and seem unwilling to touch down. The breeding birds, of course, have to have a nest site, but many of the non-breeding, younger birds do not appear to have a site where they can spend the night. These birds can be observed circling in the evening over reservoirs and then rising upwards at dusk. Radar observations show that they spend the whole night aloft. Since the same birds seem to be involved each night, it is possible that individuals may not land at all during the whole of the summer. Since roosts have not been noted in their winter quarters, it is just possible that Common swifts do not land at all except to breed and may spend their early non-breeding years totally aloft. It is not known how they are able to do this or to how many species of swift this may apply. Individuals of other species are known to roost in caves and rock crevices. The dusk ascent is thought to be associated with the need to be above the level where there is any danger of flying into obstacles.

Many birds cannot sleep deeply since they are quickly on the wing if disturbed. One suspects that it is necessary for many of them to sleep lightly for fear of predators. However, those birds such as the hummingbirds that go torpid become so deeply asleep that they may take several minutes to awaken since it is necessary for them to re-heat their bodies before they can become active again.

FEEDING

Many birds need to drink frequently. The majority of species do this by dipping the beak into water, filling the mouth and then raising the head to let the water run down the throat, as shown in the Song thrush *Turdus philomelos* (1). The pigeons differ in being able to drink continuously, sucking the water up with a pumping action as in the Turtle dove *Streptopelia turtur* (2).

The Golden eagle *Aquila chrysaetos* drinking.

Eating and Drinking

As a result of their lack of teeth, birds feed rather differently from mammals. The food is not chewed at all, but transferred to the gizzard where it is ground up. Many birds eat their prey whole. At times this may involve the swallowing of lizards, snakes, large insects or fish that are large in relation to the size of the bird. The majority of birds, however, take smaller prey than this; finches, warblers and thrushes for example take prey that are usually of sufficiently small size for them to be easily swallowed. Others such as the gulls and many birds of prey tear up larger prey with their beaks. Yet others such as the ducks and game birds may eat foliage.

Birds do not usually prepare their food, but there are exceptions. Many bee-eaters remove the stings from their prey before swallowing them. The bee is beaten against the perch and then vigorously wiped along the perch removing the sting. Birds that eat large insects, for example caterpillars which have powerful biting mouthparts, usually peck the head of their prey. This prevents the possibility of the insect biting the bird after it has been swallowed. In some cases the head capsule of the insect may be completely discarded. Occasionally birds remove the gut of caterpillars.

Feeding is a dangerous occupation since the bird must concentrate upon it and therefore run the risk of not noticing the approach of a predator until it is too late. In some cases the use of the crop may be advantageous since it enables the bird to feed in an exposed site for a very short period and then to retire to a safer place where it can digest the food that it has collected. Another situation when feeding may be dangerous is when sea birds come down to catch fish driven to the surface by larger fish. The birds risk becoming the prey themselves. Drinking is often dangerous too. Some birds obtain most of their water from their food, especially the insectivores and birds of prey which may never need to drink, but many other species must come down to water. In doing so the birds expose themselves to predators. This is especially true in the drier areas of the world where birds must congregate in large numbers at the few water holes available. The birds of prey know only too well where these are.

Many small birds may satisfy their needs from the dew or rain by merely sipping drops off the vegetation. Others such as the swallows and swifts collect water by accurate dives across the surface of lakes and rivers. Most birds use the same method as does the domestic hen; the beak is lowered into the water, the mouth filled and the head raised so that the water runs down the throat. The pigeons, sandgrouse and buttonquails are able to drink by dipping the beak into the water and sucking it up with a pumping action.

Sea birds face special problems since the available water is very salty. When they drink seawater, the majority of the salt is transported, through the blood supply, to the nose where it is transferred to large nasal glands which eliminate most of the salt from the body—their kidneys are relatively inefficient in this respect. When it has drunk a large quantity of salt water, a sea bird looks as if it has a cold. Droplets of highly concentrated salt run to the tip of the bill and are shaken off with a flick of the head.

The Pine grosbeak *Pinicola enucleator* feeds largely on pine seeds. The male is red and the female greenish-brown.

The bill in seed eating birds are modified to cope with a variety of size and hardness of seed coats. Short, stout bills are required to crack heavy seeds.

A male Goldfinch *Carduelis carduelis* forages for thistle seeds.

Seed Eaters

Compared with mammals, birds do not always digest plant material efficiently; they do not have the ability to break down cellulose and digest leaves and grass in the same way that mammals do. Even those species that feed to a large extent on grass, such as the geese, do so by consuming great quantities of vegetation from which they extract relatively little of the available nutrients. The parts of plants which birds can and do eat in quantity are the seeds and fruits. A wide variety of birds consume one or other of these as a regular and major component of their diets. Amongst non-passerines one might list many of the ratites, the tinamous, a number of the ducks, the game birds, a number of gruiform birds, the sandgrouse, the pigeons, the parrots and the woodpeckers. Amongst the passerines, some tits, nuthatches and crows eat seeds for long periods of the year; however, the seed eaters *par excellence* are the finches of the four families Emberizidae, Fringillidae, Estrildidae and Ploceidae. Together there are some 600 species within these groups and the large majority are seed eaters for a major portion of the year. Not only are they very numerous, in terms of species, but also many of the species are exceedingly abundant; for example the pest of African grain crops, Quelea, may occur in colonies or roosts of many millions and devastate an area.

Seeds are hard structures and many are relatively difficult to break open and eat; often they are covered by a very thick outer shell or by a spiny case. A few species such as the Emu and the proverbial Ostrich seem able to swallow exceedingly spiky seeds and to digest them somehow or other. Most of the other birds that tackle the stronger seeds have ways of breaking into them: many such as the ducks and pigeons take only smaller seeds without strong coverings so that the problem does not arise to the same extent. Nobody who has seen one of the larger parrots opening seeds would readily put his finger near its beak! Indeed some of the finches can exert a considerable crushing force and, for its size, even the Blue tit has a powerful bite.

The larger parrots and macaws can crack open very large seeds with great ease; the bill of the Palm cockatoo is so deep and powerful that it can open the hard nuts of palms with relative ease. Some of the finches have equally remarkable strength. The Hawfinch opens cherry and olive stones to get at the seeds inside; it has been demonstrated that a cherry stone requires a crushing load of from 65–80 lb (30–36 kg) to break it open while the equivalent power required to open an olive stone is 106–159 lb (48–72 kg). Yet this two-ounce (56 gm) bird is able to achieve these strengths and split the stones. Hawfinches have immensely heavy, powerful skulls and beaks with extremely large muscles; the mandibles are protected from dislocation by a strong ligament that is partly ossified.

It is normally accepted that closely related species survive alongside one another by virtue of each species taking different foods; in this way they divide up the resources of the habitats. In the finches the different species tend to take seeds of different sizes, the larger species taking the larger seeds. The bills of the finches are specially adapted to deal with seeds and each size of bill is best suited for husking seeds of different sizes. The sharp edge of the lower mandible fits into a V-shaped cleft in the upper mandible. Using the tongue, the finch positions the seed in this cleft so that the joins in the husk or stone are in a position against the sharp edge of the lower mandible.

The shape of the bird bill has been modified to take advantage of a large variety of foods. (1) The Galapagos Woodpecker finch *Camarhynchus pallidus* uses a twig to probe for insects, (2) the European Nightjar *Caprimulgus europaeus* has bristles round the mouth which help to trap insects, (3) the North Atlantic gannet *Morus bassanus* has a stout, pointed and conical bill and dives from a considerable height into the water, (4) the anhinga *Anhinga anhinga* impales the fish with its sharp bill, (5) the American greater flamingo *Phoenicopterus ruber* has marginal hooks for filter feeding, (6) the African Spoonbill *Platalea alba* feeds while wading, sweeping the partly open bill from side to side.

The Black or Palm cockatoo *Probosciger aterrimus* uses its powerful beak to crack open hard palm nuts and extract the contents with the pointed tip of the bill.

The Hawfinch *Coccothraustes coccothraustes* (1) has a very powerful beak capable of splitting cherry stones while the Redpoll *Carduelis flammea* (2) with its weaker bill eats small seeds such as those of birch. The Australian Star finch *Bathilda ruficauda* (3) and the South African Waxbill *Esrilda melanotis* (4) are both members of the Estrildidae a family of small finches that feed mainly on small grass seeds.

After part of the husk has been cut through by the mandibles, the seed is rotated and another crack made, until all the husk has been removed. The groove in which the seeds are held is wider at the back of the skull than at the front so that seeds of different sizes can be accommodated. If the seed is too large it shoots out of the cleft when pressure is applied. Hence there is an upper limit to the size of the seeds that each species can handle efficiently. Since large finches find it uneconomic to eat small seeds, each species tends to be restricted in its diet to a range of seed sizes related to the structure of its bill.

Seed eating birds face other problems in relation to their diet; they need powerful gizzards with a good supply of grit in order to break up the seed. Seed eaters usually possess a crop, a bag-like extension of the side of the lower throat in which food can be stored. Those birds that bring seeds back to their young carry them in the crop. Many of the birds, especially the smaller finches, go to roost in mid-winter with a crop full of seeds, enabling them to have a 'snack' in the middle of the night and so increase their chances of survival. Lastly, the possession of a crop enables the birds to feed rapidly in exposed places and digest the seeds later in safety.

Relatively few of the seed eating birds eat seeds the whole year round. For example the tits are largely insectivorous during the summer season and many of the finches raise their young on insects as well as seeds; there is a tendency for birds that have late broods to feed the young larger quantities of seeds than they brought to their earlier broods. This may reflect the increase in the number of available seeds, but caterpillars are becoming scarcer at this time as well and this may, in part, account for their diminuition in the diet. The full reasons for feeding insects to the young are not known, but insects are probably richer in certain proteins necessary for animal growth than are seeds. In addition, insects contain large quantities of water which are essential to a growing chick; seeds do not. The periods of the year when birds change over from a diet of seeds to one of insects and back again may be difficult ones for the birds. The digestive tract is more powerful and muscular when the bird is eating seeds than it is when the bird is eating insects; little is known of what happens during the period of changeover from one diet to the other.

Four different seed eaters. (1) Cardinal *Richmondena cardinalis* of North America, (2) Evening grosbeak *Hesperiphona vespertina* also of North America, (3) Greenfinch *Chloris chloris* of Europe and (4) Red-cheeked cordon bleu *Uraeginthus bengalus* which occurs on the southern side of the Sahara from Senegal to the Sudan.

Two of the most northerly seed eaters, the Snow bunting *Plectrophenax nivalis* and the Lapland bunting *Calcarius lapponicus*. Both these birds breed in the high Arctic though the Snow bunting also breeds in mountains further to the south. Both migrate southwards for the winter.

Some finches remain on a diet of seeds the whole year round and feed their young on them. Their breeding seasons closely match the timing of their main food stocks of seeds. In many parts of Britain the Crossbill feeds its young on the seeds of pine cones, finding them most plentiful when the cones open in spring. In order to have its young in the nest in March and April when these seeds are available, the Crossbill lays its eggs before this date, often in February or early March; hence the females may be incubating during some of the coldest weather of the winter. In many parts of continental Europe, the Crossbills feed their young on the seeds from spruce cones which open even earlier; under these circumstances the birds may be found breeding at almost any time during the winter. As a result, the Crossbill has perhaps the most variable breeding season of any species of European bird. By way of contrast, the Goldfinch brings very small seeds of herbaceous plants to its young and often does not start breeding until May, having young in the nest from June onwards when the new crop of seeds is plentiful. If conditions are suitable the Goldfinch may go on nesting through until late summer; it is one of the latest European passerines to nest.

Seeds keep well and as a result, many seed eating birds store seeds so that they can find them during the winter when food is more difficult to come by. Jays and Old World nutcrackers store large seeds such as acorns and hazel nuts as do the Acorn woodpeckers. Smaller birds such as tits and nuthatches store small seeds in crevices in the bark from which they retrieve them later. During late summer and early autumn the birds may spend a high proportion of their time storing seeds.

53

The Toucan barbet *Semnornis rhamphastinus* (1) lives in the mountains of northern South America. Like other members of the family it eats large quantities of seeds and fruits though, like many finches, it takes insects to its young. Head of Toucan barbet *Semnornis rhamphastinus* (2) The powerful beak has serrations on the side which enable the bird to grip and cut into fruits easily. Barbets also use their bills for tearing wood when making nesting holes.

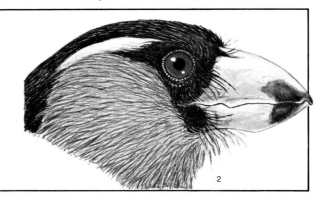

The Green imperial pigeon *Ducula aenea* of India and South East Asia takes very large fruits which it can swallow because it has a distensible gape. Such fruits often have large stones which the birds void undamaged.

Fruit eaters. (1) Knysna turaco *Tauraco corythaix* from Africa, (2) Bartailed trogon *Trogon collaris* from South and Central America – many trogons also eat insects which they catch on the wing, and they take fruits by hovering alongside branches, (3) Toco toucan *Ramphastos toco* from South America, (4) Yellow-bellied fruit pigeon *Leucotreron cincta* from the East Indies, (5) Double-toothed barbet *Lybius bidentatus* from central and east Africa and (6) Blue-crowned hanging parrot *Loriculus galgulus* from South East Asia. ⟹

Fruit Eaters

Seed eating birds remove the offspring from a plant. Because of this, plants have evolved many mechanisms which make it more difficult for animals to remove seeds. For example, seeds may have hard shells or the trees may have short, well-synchronized seeding periods so that the animals have more food than they can possibly eat at one period and a dearth of food at another. From the evolutionary viewpoint, the strategy of a fruiting plant is quite different; we may say that it 'wants' the bird to eat the fruit in order that the seeds may be spread around. Although the fruits are highly digestible, the seeds are extremely resistant to the digestive juices of birds and usually pass through the gut undamaged.

In order to encourage the bird to eat and so distribute the seeds, the plant provides the fruit as a 'reward'. However, in order to have as many fruits as possible the plant grows fruits that are only just nutritious enough to attract birds; if they were less nutritious the birds could not survive on them and if they were more nutritious the plant would not be able to set so many seeds. Hence fruit eating birds eat a diet that is often poor in nutrients and they may have to spend long periods of the day feeding in order to get sufficient food. In further contrast to seed bearing plants, fruiting plants often bear fruits over long periods of the year in order that all their fruits may be taken by the birds. The relationships between fruit ripening and seed ripening have not been well worked out, but many fruits are bitter and distasteful as well as green in colour until the seeds are ripe; at this point the sugars are put into the fruit and it becomes highly coloured as a 'signal' to the birds that the fruit is ready to be eaten.

Fruits are often relatively large in size and, as a result, many of the fruit eating species have wide bills and gapes, enabling them to swallow the fruits whole; the toucans not only have a large bill, but a long one which enables them to reach small fruits from a strong perch. Once swallowed, the soft fruit is relatively rapidly broken down and digested. Although small seeds are passed through the digestive system, the large seeds of some of the tropical fruits are regurgitated.

In temperate areas fruits are not available all the year round so that many species that eat fruit at one time of the year may have to have other diets at other times of year. Many of the insectivorous migrants hunt for fruit in late summer and may concentrate upon the rich supplies of blackberries during the period when they are laying down the fat for their migration.

In Europe many fruits ripen at the time that small migrants are most abundant in the area. For example, plants may flower first in southern areas of Europe such as the Mediterranean and flowering occurs progressively later the further north one goes; however, the same does not hold for the fruiting seasons of many plants. The fruits ripen first in the northern areas, fruits in the southern areas maturing so slowly that they ripen after those in the north, but at the same time as the migrant warblers are passing through. It is difficult to escape the conclusion that the plants are timing their fruiting so as to coincide with the presence of the largest number of fruit eating birds.

In the tropics fruit may be available all the year round and several groups of birds feed largely on such a diet. The manakins and cotingids of South America and the fruit pigeons of Africa and southern Asia are good examples of such species, but many other less specialized species will take fruits when they are in abundance.

One tropical fruit eating species which deserves special mention is the Oilbird of northern South America. Although probably related to the insectivorous nightjars, it has taken to a diet of fruit. Like its relatives it is nocturnal, spending the day in dark caves where it finds its way about by echo-location. The Oilbirds leave their caves at night and set out in search of fruits. They feed mainly on the fruits of palms and of species of the family Lauracae, all highly aromatic fruits. Since the Oilbird has particularly well-developed olfactory lobes to the brain, it seems virtually certain that they possess a good sense of smell and track down these fruiting trees by scent.

Insect eaters. (1) Flamed minivet *Pericrocotus flammeus* from India to South East Asia, (2) Firecrest *Regulus ignicapillus* from western Europe, (3) Bearded tit or Reedling *Panurus biarmicus* from Europe to central Asia, (4) Black-billed scythebill *Campylorhamphus falcularius* from South America, (5) Paradise flycatcher *Tersiphone paradisi* from India to South East Asia, and (6) Raquet-tailed drongo *Dicrurus paradiseus* from India and Malaya.

Insect Eaters

Although typically one tends to think of the small passerine insectivores, a wide variety of birds eat insects. Many of these are, at first sight, relatively unspecialized for this purpose—those such as the warblers having small all-purpose bills. One reason for this is that many insectivorous species turn to other diets at other times of year. It has already been mentioned that tits and other temperate birds such as the warblers eat fruit extensively prior to migration. For all-too-obvious reasons it is not possible to be a full-time insectivore in temperate areas.

The truly specialized insectivores that take insects the whole year round may, broadly, be divided into two types—those with stubby bills and huge gapes and those with long pointed bills. The latter group, which includes birds such as the bee-eaters, catch large flying insects and then return with them to a perch where they prepare them for eating, if necessary beating out the sting of the bees. Bee-eaters occur throughout much of the warmer areas of the Old World, with one species migrating for some distance up into the temperate areas. In South and Central America there is a remarkably similar group of birds, the jacamars, which feed in the same way.

The birds with stubby bills and broad gapes include a few that take large insects, such as the nightjars and the puffbirds, but many others take much smaller prey. These include the swifts and swallows. Some of these species take very tiny prey such as aphids and young spiders that are being blown along on their gossamer threads. When raising young, swifts take back large bolusses of insects to their brood. It may take some hours to collect such a large ball of small insects and some young swifts may only get fed four or five times a day or even less frequently if the weather is cold and insects are not plentiful. All these birds that feed on aerial insects are dependent on good supplies the year round; they do not change their diet. Almost all those that hunt prey in the temperate areas depart to spend the winter in more tropical climates.

Nightjars, (1) (Capirmulgidae), swallows, (2) (Hirundinidae) and swifts, (3) (Apodidae) have extremely broad gapes which enable them to scoop insects out of the air.

56

Birds that catch insects on the wing. (1) European bee-eater *Merops apiaster* from southern Europe and west Asia, (2) Rufous-tailed jacamar *Galbula ruficauda* from Central and South America, (3) Vermilion flycatcher *Pyrocephalus rubinus* Central and South America and (4) Puerto Rican tody *Todus mexicanus*.

The Great reed warbler *Acrocephalus arundinaceus* breeds in Europe and southwest Asia. Like almost all insectivores it migrates south outside the breeding season, spending the winter in tropical Africa. Here, a parent bird shades its young from the sun.

In North America a nightjar, Nuttall's poorwill, hibernates to overcome this difficulty though even this species may not hibernate for the whole winter; it may come out to feed on occasions when the weather is favourable.

A wide variety of other species of birds take insects, though not quite as dramatically as the swallows, bee-eaters and flycatchers which hawk them on the wing. The warblers feed primarily on insects which they glean from the foliage. Treecreepers and nuthatches climb up and down the trunks of trees searching for insects hidden behind the bark; the nuthatches may probe deep into the bark in their searches. In South America the woodhewers have evolved a wide range of birds that, like treecreepers, probe amongst the bark of trees. Perhaps the most specialized of insectivores that hunt for their food in the trunks of trees are the woodpeckers which drill holes into the burrows of beetle larvae and withdraw the grubs with their long tongues; the tip may be barbed or sticky to help them grip their prey. In the Galapagos Islands the Warbler-finch uses a sharp thorn to probe in holes for grubs, spearing them and pulling them out; it is one of the few animals known to use a tool regularly.

Many large birds also feed on insects. Birds such as rollers, hoopoes and hornbills take many large insects in their diet. Storks and herons may feed on large grasshoppers; the Cattle egret has acquired its name from its habit of closely following the cattle so that it can pick up the insects disturbed by them as they walk through the grass. Many of the marsh-dwelling terns eat insects. Birds of prey too may feed on insects: some of the smaller falcons include a high proportion of insects in their diet and even larger birds such as kites may descend on swarms of locusts and devour them. At times of great abundance such as these, many birds that do not regularly make use of insect food will join the hunt; for example, large numbers of species may be seen feeding on termites when these hatch.

57

The Red-throated diver *Gavia stellata* nests on islets or beside freshwater lochs and feeds on the sea; it is often seen flying between the two places, bringing food to the young.

The Puffin *Fratercula arctica* is a highly colonial fish eating bird. It digs its burrows in soft soil, often preferring burrows already made by rabbits or other birds. The parents bring as many as 20 or 30 small fish to the young at a single feed.

Common eider *Somateria mollissima* is a sea-duck that is widespread along north temperate coasts. It feeds in shallow water on a wide range of shellfish, crabs and mussels.

Fish and marine invertebrate feeders. (1) Oyster-catcher *Haemotopus ostralegus* eats a wide range of shellfish and crabs and also takes worms and insects inland, (2) Turnstone *Arenaria interpres* turns over small stones and seaweed in its search for invertebrate food, (3) Arctic tern *Sterna paradisea* takes a wide variety of small fish, (4) Black-throated diver *Gavia arctica* takes larger fish, in the breeding season these may be fresh water species from near the nest, (5) Razorbill *Alca torda* feeds its young mainly on small sandeels and (6) Rockhopper penguin *Eudyptes crestatus* is widespread in the Antarctic. ⇨

Fish Eaters

Species of six orders of birds (penguins, divers, grebes, petrels, pelicans and herons) feed predominantly on fish, though not all the individual species do so. In addition to these a number of ducks, a few birds of prey, most gulls and terns, skimmers, auks and kingfishers feed largely on fish, as also do a few species of owls. Curiously no passerines do this, though the Dipper may eat eggs of various fish.

The different species hunt their prey in a wide variety of ways. Some dive and swim after them catching them from behind; these include the cormorants, mergansers, auks, penguins, divers, grebes and petrels. Others, including pelicans, Gannets, terns and kingfishers, dive upon them from above; all these must chase their prey briefly except for a few of the terns that pluck their prey from the surface. The fish eating birds of prey and owls plunge down on the prey and catch them in their talons. Herons stalk them along the bank or in the water and then pounce on them.

Fish are extremely slippery prey and birds have evolved several adaptations which reduce the chances of their escaping. Some, such as the petrels and cormorants, have a sharp hook on the end of the upper mandible with which they grab their prey. Others, such as the herons, darters, kingfishers and penguins, use the open mandible to 'spear' the prey, giving them two chances of striking home, though more often they catch the fish accurately between the mandibles. The darters have two specially adapted neck vertebrae which enable them to catch their prey more easily; the birds swim with their necks folded back, but when they reach forward to try and catch a fish, the configuration of these vertebrae enables them to 'snap' the neck over at great speed. Similarly the long necks of the herons enable them to reach forward a great distance when they stretch out to strike at prey.

Once captured, the prey must be held firm so that it cannot escape. Again, a wide variety of methods are used. Many herons have backward facing serrations along the sides of the bill, penguins have them mainly on the tongue. Mergansers have tooth-like extensions to the sides of the bill which they clamp into their prey. Some such as the auks and cormorants may bite the prey hard on its initial capture in the hope that it will not be able to struggle any further. The owls, Ospreys and sea eagles have particularly long talons which sink into their prey and greatly roughened pads on their toes which enable them to prevent their prey from slipping. Most of these fish eating birds, including the owls, have unusually long legs which are bare of feathers; presumably this reduces the amount of water-logging when the bird strikes the water.

Some of the terns take their prey without ever settling on the water; they just snatch them off the surface. Indeed a number of sea birds are only poorly water-proofed and do not normally settle on the water. Such species include not only some of the terns, but also the frigate birds and some of the storm petrels. Whether they rest or how they do so is not known; certainly since they only make landfall in the breeding season the storm petrels do not come to land to rest.

Another group of species which do not usually catch their prey by settling on the water is the skimmers; these species have a remarkable way of catching fish. They feed on tiny fish and prawns that lie just below the surface of the water. A skimmer's beak is unusual in that the lower mandible is half an inch or so longer than the upper one and also in that it can raise its upper mandible well out of the way of the lower mandible. The bird flies along maintaining a very precise level just above the surface of the water with the tip of the lower mandible cutting through the water. As it makes contact with a small fish beneath the surface the bill snaps shut as a result of a reflex action and the fish is caught. It does not seem that sight is involved in the capture though it must be in the maintenance of the bird's position above the water. Skimmers will even fish in drying pools only an inch deep, so accurate is their flight.

Sight is important for predatory birds, but fish eaters have two problems to contend with that other species do not encounter. A heron aiming at a fish underwater has to be able to allow for the refraction of the water, since the fish is not exactly

The American darter or snake-bird *Anhinga anhinga* catches fish by stabbing with its beak open, thus doubling the chance of successfully spearing its prey. It then surfaces and turns the fish round so that it can swallow it head-first.

The Shelduck *Tadorna tadorna* searches through fine estuary mud for small snails. It uses a scything action while hunting and may leave tracks in the mud.

The King penguin *Aptenodytes patagonica* is one of the largest living penguins. Penguins eat crustaceans and squid as well as fish and may dive to considerable depths while hunting.

where it appears to be. No one is sure exactly how they do this: it may be that the young have to learn how much to allow for when they are fishing with their parents; in some species even birds of one year old are not as successful at fishing as are the older individuals so that the learning process may be long. Birds swimming after fish underneath the water have a different problem. The optical characteristics of water are different from those of air—as anyone who has opened his eyes underwater in a swimming pool will testify. Mammals such as seals have evolved eyes that suit the underwater conditions better than those in air, hence their, at times, apparent blindness when one approaches them. Some diving birds have come up with a better solution. Birds have a second, inner eyelid—the nictitating membrane. In diving species the central area of the membrane is clear but thickened; the membrane is kept across the eye while the bird is underwater and acts as a supplementary lens which makes the eye suitable for seeing underwater without the loss of good vision when the bird is in the air.

Fish eating birds have a wide variety of ways of bringing the fish back to their young. Some such as the skimmers bring back a morsel of prey each time that one is caught; this is a time-consuming operation and severely restricts the distance from the colony at which they can profitably feed. Other birds such as some of the terns bring back a small number of prey in the bill. Many of the auks do this also, though they may return with still larger numbers of prey. The Puffin is noted for its beakful of food; as many as 30 or more small sand eels may be brought in on a single visit. The Puffin catches the prey underwater, nipping it between the two mandibles and then transferring it so that it is held between the tongue and the upper mandible, thus allowing the bird to open its beak and catch further prey. Others such as the Gannet may bring the food back in their crop and the pelicans use their pouch. These birds usually travel further in search of food and so would waste too much time travelling if they did not bring back large quantities at irregular intervals. The extreme example of this habit is reached in certain oceanic sea birds such as some petrels and shearwaters where the birds may not return to the nest more frequently than every four or five days. In order to bring back the maximum amount of food they partially digest the fish they catch. Since fish are about 70 % water, by doing this the birds can get rid of the water in the prey and bring back a full load of food which, weight for weight, is much more nutritious than if they brought it back undigested.

Although one tends to think of all sea birds as fish eaters, a number of species may specialize in other prey. Many of the smaller storm petrels patter along the surface of the water taking small crustaceans or other plankton. Some of the larger shearwaters and petrels specialize in feeding on krill, the widespread shrimp-like animals. Some albatrosses take jellyfish, including some of the venomous ones, having apparently developed some form of immunity to their stings. Albatrosses and penguins also take a large number of squid in their diet as do some of the terns and smaller shearwaters.

The feet of a vulture (1) and an eagle (2). The vulture can walk and run well on the ground but does not have the powerful gripping talons of the eagle. The eagle, however, cannot walk on land as well as the vulture.

The Palmnut vulture *Gypohierax angolensis* is an unusual bird of prey in that it has adapted to feeding on the fleshy parts of the fruits of the Oil palm.

The Everglades kite *Rostrhamus sociabilis* feeding exclusively on large aquatic snails. Its specific name *sociabilis* was given to it because of its colonial nesting habits.

The Secretary bird *Saggitarius serpentarius* is an aberrant bird of prey which feeds largely on snakes. It strides around on its long legs and kills the snakes with powerful blows from its feet. When attacking a snake it holds its drooped wings in front of itself, apparently to avoid being struck in the body by its poisonous adversary.

Birds of Prey

Two orders of birds, the Falconiformes and the Strigiformes, are usually classified as the 'birds of prey', often being referred to as the diurnal and the nocturnal birds of prey respectively even though a few of the owls are also diurnal. Although not closely related, the two groups have evolved a number of remarkable similarities that enable them to take their prey. There are similarities in the shapes of their bills and talons, both of which perform the same functions in the two groups, namely those of grasping their prey and of tearing it up to eat it. The positioning of the eyes in both groups is also similar, facing well forwards; possibly this increases the stereoscopic vision so essential to a bird that hunts moving prey.

The size of the prey taken—and the savageness of the larger birds—has usually been grossly exaggerated. Eagles may occasionally attack sheep, but almost always the sheep is seriously ill or dying before the eagle will risk doing so. Carrying off lambs or even small children are way beyond their capabilities; they could not hope to fly with such a load. As a result of this reputation however, the birds have been greatly and almost always unnecessarily molested and even exterminated. Sadly this habit still goes on, not only in the uneducated parts of the world but also in Europe and North America.

The largest birds of prey are the eagles, condors and vultures. The largest species may have wingspans of as much as eight or nine feet (about 2.5 m); a few much larger records are almost certainly exaggerations. Not all these birds kill their prey and most are not above scavenging from carcasses if they get the opportunity. Indeed these are the staple diet of the African vultures which usually, contrary to legend, feed only on freshly dead prey, if only because it is so swiftly consumed that they would get no other chance. The vultures do not carry food in their feet, but may so gorge themselves that they have difficulty taking off. The South American vultures, but not apparently the Old World species, have strong powers of scent and can locate decomposing bodies by this means; since some of these birds hunt over dense forest presumably they would have no chance of finding carrion there by any other means. One of the largest vultures, the Lammergeier, has learned to drop bones from a height onto rocks so that they break open and the bird can extract the marrow.

The larger eagles take a wide variety of prey, though on average much of this is smaller than believed; large objects tend to take longer to consume and so are noticed more frequently. Hares and rabbits are common prey for many species. The Wedge-tailed eagle of Australia takes some small wallabies, but now in many areas feeds largely on introduced rabbits. The Golden eagle takes many birds such as grouse and Ptarmigan. The White-tailed eagle takes many sea birds, and some tropical eagles specialize in taking monkeys from the tree-tops. The long-legged Secretary bird (usually put by itself in a separate suborder of the Falconiformes) is well known for its habit of taking snakes. A few other eagles also specialize in taking snakes as for example the Short-toed eagle—often called the Serpent eagle—which occurs through much of southern and western Europe and western Asia. Hence the prey taken is quite different for different species, but few prey are excessively large.

The Osprey *Pandion haliaetus* is a widespread, fish eating bird of prey. It has long, unfeathered legs and roughened pads on the toes which help it to grip its slippery prey.

Many predatory birds move their heads from side to side before attacking their prey; apparently this enables them to judge the distance more accurately. The bird shown here is a Black-and-white hawk eagle *Spizastur melanoleucus* from Central and South America.

The Peregrine falcon *Falco peregrinus* attacks an American bittern *Botaurus lentiginosus*. Although the Peregrine does not often take prey as large as that figured here, from time to time it takes very large prey, such as geese.

Many of the smaller eagles have similar diets to the larger eagles though they take still smaller prey. The falcons are noted for fast flying and many of them swoop onto their prey at speeds which they could not reach in level flight. Many of the faster falcons take other birds as food, though a few of the smaller ones take insects. In contrast the goshawks, also bird eaters, have broad wings and fly much more slowly; they have much greater powers of quick manoeuvre and can chase small birds through the thick branches of a forest, something a falcon could not do. The kestrels are relatively slow-flying falcons with the ability to hover in light winds over grassy meadows where they hunt for small mammals on which they drop from a considerable height.

A number of birds of prey are specialized for odd careers. The African Bat-hawk hunts bats in the twilight, and hawks of the genus *Daptrius* have become vegetarian. However, taken as a group, it is the predatory habits and their speed that has attracted man and certain species have been tamed and used for falconry for many centuries. Falconry dates from over 1,000 years BC and at times was the prerogative of royalty.

The method used by birds of prey in hunting require considerable skill and, like most such, the hunters can meet with bad luck or scarcity of prey. Success at hunting affects the breeding of the birds of prey. They usually have only a small number of young, say one, two or three, though a few of the smaller species may lay more eggs. The young hatch one after the other rather than all together; hence during growth there is considerable disparity in size between nestlings in the same brood. If food is scarce the largest easily gets sufficient and the smallest quickly perishes having taken little food that might otherwise have been given to the larger. If the birds were all of equal size, then all might have been weakened. Hence this habit of hatching asynchronously increases the chance that some young may be raised successfully even when food is scarce. Once the young have left the nest they are cared for by their parents for some time while they develop the necessary hunting skills. Some of the largest eagles and condors look after their young for more than a year and so only breed every second year. The young birds may not breed for many years until they have perfected their skills to the extent where they can get sufficient food not only for themselves but also for their brood.

In many species the two sexes differ markedly in size. Apparently such differences have been evolved since they enable the two birds of a pair to hunt for a different range of sizes of prey and so increase the potential food available to the pair.

The owls are in many ways similar to the diurnal birds of prey, except that most of them hunt at night. They have exceptionally good night vision, they have high numbers of rods—the light sensitive cells of the eye—and few cones—the cells associated with colour vision; hence they see well in poor light but probably can only see in black and white. The ears of owls are positioned asymetrically on the head; apparently this helps them to locate a sound with great accuracy since something heard most clearly with one ear at one position of the head will be heard more clearly by the other ear when the head is in a different position. Using hearing, some owls can locate the position of a prey with an accuracy of at least one degree in both the horizontal and vertical planes and probably a good deal more accurately than that. To increase its chances of striking its prey, the owl spreads its talons as widely as possible along the direction that the animal is moving.

Many owls specialize in catching small mammals while others take birds. The European Tawny owl eats many earthworms. On damp nights these come to the surface in the dark and rustle on the leaves in the same way that a mouse would do, and under such conditions the owls take them in large numbers. Like the diurnal birds of prey, owls tend to have relatively small clutches and the young hatch asynchronously. When food is scarce, clutches may be small or the birds may not breed at all. However, in a few cases such as the Short-eared owl and the Snowy owl which feed on voles and lemmings, the birds may have large clutches in years when their prey are very numerous; as many as six or eight eggs may be laid and raised.

Birds of prey. (1) Steller's sea eagle *Haliaeetus pelagicus* an inhabitant of the Pacific coast of Asia eating a Steller's eider *Polysticta stelleri*, (2) Swallow-tailed kite *Elanoides forficatus* which is found from southern USA to South America, (3) Bateleur eagle *Terathopius ecaudatus* from Africa eats a wide variety of small animals and also carrion, (4) Scops owl *Otus scops* and (5) Collared red-thighed falconet *Microhierax caerulescens* from Eurasia and Africa and from India and South East Asia respectively are very small birds of prey that feed mainly on insects though the owl may also take very small mammals and reptiles.

The Nuthatch *Sitta europea* takes a wide variety of insects in summer but feeds mainly on seeds and nuts in winter. It wedges nuts into a crack and hammers them open with its powerful bill.

Many species store seeds in autumn in order to increase their winter food supply. The species shown here are (1) Acorn woodpecker *Melanerpes formicivorus* from western USA, and (2) Grey jay *Perisoreus canadensis* from north Canadian forests. The woodpecker wedges nuts into holes it has made in the trunk of an oak tree, the jay sticks insects and seeds into crannies with the help of its own saliva.

The finfeet are represented by three species in different parts of the tropics. They take a wide variety of molluscs and crustacea and occasionally flying insects. This species is *Heliopais personata* from Asia.

Omnivores

As will have been apparent from the previous sections a great many birds take more than one type of food. Many show seasonal variation while others will not ignore a temporary abundance of any food that they can eat. Nevertheless there are birds that take a wide variety of foods at all times of the year, the jacks-of-all-trades. The Common starling is perhaps a good example of such a species; it may live in rural or urban areas, dig for small animals such as worms and wireworms in the meadow or plunder bird tables for food put out for other birds. In many areas they retire to the woods at the end of their nesting season, taking their fledged young with them to reap the caterpillars that have not yet completed their development. Soon after that they may return to gardens for the early soft fruits that are ripening; in places they may be a very serious threat to fruit growing.

The Common starling owes its great success in spreading over the wide areas of the world where it has been introduced to its ability to tackle such a wide variety of foods; in large measure it owes this ability to its 'all-purpose' beak. The medium length, straight beak enables it to probe the soil, pick caterpillars from leaves and reach and pull down fruits. In addition its strong feet enable it to perch easily in many places and on many types of twig. The Blackbird too is almost as successful at eating a wide variety of foods and has a similarly shaped beak.

Some of the gulls have also shown themselves able to cope with a wide variety of foods. The Herring gull has a longish bill with a slightly hooked tip. With this it is adept at catching fish; it probably did this most of the time before urban man appeared on the scene. The young gulls, in their brown plumage, stay on the shore much more than the older birds who are out at sea. Apparently the young gulls, being inexpert at fishing, augment their diet with quantities of odds and ends scavenged off the beach. A boat trip across the North Sea will be sufficient to show that the young gulls, although often prominent followers of ships close inshore, mostly drop out when the open sea is reached and only white birds follow the boat the whole way across. The hooked tip of the gull's beak serves not only to enable the adult birds to catch their prey, but also to help the young ones tear up dead fish and other offal on the beach. With this background of scavenging at least for part of the time, Herring gulls were well placed to make use of sources of food made available by man. Firstly they took the offal from fishdocks where the fish were cleaned, then they moved in and scavenged on the rubbish dumps that were placed on the outskirts of towns to deal with man's ever-growing piles of rubbish. In addition they discovered that the plough turned up huge quantities of earthworms and so they started to follow tractors across the fields. In recent years many gulls have spent more and more time in and around the coastal cities and are now spreading inland further and further and are also tending to remain there for longer periods each year. As a result of their ability to use these varied sources of food, the gulls have increased greatly in numbers until they have become quite a serious problem in some areas. They are therefore a good example of a species that has gained from the presence of man, unlike many others that have suffered from his influence.

Other scavengers are also good at eating a wide variety of foods. The Black kites normally scavenge dead animals or fish, but they too have learned the values of rubbish dumps; at other times they will turn to eating anything available and may descend on swarms of locusts in large numbers. As with gulls and the Common starlings, Black kites may be numerous in areas occupied by man.

All these birds could be called omnivores. There are, however, few birds that are truly omnivorous: seed eaters tend to remain seed eaters (though as we have seen, they may take insects in the breeding season) and relatively few other birds eat seeds in addition to their normal diet. It appears that either the bills, the digestive systems or the digestive enzymes of birds limit them to taking only a section of the full range of foods taken by all birds.

Omnivores. (1) Carrion crow *Corvus corone* from Eurasia, (2) Magpie *Pica pica* from much of the north temperate areas of the world, (3) House sparrow *Passer domesticus*, (4) Starling *Sturnus vulgaris*, (5) Spotted bowerbird *Chlamydera maculata* from Australia and (6) Little king bird of paradise *Cicinnurus regius* from New Guinea; bowerbirds and birds of paradise are closely related and take a wide range of fruits and insects. As a result of their omnivorous habits (3) and (4) have successfully followed man's civilization.

The Hoatzin *Opisthocomus hoatzin* is an unusual bird in that it feeds mainly on the leaves of certain riverine bushes. Here one of its young is seen reaching for food that the adult is about to regurgitate from the crop.

Specialized feeders. (1) Cattle egret *Bubulcus ibis* catches many large insects disturbed by big-game, it has spread through many parts of the world making use of man's cattle for the same purpose. (2) The Everglades kite, *Rostrhamus sociabilis*, and (3) Limpkin *Aramus guarauna* both live in American swamps feeding on large snails.

Specialized Feeders

As we have seen, most birds are specialized to some degree in the types of food they take or in the way that they take it. However, there are species that have particularly specialized ways of feeding; such methods often involve a highly specialized beak and this usually prevents them from being able to take a wide range of other types of food. Some birds, for example, are wholly dependent on a single species or group of species. The Limpkin, an American bird related to the rails but looking rather like a cross between a rail and a heron, feeds on large snails which it takes from shallow marshy ground. It apparently feeds on almost nothing else and even brings snails to the young which, at least at times, swallow them whole and later regurgitate the shell. Curiously, another species of bird is also dependent on these large snails. The Everglades kite, a rare bird in the USA but more numerous in tropical America, takes these large snails when they are near the surface; it picks them up in its feet and flies with them to a perch where it hooks the snail out of its shell with the long, curved tip of its upper mandible.

The African oxpeckers specialize in taking the ticks and mites off big game animals and, since the advent of man, have extended this habit to 'looking after' domestic cattle also. Not everyone believes that they are wholly beneficial since although they remove the parasites from open wounds in cattle they also sometimes eat the flesh and fat around the wound and so, it is believed, may extend the period for which the wound is open or even considerably enlarge it. Oxpeckers hang on the sides of large animals in the same way that woodpeckers hang on trees, and their feet are so adapted to perching in this position that they are not normally seen elsewhere.

It may not always be the bill that is specialized for taking an unusual diet. The

The hummingbirds of the New World and the sunbirds of the Old World, here depicted by (1) Purple-crowned fairy *Heliothrix barroti* and (2) Regal sunbird *Cinnyris regius* are highly specialized for the feeding on nectar. (3) The Dipper *Cinclus cinclus* feeds on insects which it catches in fast-flowing streams.

The Dipper *Cinclus cinclus* is adapted to take insects from the bottom of fast-flowing streams. It runs along the stones, at times flapping its wings to aid its progress. It is the only passerine bird that could be said to be a 'waterbird'.

honeyguides of Africa have a relationship with the Honey badger whereby they lure the animal to a bees' nest that they have found and once the badger has opened the nest they share the contents with him; they may also lure hunters to the nest. The unusual factor in the diet of these birds is that they eat not only some of the insects but also the bees' wax; this is not normally digestible by birds, but the honeyguides must have some special means of breaking it down. One species has even been recorded eating candles from a church altar!

In the warmer parts of the world there are a number of groups that specialize on feeding on nectar. In the New World the most striking group is the hummingbirds, over 300 species of tiny, brilliantly coloured birds. Their powers of hovering at flowers to obtain the nectar are well known: the smaller species may beat their wings as fast as 80 times per second. In Africa and much of the Oriental region we find the sunbirds which have a total of a little over 100 species. Again these birds are often brilliantly coloured and very small. They too may hover at flowers to obtain nectar, but they are not so proficient at doing so as are the hummingbirds. In the Far East, especially in New Guinea and Australia, another group of birds take nectar. They are the honey-eaters; about 170 species in all, these again include a number of small species, but lack the brilliant metallic hues possessed by many of the sunbirds and hummingbirds. In order to eat nectar many of these birds have the tip of the tongue divided into many hair-like processes. The white-eyes can roll the tongue into a tube. With this they 'brush' up the nectar and then suck it into their mouths. Even some of the lories and lorikeets of the Far East, have brush-tips to their tongues.

Specialization carries with it inherent dangers. Such birds are dependent wholly on a very special diet and if this becomes scarce or disappears then they face extinction. The very nature of their specializations does not enable them to switch easily to another type of food. Highly specialized birds have rarely been able to take advantage of man in this changing world; more often they find any change is for the worse. It is the omnivores such as the Common starling or the grain eaters such as the House sparrow that have benefited from the presence of man and have increased and spread widely.

67

HABITATS

Polar Regions

The polar areas of the world may be roughly defined as those where the mean temperature does not rise above 50°F (10°C) in the warmest month, and in which snow and ice cover the ground for long periods of the year. The polar regions of the south and north—the Antarctic and Arctic—differ in that the former area is frozen land surrounded by sea, whereas the latter is an area of frozen sea surrounded—in several places—by extensive land masses. These land masses support a variety of plant life during the short northern summer, but the Antarctic does not have a flora of equivalent richness.

Plant life forms the basis of all food chains. In order to grow, plants need sufficient light, warmth and nutrients; the first two of these are scarce in polar regions. Throughout the winter months there is little or no sunlight and thick layers of snow may cover the plants, cutting out what little light there is. As a result, plants in polar regions can grow only for short periods of the year. The animals which feed on these plants can likewise flourish only during these short periods.

In such inhospitable lands most birds cannot find food outside the summer period. In winter either there is no food at all or what there is lies covered with snow and ice and is totally inaccessible. An additional problem for the birds at such low temperatures is that they need very large amounts of food in order to provide the fuel to maintain their body temperature. It is not surprising therefore that most birds living in polar regions do so for only the short period of the summer months. Even so, their visit may be fraught with difficulty. The timing of both the spring thaw and the autumn freeze is very variable and so the breeding season tends to be a race against time in order that the birds may be able to raise their young and get away before winter returns. Many geese arrive in the Arctic with sufficient reserves to lay their eggs almost immediately and even to incubate them before food becomes available in the area. Hence they are able to start breeding well before they could if they were dependent on finding the necessary food on the breeding grounds. Many waders do not have time to moult after breeding and pause to do so on their southward migration. In some years a thaw may not come at all or comes so late that the birds fail to breed.

The presence of extensive land masses close to the pole in the Arctic, but not in the Antarctic, probably explains some of the differences between the birds found in these two areas. The Arctic tundra is covered with open valleys, streams and lakes in which plant life abounds. These areas are visited in summer by large numbers of birds which could not find a place for themselves in the Antarctic. Hence in the north there are many waders and wildfowl together with a few passerines, while few such birds visit the Antarctic.

The other habitat much favoured by birds of these regions is the sea, which is rich in nutrients and supports diatoms (microscopic plants), crustaceans and small fish. As a result we find an abundance of sea birds rarely matched in any other area of the world. The Antarctic is particularly rich in species, including large numbers of procellariform birds and, of course, the penguins.

The Adelie penguin *Pygoscelis adeliae* builds a nest of pebbles, probably in order to keep its two eggs above the ground so that they are not swamped by melting snow and ice.

The Sheathbill *Chionis alba* is a common scavanger in penguin colonies, taking eggs and unguarded small young and any food spilled during regurgitation, as is seen here.

Many polar species are white in colour, presumably as camouflage against enemies. Two high Arctic gulls, (1) The Ivory gull *Pagophila eburnea* and (2) Ross' gull *Rhodostethia rosea*. (3) The Antarctic Sheathbill *Chionis alba*, (4) McKay's bunting *Plectrophenax hyperboreus* from the Bering Straits, (5) Snow petrel *Pagodroma nivea* from the Antarctic, (6) Snow goose *Chen hyperborea* which breeds in Arctic Canada and (7) an adult Emperor penguin *Aptenodytes forsteri* standing by a creche of young. ⟹

Temperate Forests

Temperate forests once covered huge expanses of the northern hemisphere but being on soil that made good farming land they have been progressively reduced. These forests are very different in type and may be divided into coniferous and broad-leaved woodlands. The most northerly forests are coniferous, and conifers are also to be found in the higher, cooler zones on mountains where lower temperatures again prevail. To the south of the conifers lie the broad-leaved woods and these may again be subdivided into two: the northern broad-leaved trees such as the oaks, beeches and maples are deciduous, while the more southerly ones, occupying such areas as the Mediterranean and southern USA, are evergreen. As their name suggests, these forests occur in places where the climate varies greatly around the year.

Although the temperate forests of the northern hemisphere are much more extensive than those of the southern, the latter are very important habitats for a wide variety of animals. There are four main areas of broad-leaved temperate forest in the southern hemisphere: there is a restricted area of Mediterranean-like forest on the southern tip of Africa; secondly, Australia, with its rich and unique fauna, has a variety of sclerophyll forests—the trees are primarily eucalypts, some growing as high as 300 ft (90 m); and lastly, both South America and New Zealand have extensive areas of Southern beech *Nothofagus* forests which contain a large number of animals and birds that occur nowhere else. The inroads presently being made into these latter forests are of considerable concern to conservationists.

In forests the large trees are constantly striving to get as much light as they can in order to grow well or to set seeds and fruit; they grow upwards and outwards, reaching for the sky and forming a closed canopy. As a result, in a mature woodland little light may reach the forest floor and plant growth there is poor. Most of the bird life follows this trend with many more species living in the trees than on the ground.

The Eagle owl *Bubo bubo* is found over a large area of the Old World and north Africa. It eats a wide variety of prey, some quite large. Here it is seen swallowing a hedgehog. It will later regurgitate the spines.

Nutcrackers occur in the temperate forests of both the New World and the Old World. (1) Clarke's nutcracker *Nucifraga columbiana* from western USA and (2) the Eurasian Nutcracker *Nucifraga caryocatactes*. Both species store seeds for winter use.

The temperate forests of the Old and the New Worlds have many similar species of birds. (1) Sparrowhawk *Accipiter nisus* from the Old World, (2) Sharp-shinned hawk *Accipiter striatus* from the New World; both hunt small birds amongst the forest trees.

Woodpeckers are common in temperate forests. Here a pair of Great spotted woodpeckers *Dendrocopus major* tap to one another at a potential nest chamber they have made. The male has the red on the back of the head.

Two features of temperate forests have overwhelming effects on the bird life in them. Firstly, the food supply varies markedly with the seasons; even the evergreen trees put on their new growths in the spring and usually produce their fruits in the autumn. The insect larvae grow best on the young tender leaves and so appear soon after bud-break. In European broad-leaved woods these caterpillars grow up very rapidly and soon disappear to pupate—often in the ground out of the reach of birds; those present in conifers grow a little more slowly and so are available to the birds for a longer period. Later in the summer, flying insects are more abundant, but both these and most other small animals become scarce as soon as the first autumn frosts occur. The insect eating birds then face a dilemma. Either they must go away or they must change their diet. Many, such as the warblers, leave the northern woods at this time and migrate southwards to spend the winter in much milder areas in or near the tropics. Others such as the finches and tits may stay, living largely on seeds. The thrushes also switch from worms and other small animals to fruits, at least when the ground is too hard to permit them to forage for the former. Hawthorn berries are a well-known winter diet for these birds.

Very few birds are resident in the northernmost forests; these are too cold and too thickly covered with snow for most birds to be able to survive and so they must move further south, though not as far as their insectivorous cousins. Another factor also governs whether or not these birds will migrate. The trees in temperate forests produce huge crops of seeds, but only in some years; in others there may be a great scarcity of seed and the birds may be forced to leave. Such sporadic fruiting occurs in many tree species, both conifer and broad-leaved. Years of great plenty are almost always followed by a year of crop 'failure', when no seeds are produced. It is not unlikely that such periodic fruiting has evolved as an adaptation against the seed eating birds and mammals; in one year there is no seed and the animals die in large

(1) Lesser spotted woodpecker *Dendrocopus minor* and (2) Red-headed woodpecker *Melanerpes erythrocephalus*; both these are birds primarily of deciduous woodland, though the latter is larger than the sparrow-sized former species.

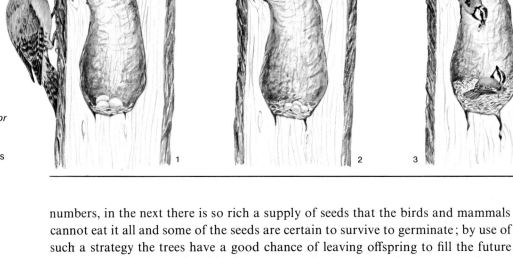

The Great spotted woodpecker *Dendrocopus major* occurs in forests throughout much of Eurasia. It searches for food by climbing trees in a spiral, supporting itself on its stiff tail feathers. Its flight is strongly undulating.

The Tawny owl *Strix aluco* may defend itself and its nest by fluffing its feathers up so as to make itself look as threatening as possible while hissing at the same time.

The wryneck *Jynx torquilla* is an aberrant woodpecker which is found in Europe and Asia; it occurs primarily in broad-leaved deciduous forests. Most of the birds that breed in the north of its range migrate south for the winter.

numbers, in the next there is so rich a supply of seeds that the birds and mammals cannot eat it all and some of the seeds are certain to survive to germinate; by use of such a strategy the trees have a good chance of leaving offspring to fill the future woodlands. Whether such an idea is true or not, the numbers and movements of many birds of north temperate forests are markedly affected by the seed supply; waxwings, nutcrackers, crossbills and many other finches, nuthatches and tits move south in great numbers when seed crops fail.

Another bird was once dependent on seed crops—the Passenger pigeon which is now extinct. This bird once roamed the North American continent in huge flocks in search of the seeds of beech and oak. Some estimates suggest that there were as many as 1,000 million Passenger pigeons in a single flock. This gives some indication of how abundant seeds must have been. The pigeons nested colonially in great numbers and were easy game for hunters. However, the removal of the forests in order to create farmland must have greatly reduced their populations long before man, as a hunter, made serious inroads into their numbers.

When seeds are readily available, many birds may store them in large quantities so that they can find them more easily during midwinter when days are short and searching times reduced. Tits, jays, nutcrackers and nuthatches are among those that store food in this way. Many, such as the European jay, store large quantities of acorns in the ground, where some remain unfound and germinate in spring. Jays are important in the dispersal of these heavy seeds and may be the main agent in the uphill dispersal of the heavy acorns. The tits in Scandinavia tend to store their seeds in the bark of trees and crevices in branches since the ground is covered by deep snow in winter. Among the food-storers pride of place must go to the Acorn woodpecker of the western USA. This bird lives in small parties in open oakwoods. The party selects a tree or trees and drills large numbers of holes in the trunk; an acorn is placed in each hole and these storage trees are jealously guarded throughout the winter; indeed if a party loses its 'larder' it may well starve. The same trees are used as stores for many years.

Woodpeckers are an important part of the avifauna in temperate woodlands. Mostly they drill for, and extract beetle larvae from dead or damaged timber with their long tongues which have barbed or sticky tips. Many of them also eat seeds such as hazel nuts and acorns. In summer some species may not distinguish between insects and small birds. Broods of tits in holes in trees may be dug out and fed to the young woodpeckers. Another American species of woodpecker, the Sapsucker,

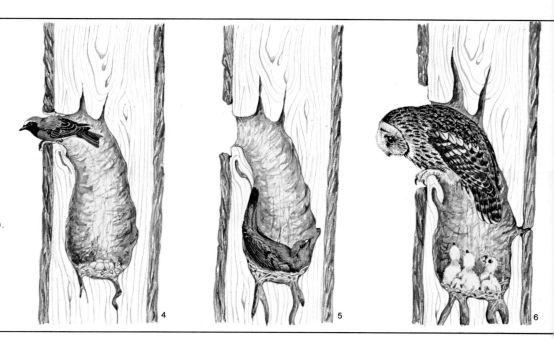

Many birds nest in holes in trees and at times these may be in short supply. Some birds, such as the Green woodpecker *Picus viridis* usually excavate a new hole for themselves each year (1). These may be used by Nuthatches *Sitta europea* which partly fill the entrance with mud to prevent other larger birds entering and evicting them (2). Tits, such as the Blue tit *Parus caeruleus* may use the hole also (3). When the entrance becomes slightly larger again (4), the Redstart *Phoenicurus phoenicurus* may nest. As the hole starts to decay and the entrance becomes still larger, birds such as the Stock dove *Columba oenas* (5) or the Tawny owl *Strix aluco* (6) may use the site.

Jays are important members of the avifauna of many temperate forests where they store tree seeds for food in winter; since they fail to find many of them, they help to sow future trees. This species is *Garrulus glandarius*, found over much of Eurasia.

The Honey buzzard *Pernis apivorus* occurs in woodland throughout much of Eurasia. It is unusual for a bird of prey of its size in that it takes a large number of insects, including larvae from wild bees nests.

drills a series of holes in live wood and, as its name suggests, feeds on the sap that runs from these; it may also take the insects that gather on the sap. Woodpeckers nest in holes in trees, normally ones that they have excavated for themselves, often in sound timber.

Holes in trees provide nesting sites for a very wide variety of birds and are particularly valuable since they are relatively safe from predators such as large birds and most ground mammals. In addition to the woodpeckers, owls, tits, Jackdaw, Redstart, nuthatches, some flycatchers, doves and some American warblers all nest in holes in trees. In the relative safety of such sites they tend to have larger broods than do their relatives nesting in more exposed sites; although the large broods need more food, this can be brought to them over a longer period and hence the young birds raised in holes tend to stay there a little longer than birds reared in open, cup-shaped nests. Although many other birds build their nests in trees, a number perhaps surprisingly descend to the forest floor for nesting, especially if this has thick vegetation of brambles, ferns or mosses.

Although towards the poles the temperate forests are extremely cold in winter, the same is not true of forests nearer to the tropics where the winters may be relatively mild and many birds are resident the whole year round. For example, many honeyeaters and parrots are resident throughout the year in the forests of southern Australia. Some even breed in winter. Not all these birds are nectar feeders; many of the parrots eat seeds and many of the honey-eaters eat insects. However, some flowers and insects are available throughout the winter and these are plentiful enough to allow these birds to breed.

In the forests of the Mediterranean and of the southern USA the weather is much less harsh in winter than is the case further north and insects can still be found in these evergreen woodlands in winter. Some of both the European and the American warblers spend the winter in these habitats; others go much further afield—into Africa and Central America respectively.

The wide range of animal life in temperate forests has resulted in a number of predatory birds. The sparrowhawks *Accipiter* are specialists at catching birds by chasing them among the branches. Though relatively slow compared with the falcons, their great manoeuvrability makes them experts in this habitat. Many owls live in woodland, and kill both small birds and mammals by hunting them in the dark. They live in relatively restricted territories which they come to know so well that they can fly around even on a very dark night; they locate their prey by sound.

Tropical Forests

Tropical forest birds. Trogons are found in most tropical forest areas of the world; this species (1) the Coppery-tailed trogon *Trogon elegans* is from Central America. There are some 320 species of hummingbirds all of which come from the New World. The species shown here (2) are, from left to right, the Sappho comet *Sappho sparganura*, the Scale-throated hermit *Phaethornis eurynome* and the Ruby and topaz hummingbird *Chrysolampis mosquitis*. Most birds of paradise occur in New Guinea; the two shown here are the Superb bird of paradise *Lophorina superba* (3) and the Enamelled bird of paradise *Pteridophora alberti* (4), so-called because of the enamel-like blue gloss on the elongated head feathers.

The Quetzal *Pharomachrus mocino* is a trogon. The male is unusual in having very long tail feathers. The species is found in tropical forests of Central America where it nests in holes in trees.

Tropical forests are one of the most exciting and richest habitats in the world. The huge, towering trees and the stillness inside the forest have a quality all of their own. True tropical forests are found only in the equatorial regions of the earth in areas of high rainfall—central America, Malaysia and the Far East, small areas of northeastern Australia and the huge forests of Central and South America, in particular the vast Amazon basin. A common factor in these areas is the high year-round temperature and the heavy rainfall; the latter is also usually spread right round the year. Although there may be wetter and drier periods of the year, there are not prolonged dry seasons; these would result in different, more seasonal woodlands. The warmth, with few extremes of temperature, makes relatively small demands on warm-blooded creatures and the high humidity results in a perpetually damp climate with little chance of fire spreading any distance. Tropical rain forests probably owe their continued presence today to their resistance to fire, for elsewhere man has used fire widely as a way of clearing forests.

The majority of the trees in tropical forests are evergreen; though some species shed all their leaves together they are usually leafless for a very brief period. The trees are often very large, the closed canopy being some 100 or even 120 ft (30–36 m) above one's head with even larger emergent trees towering over this. As a result, little light reaches the forest floor and there may be relatively little plant life there, possibly only a few small shrubs and many small saplings of the large trees.

Many of the trees in tropical forests have much in common with each other. They are straight and tall, with few side branches until 60 or 70 ft (18 or 21 m) above the ground, a result of their rapid race against other small trees to fill the space left by a dying canopy tree. Many have large buttresses or stilt roots at their base—outward projections that enable the tree to be more firmly rooted in the soil. The

Tropical forest birds. Woodcreepers are birds that are found mainly in the tropical forests of the Americas; they climb up tree trunks, foraging for insects in a manner similar to treecreepers. The Barred woodcreeper *Dendrocolaptes certhia* (1) is the size of a large thrush. The Long-tailed hawk *Urotriorchis macrourus* (2) occurs in the forests of western Africa. The two species of rock fowl are found in highland forests of west Africa where they build mud nests on cliff-faces, the Grey-headed rock fowl *Picathartes oreas* (3) and the Bare-headed rock fowl *Picathartes gymnocephalus* (4). Pittas, such as the Garnet pitta *Pitta granatina* from South East Asia (5), live on the forest floor.

Many New World orioles build hanging nests in groups around wasp nests from which they gain protection from predators such as monkeys. The nests may even resemble the structure of a wasp nest. This species is Wagler's oropendola *Zarhynchus wagleri*, a crow-sized bird.

mature leaves are dark green with 'drip tips', pointed ends which are said to enable the rain to be rapidly shed from the leaf. The young leaves are often pink or red and hang vertically to avoid the sun's rays until they are fully developed. With these and other characters the tropical forests of the different parts of the world have a great deal in common even though the actual tree species may belong to totally different families. Unless he is an experienced botanist, the observer could find himself in any tropical rain forest in the world and be hard put to know where he was.

Rain forests are noted for the rich variety of species of both animals and plants and the trees that form the forest are no exception to this. There may be as many as 600 different species of tree in a single square mile (2.5 sq km) of rich rain forest. Because of this great diversity there tend, of course, to be relatively few individuals of any given species. This is a considerable contrast to a temperate woodland where the majority of the tree species may belong to perhaps half a dozen different species. Some idea of this diversity can be obtained by looking out over the top of one of these forests; perhaps this week one may see that a tree with orange flowers is in bloom and that these orange-flowered trees are widely scattered over the forest, but very few in number; next week the same may be true for a purple-flowered tree and then a red one and so on, each tree being relatively uncommon but all the individuals of that species flowering together.

Such successional flowering has important effects on the avifauna. Although all the individuals of a given species of tree tend to flower within a fairly short period, there are usually some species in flower or fruit at all times of the year. As a result, birds specialized to feed on nectar can exist. Even if there were no flowers or fruits for only one month of a year many of these birds could not survive. Among the most specialized are the hummingbirds of South America, the sunbirds of Africa and Asia, and the honey-eaters of Australasia. Many of these take insects in addition to a nectar diet, but nevertheless they need a reliable source of food that can only be

The White-faced antcatcher *Pithys albifrons* belongs to a large family of antbirds which occur in Central and South America. Most species live low down in the forest or even on the ground.

The Magnificent bird of paradise *Diphyllodes magnificus* is another inhabitant of New Guinea. The male bird clears a display ground some 20 ft (6 m) across, removing also the leaves of the saplings above so that more light filters through.

Like many other hornbills, the Giant hornbill *Buceros bicornis* from India and South East Asia walls the female into a nest cavity. The male feeds her through the small crack during the laying and incubation periods and through the early part of the nestling stages.

Silvery-cheeked hornbills *Bycanistes brevis* may travel ▷ long distances for food. Here a pair attack a snake, a habit that does not, however, occur very often.

found in such relatively stable areas as the tropics. The same applies to fruit eaters such as the fruit pigeons and the cotingids; they could not exist in areas without a plentiful supply of fruit in every month of the year.

The birds show some of the features described for the trees. Within the rain forest there are large numbers of different bird species, but by and large each species tends to be rather rare. Further, their breeding seasons show similarities to those of the trees in that although each individual species tends to breed only at certain times of the year some are breeding in every month. The length of each species' breeding season may be long compared with the breeding season of most birds in temperate areas, but nevertheless each species has a well-marked period when breeding does not take place; at this time the adults may moult to replace their worn plumage and generally prepare for the next breeding season. Hence if one goes into the forest in each month of the year, one may be able to find some species breeding on each visit, but not the same species on every visit.

People who walk through tropical forest often think that the forest is rather empty of birds. This is to some extent true; birds are not very common compared with the high densities of birds that one may at times find in other habitats. It is also partly a false impression. Firstly, most of the life in such forests goes on above one's head—most birds are in the canopy where the leaves, flowers, fruits and insects are and only a few ground- or trunk-foraging birds are to be found by the pedestrian observer. Climb up and sit in the canopy—especially near a flowering or a fruiting tree—and the story will be quite different. Another feature of the forest birds may aid this impression of scarcity. Many of the smaller birds go about in foraging flocks of 20, 30 or sometimes many more birds, a variety of species all foraging in the same flock. These travel steadily through the forest in each other's company. Suddenly, the air is full of birds and, just as suddenly, before one has had an opportunity to look at or identify them all, they have disappeared. After that one may walk for an hour or two and hardly see a bird, and then, another flock. The reasons why birds live in these mixed parties are not fully known, but the birds may be of use to one another by being on the look-out for potential predators—more watchers are better than one. In addition, some birds catch insects disturbed by others and so may gain from being in a flock.

Nonetheless birds are not as abundant in these forests as they are in many temperate regions. One possible reason for this may be that there are other animals which though relatively rare in temperate regions are common in the tropics. For example

Keel-billed toucans *Ramphastos sulfuratus* mobbing ▷
an Ornate hawk-eagle *Spizaetus ornatus*. As with
small birds of temperate woodland, toucans will join
together to mob a predator or potential enemy.

The Bare-headed rock fowl *Picathartes gymnocephalus*
from west Africa builds its nest of mud on a rock
wall; it may nest in groups. The birds hop along the
forest floor catching insects and other small animals.

The Sulphur-crested cockatoo *Cacatua galerita* occurs
over extensive parts of the eastern half of Australia.
It lives in rather open forest from the tropics to the
temperate areas, and nests in holes in trees.

The Superb lyre-bird *Menura superba* lives in cool
sclerophyll forests of the southeastern part of
Australia. The males display from small mounds that
they scratch up. They are remarkable mimics of the
other birds. The female builds a large domed nest of
twigs and lays a single egg.

frogs and lizards abound in rain forest, living in the tops of trees where they must
take a heavy toll of insects. Possibly because of this competition for food there cannot
be so many birds as where these competitors are absent. This is a guess, but the
fact remains that these rich forests do not harbour the high number of birds that one
might expect; the richness is in species rather than in numbers.

Birds in the tropics tend to lay rather fewer eggs than those in temperate areas
and birds in the rain forests tend to have the smallest clutches of all. Many reasons
have been suggested for this but conclusive proof is lacking. Firstly, the birds have a
shorter day in which to feed in the tropics than is the case in the temperate areas in
the breeding season and so could not collect so much food each day for their growing
young. Secondly, food rarely becomes so plentiful in the rain forest as in the spring
flush of insects in temperate regions so that the parent birds may have to search harder
and for longer in the tropics than in the temperate areas in order to find food.

Birds nesting in tropical forests face enemies that are less common in the temperate
regions; among the enemies of nests, snakes and monkeys rank high. Many of the
smaller tropical birds hang their nests from slender tips of branches or from creepers
to make them difficult to reach; also they build a domed nest so that the potential
predator cannot see whether there are eggs or not. Some birds build their nest close
to a colony of wasps so that prospective raiders will have to face a barrage of angry
wasps to get their prey; somehow or other the birds themselves seem to safely avoid
antagonizing the wasps.

Many groups of birds are specialized for living in tropical forests. The South
American family of woodhewers Dendrocolaptidae has produced a wide range of
treecreeper-like birds which forage on the enormous area of trunks in the forests.
These birds range in size from about that of a sparrow to about the size of a crow and
have a wide variety of beak shapes for probing and pecking into the bark of trees.
The trogons, including the beautiful Quetzal of Central America have a wide
distribution in the tropics; they sit just below the canopy and make quick flights out
after passing insects. In several parts of the world birds follow the big movements of
ants around the forests. Some of the ant thrushes Formicariidae of South America
specialize in this; they do not often take the ants, but rather specialize in catching the
other insects that dash for safety from the approaching columns of ants.

Sadly, huge areas of tropical forests are currently being cleared by man; often
they are not in fact good areas for cultivation. Once cleared of the big trees the heavy
rain usually washes the nutrients out of the soil and within a year or two the land is no
longer fit for cultivation; the farmer must move on and clear another area.

77

Grasslands

Grasslands occur mainly in areas of relatively low rainfall; they lie between the deserts and the forests and grade into both. The temperate grasslands are mostly in the centres of large continents, away from the rain-bearing sea-winds. The great prairies of North America, the pampas of South America and the steppes of central Asia are of this type. Since they are distant from the warming influence of the oceans some of these places are very cold in winter. The great savannahs of central Africa and the grasslands of Australia are different in that they are warm the whole year round. In Africa the high temperature induces high evaporation and this, coupled with long periods of little or no rain, produces the grasslands. Trees find such conditions difficult especially since extensive fires may burn the dead grass in the dry season and cause them severe damage. Such fires may be caused by lightning strikes, but the grasslands of India and perhaps much of the Australian eucalypt woodland are partly the result of man's burning activities.

In grasslands totally devoid of trees, the number of bird species is usually low; once there is a scattering of trees a much wider variety of bird life is found. Many more birds are found in areas which are within easy flying distance of water, for most birds seem to need this addition to their diet.

A striking group of birds occurs in grasslands—the Ostrich, rhea and Emu, in Africa, South America and Australia respectively (though fossils show that the Ostrich was once widespread in parts of the Palearctic). These huge flightless birds have many features in common, but there is some dispute as to whether or not they

Two unrelated grassland species have remarkably similar plumage. The Eastern meadow-lark *Sturnella magna* (1) of the USA and the Yellow-throated longclaw *Macronyx croceus* (2) of Africa look remarkably alike although the meadowlark is much larger than the longclaw.

Grasslands provide living places for several species of large cursorial birds. The Old World has some 22 species of Bustard including (1) the large Kori's bustard *Choriotis kori* from east and southern Africa. These birds are omnivorous. The Carmine bee-eater *Merops rubicoides* often rides on bustards, catching insects flushed by them as they walk through the grass. (2) The Secretary bird *Sagittarius serpentarius* also of Africa, runs on the open grassland and catches reptiles. (3) The Crested seriama *Cariama cristata* lives on the pampas of South America; it is an aberrant gruiform bird. Like the bustards, cariamas are omnivorous.

Birds of grassland. (1) Black-tailed godwit *Limosa limosa* nests in damp grasslands and spends the winter in estuaries, (2) Meadow pipit *Anthus pratensis* nests in open rough grassland and on moorland, (3) Lapwing *Vanellus vanellus* nests on rather drier grasslands; many of the birds from central Europe move westwards to damper areas for the hottest part of the summer, they may also leave for milder areas if the grasslands freeze in midwinter. Kestrels also live in grasslands, hunting small mammals. Shown here are the American kestrel (often called a 'Sparrowhawk') *Falco sparverius* (4) and the Kestrel *Falco tinnunculus* (5) from Eurasia and Africa.

Although living in grassland, the Kestrel *Falco tinnunculus* needs trees for nesting in. If cornered in its nest it may lie on its back and defend itself with its powerful talons.

are closely related. They live in grasslands or open forest where their large size combined with long legs and necks gives them the opportunity to spot danger from afar and to make a rapid getaway, at speeds of up to 40 mph (64 kph). They all feed primarily on vegetable diets and although they drink when water is available, they are able to extract some of the water they need from seeds and berries. Other powerful runners occupy the grasslands, though these can also fly if they have to. They include the bustards and the guineafowl.

A number of smaller birds also occupy the grasslands, among them the partridges and quail, the sandgrouse and some waders—in particular the stone curlews, dotterels and coursers—and some American orioles and Old World pipits and larks.

Another group that is particularly abundant in grassland deserves special mention —the finches. These birds live primarily on a diet of seeds though some of them feed on insects and many bring insects to their young. From the time that the seeds start to ripen (when many of the birds begin to nest) until the start of the next rainy season, there are large quantities of seeds. Only when rain has fallen and the seeds have started to germinate is food in short supply, and this apparent time of 'spring' is when some finches suffer the greatest hardships. To avoid this difficulty, many may wander from area to area avoiding the periods of dearth or switch from the seeds of one plant to those of another. In the grasslands of central Africa some species may follow the passage of the rain northwards and southwards, arriving in each area when the grass seeds have begun to ripen.

By their very nature the finches have sometimes come into severe conflict with man. Our cereal crops are grown in the grassland areas of the world, or in extensions of them where we have removed the forests. To these birds, man's extensive crops are just another seed to eat and they descend on them in thousands or in millions. In no area is this problem so acute as in Africa where colonies of many millions of a small finch, the Quelea, do untold damage. They take many crops but are especially partial to millet, possibly because in some areas this ripens at a time when there are few natural grass seeds available.

Deserts

We tend to think of deserts as areas of great heat and they may be, but they may also be extremely cold at night or in the winter. This is because they tend to occur far from rain-bearing winds which modify the climate on land near the sea by bringing warming winds in winter and cooling winds in summer. Since such winds have spent their warmth or moisture before they reach the desert areas, the extremes of temperature are not moderated in this way. Rainfall is not only slight but its timing is often unpredictable, hence animals must survive as best they can from one period of rainfall to the next. Because of water shortage the growth of plants is slow and if damaged by over-grazing they may take many years to recover. The sandy areas such as the great Sahara Desert of North Africa are, in many places, man-made. As a result of over-population and over-grazing by man's herds, especially by the all-destructive goat, the slow growing plants are being progressively eliminated and their slender hold on the poor soil removed so that the desert is allowed to spread.

Few natural deserts are sand blown wastes devoid of life. Most have grasses and small plants and many are even rich in plants and trees. Such places often house a wide variety of animals though these may not be conspicuous. For both the animals and plants, water conservation is of overriding importance. The desert adaptations of the plants are well known; in those such as the cacti, limited leaf surfaces reduce evaporation and the large stems have the ability to store water. Other plants are ephemeral, they grow rapidly from seeds once rain has fallen, set seed and die leaving the next generation of seeds to survive the dry period until the advent of more rain.

The rate of water loss by animals is related to their exposure to the sun and so animals take what steps they can to avoid unnecessary activities in the heat of the day. They may lie inactive in the shade of a bush or a rock or even shelter down burrows where the changes in temperature are less marked. The closer one is to the sandy soil, the hotter it is; only a few inches above the surface the temperature is markedly lower. This may in part explain why desert animals, including birds, have relatively long legs, for it is clear that the higher they can stand or walk, the less water they will lose.

Compared with mammals, the birds of deserts are not especially well adapted to such areas. Mostly they do their best to avoid exposure to the sun in the full heat of the day; they take a siesta and are most active in the early and later parts of the day. A few are able to go without water for long periods; some small finches can obtain much of their water supplies from their vegetable diet. When food material is digested, water—so-called metabolic water—is formed and the birds may be able to exist on this. However, most desert birds need to get water and must therefore live within flying distance of a source; normally they come both night and morning to the water holes. Huge flights of sandgrouse may be seen coming in to water during the evening in some parts of Africa. If these areas of water dry up the birds must move away. As a result, the birds of desert areas may be nomadic, settling to breed after rain and remaining as long as the area is suitable then, when the land dries out, departing in search of better areas.

Desert birds also have a problem with their nests since the eggs and young must be shielded from the worst of the sun's heat. Some of the smaller birds such as wheatears seek shelter for their nests down burrows or in crevices in rocks. Others such as some of the waders may have to stand over their eggs or young during the heat of the day in order to shield them from the intense heat. Since the young birds cannot fly to water, the parents may bring the water to them; when drinking, sandgrouse soak their breast feathers in the water and bring this water to the young. The feathers are specially adapted to absorb and hold large quantities of water. Kittlitz' plover in South Africa has been recorded burying its eggs in the sand during the heat of the day, and the Indian Yellow-wattled plover brings back water on its belly feathers to dampen the eggs and so help to keep them cool.

Waders that live in deserts. (1) Cream-coloured courser *Cursorius cursor* lives in very dry areas of North Africa and the Middle East and western Asia and (2) Collared pratincole *Glareola pratincola* which is widespread through the drier parts of the Old World. It is often found near dried up areas near water.

The Hoopoe lark *Alaemon alaudipes* lives in the deserts of North Africa and the Middle East. It has striking display flights during which the male spirals upwards and then glides down again.

Desert birds. (1) Pallas' sandgrouse *Syrrhaptes paradoxus* breeds in the steppe country to the east of the Caspian Sea, but has occasionally visited Europe in large numbers, (2) Pygmy seedsnipe *Thinocorus rumicivorus* is one of the four species of seedsnipe and aberrant is an wader. They live in the very dry grasslands of South America. (3) The Bar-tailed desert lark *Ammomanes cincturus* from the Sahara and the deserts of the Middle East, (4) Road runner *Geococcyx californianus* a ground-dwelling, aberrant cuckoo from southern USA and Central America and (5) Black vulture *Coragyps atratus* which occurs in deserts and a wide variety of other habitats in southern USA, Central and South America.

The Lammergeier *Gypaetus barbatus* lives in mountainous areas, where it scavenges like other vultures. It has learned to drop bones onto rocks so that they break enabling it to extract the marrow.

The Wallcreeper *Tichodroma muraria* inhabits high mountains of Europe, the Middle East and through to the Himalayas. It climbs up rock faces searching for its insect food.

Choughs *Pyrrhocorax pyrrhocorax* live in mountainous areas or on rocky cliffs. Outside the breeding season they commonly live in flocks, often of several hundred birds.

Mountains

Great mountain ranges or immense isolated mountain peaks occur in most continents. The mountain tops present considerable challenges to the animals which try and live on them. Two vital needs, oxygen and warmth, become scarcer with increasing altitude. Above about 16,000 ft (4,875 m) the air is rarefied and oxygen notably scarcer than at lower altitudes; many animals living at such heights have a higher proportion of red cells in their blood than animals of lower areas—this helps them to supply the body with oxygen in these difficult conditions. Temperature drops by about 3°F for each rise of 1,000 ft (6°C per 1000 m). Even on equatorial Mount Kenya one may find snow all the year round.

The effects of variations in temperature dominate the vegetation. As one goes up the mountainside one may pass from rich lowland forest through coniferous forests to poor, stunted trees, then through the treeline to alpine meadows of increasing paucity of vegetation until one reaches permanent snow. The passage up such a mountainside is like a compressed journey from the temperate areas of the world to polar regions.

In temperate areas, the mountains are subject to the same seasonal fluctuations as the surrounding land itself; as winter comes the snowline marches downwards, as spring returns the snow recedes. Many animals also show corresponding seasonal movements, spending the winter at lower altitudes than those at which they spend the summer. Because of the colder climate, birds that live on mountains tend to find themselves with a shorter summer period than their relatives in the adjacent lowlands and often have shorter breeding seasons. On high mountains in the tropics there may be little annual change in climate, but even so the animals face very rigorous conditions. High up on such mountains there may be a frost every night of the year with a sharp rise in the temperature during the day. Thus high on Mount Kenya, the daily temperature can fluctuate from 45°F (8°C) at the warmest to 10°F, or 22°F of frost (−14°C) at night, so animals find life difficult and may have to take shelter. Under such conditions many small birds roost deep down in the vegetation or down burrows in the ground since the temperature does not fall so low in such places. Some small birds such as hummingbirds and sunbirds 'hibernate' each night, becoming torpid during the cold hours and regaining their high body temperatures in the early morning in order to be able to carry out their daytime activities.

Many species of birds are restricted to particular habitats on mountains. Where the mountains are isolated, as in the case of many of those in Africa, they act like islands in a sea of lowlands; the montane birds are restricted to small groups of mountains or even to individual mountains. This coupled with their habitat restrictions may result in one particular species existing in only very small numbers and being very sensitive to changes in these habitats. In one area two closely related species may exist in neighbouring altitudinal zones. However, in an area where one of the two species is absent, the other may occupy the combined range of both species. How such partitioning of the habitat occurs is not understood.

Mountain ranges affect the lives of birds in other ways; for example, they cause changes in climate. Rain carried by winds is precipitated as the winds climb up and over the windward face of mountains; as a result this face is wet and often covered with lush vegetation. By way of contrast, the leeward side gets little rain and may have much poorer plant life. Hence the presence of mountains may have an important effect on the lowland birds as well as on the montane species. Mountain ranges have a further important influence in that they act as barriers to the passage of lowland birds and, if birds manage to cross them, the high ranges serve to keep the two populations apart. Thus isolated, the two groups may evolve differently during the course of time and may eventually become distinct species. The rich avifaunas of related species in and around the Himalayas and the northern end of the Andes testify to the importance of such barriers in the evolution of species.

Birds of mountainous regions. (1) Isidor's eagle
Oroaetus isidori from Central and South America,
(2) Golden eagle *Aquila chrysaetos* an inhabitant of
the highland areas of much of the north temperate
areas of both the Old and New Worlds, (3) Snow
finch *Montifringilla nivalis* a bird of the high mountains
of Eurasia which lives well above the tree-line,
(4) Malachite sunbird *Nectarinia famosa* lives on
high mountains in Africa, (5) Chough *Pyrrhocorax
pyrrhocorax* and (6) Alpine chough *P. graculus*.
Both these last named species are primarily birds of
mountains of Eurasia, the Alpine chough being generally
found at higher altitudes than its relative. Both
species may live at lower altitudes during the winter.

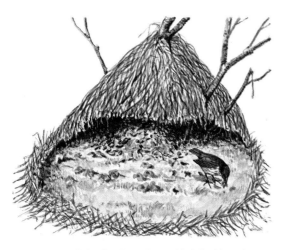

The bower of the Gardener bowerbird *Amblyornis inornatus* a species that occurs in the mountains of western New Guinea. The bird brings new fruits and flowers to the moss-covered court almost daily.

Two Australian species of bowerbirds, both of which occur in the sclerophyll forests of eastern Australia, (1) The Regent bowerbird *Sericulus chrysocephalus* and (2) the Satin bowerbird *Ptilonorhynchus violaceus*. Both these species have avenues through which they pass while displaying.

Island birds. (1) The Wattled false sunbird *Neodrepanis coruscans* is a member of the family Philepittidae. Only four species are known and all are confined to Madagascar. The honey-eaters, family Meliphagidae, are an important part of the avifauna of Australia and the south parts of the Pacific; shown here are the Cardinal honey-eaters *Myzomela cardinalis* from the New Hebrides (2) and the O-o *Moho nobilis* (3) an almost certainly extinct species from Hawaii. The Laysan teal *Anas laysanensis* (4) probably best regarded as a subspecies of the Mallard, displays the dull plumage characteristic of many island forms. The Weka *Gallirallus australis* (5) is a large flightless rail from New Zealand. ⇨

Islands

Islands may be oceanic or close inshore, large or small, barren or thickly vegetated. Such characteristics have important effects on the birds. Even large land masses, the largest of which we call continents, can from the biological point of view be considered as islands. The main factor that influences the chances of a bird getting from one island to another is the width of the sea that it has to cross without a place to rest.

The relation of an island to the continents, and the history of the island's evolution, markedly affects its bird life. Basically islands may be inshore or oceanic. The former are usually on the continental shelf of a larger land mass and probably became islands when the action of the seas eroded their connection with the adjacent land. Hence they inherited the normal flora and fauna of the mainland and may retain a varying amount of it. Oceanic islands on the other hand have formed without former connections to the mainland. Some major movement of the land at the bottom of the oceans—often a volcanic eruption—has thrown up an area near to or above the surface of the sea. This may still remain, or it may have slowly sunk again until it is crowned by a coral atoll. Such islands are, at first, devoid of terrestrial plant and animal life and these must colonize them from afar. If the nearest land masses are far distant, obviously the build-up of flora and fauna will be exceedingly slow.

Most birds need other life on which to feed before they can successfully settle, but this is not so for the sea birds. These birds use the islands only for nesting and collect their food from the sea; the barrenness of the island is of no concern to them. Indeed the absence of potential predators is a positive advantage. Sea birds may even contribute to the paucity of life; if they nest in sufficiently large numbers their massive deposits of guano cover the surface and help to discourage the growth of plants.

Once an island has emerged from the sea and erosion of the surface of the new land has begun, there is the possibility that wind-blown and water-carried seeds may reach the land and slowly, over the course of time, the island will be colonized by plants, insects and then other animals. Apart from sea birds who use the islands purely as a nesting site, most other birds require a fairly well-developed community before they can settle easily.

The chance of settlement is closely related to the position of the island. The further the island from a source of possible colonists, the more difficult it will be to colonize and the more slowly this will occur. The chances of colonization are also markedly affected by the prevailing winds; if they are towards the island the colonists will be more likely to arrive than if they have to fly against head winds all the way. In addition, not only must the bird successfully make landfall and quickly find both food and water, but also it must find a mate. In order for a pair of birds to meet on such a place, either the sea crossing must be made fairly frequently or the birds must fly in flocks. As one might expect, the abilities of different species to make such crossings vary markedly. In many oceans a particular group of birds may be well represented on most islands while several other groups are missing. Among small birds, the white-eyes seem to have been successful colonists in many areas, while among the large birds, rails have also reached a great number of offshore islands.

Within any group of islands, the size of the island markedly affects the number of bird species that are present: the larger the island the more species there are. The full reasons for this are not understood, but it is likely that the number of species present on an island is related to the richness of the flora, since islands with a richer flora have more bird species.

Extinctions are a regular occurrence on islands. All bird populations fluctuate to some extent, but the smaller the population the more likely it is that the numbers will drop to nil. The total bird populations on islands, especially on small ones, are of course low compared with those on an adjacent mainland so that the chances of extinction on islands are much higher than on the mainland.

Extinctions do not in themselves explain the paucity of birds on islands, for if one

The Hawaian goose or Ne-ne *Branta sandvicensis* (1) was almost extinct on Hawaii until many were bred in captivity. It lives on rough lava and has reduced webbing on the feet as can be seen here when compared with those of the Barnacle Goose *Branta leucopsis* (2).

The Kakapo *Strigops habroptilus* is an almost flightless aberrant parrot from New Zealand. It feeds to a considerable extent on grass seeds, often leaving well-marked trails where it has been feeding. The species is extremely scarce.

The Kagu *Rhynochetos jubatus* is an almost flightless relative of the rails. It is confined to the montane forest of New Caledonia where its future is not secure. At least partly nocturnal, its habits are not well known.

The Large cactus finch *Geospiza conirostris* is one of ▷ Darwin's finches and is confined to the Galapagos. This species has been seen to move small stones to get at seeds; it puts its head against a larger rock and thrusts the stones out behind it with its feet.

looks at the bird species that are there, one finds that they are not just a random selection of the birds present on the mainland, but rather, there are a few representatives of a wide range of families. For example, each of the islands in the Caribbean, including the large ones, has only one species of small hummingbird. Yet the Caribbean is surrounded by land where hummingbirds of many species abound. It is not even merely that only one or two of the species of hummingbird have been able to colonize the islands, for there are in all some 17 species on the islands. These and other examples make it difficult to escape the view that islands can only support a narrow variety of species, that there is only 'room' for one or two related species even if there are a number on the mainland, and that a new species can only establish itself after one of the residents has become extinct and so left a vacancy.

Island birds show some peculiarities: for example a number of them have become flightless—as have some island insects—and many others fly only very poorly. Others, related to brightly coloured stock, may have lost their bright plumage; some of the male ducks retain dull plumage like that of the female and never attain the bright colours of their mainland relatives. Both songs and plumage have probably evolved, at least in part, in order to enable each species to distinguish itself from those of other species. On a continent where there are many closely related species elaborate distinctions may be necessary, but these are not so necessary on islands where the problems of identification are much simpler.

Where, as is often the case, the colonists of islands receive few immigrants of their kind from the parental stock they will, as they evolve adaptations to their new environment, begin to differ from their relatives until, eventually, they may become a new species. This can happen even within archipelagos of islands. Here the birds on different islands may gradually evolve small differences, until eventually when they meet as a result of inter-island movements, they no longer interbreed, having become different species. Where this has happened on a number of occasions over a period of time one may find that a group of islands holds a considerable number of bird species—clearly all from the same ancestral stock. The honeycreepers of the Hawaiian islands are a good example of this; here there were once 22 species (some are now extinct) that had probably descended from a single invasion of a tanager from the New World. Perhaps less striking, though more important for another reason, are the Galapagos finches. These birds, some 14 species in all (13 in Galapagos,

The Yellow-tailed cockatoo *Calyptorhynchus funereus* lives in the forests of southeastern Australia. It may tear off the bark of trees and even rip into the wood with its powerful beak in its search for food.

The extinct Dodo *Raphus cucullatus* of Mauritius. This large, flightless bird may have been related to the pigeons. It was unable to survive in the face of man and his animals and became extinct around the end of the seventeenth century.

one on Cocos) were in part responsible for Charles Darwin's understanding of evolution. He wrote, 'Seeing this gradation and diversity of structure in one small, intimately related group of birds, one might really fancy that from an original paucity of birds in this archipelago, one species had been taken and modified for different ends.'

Speciation can occur not only in archipelagos, but on large islands; the prerequisite for speciation is that there should be two areas where a bird can live, separated by some form of physical barrier which cuts down movement between the two groups so that they can evolve sufficient differences to become separate species. This can, and has, happened within large islands such as Malagasy and New Guinea; once again the distinction between such islands and the continents is not a biological one.

A great many of the bird species on islands are represented on earth by very small populations and they are in many ways extremely vulnerable. In the natural course of events these species are relatively short-lived compared with many on the continents. They are often extremely vulnerable to small changes in their environment. Hence many are threatened today by man's activities. Of the birds that man has exterminated in the recent past, many were species restricted to small islands. Man has seldom exterminated these species intentionally, though he undoubtedly hunted the larger ones such as the Dodo of Mauritius and the Solitaire of Rodrigues. More often he has altered the natural balance on the islands, either by destroying the habitat or by introducing other animals. Introduced goats have eaten away the natural forests, and rats and cats have hunted and destroyed the birds, often ill-adapted to defend themselves against predators since many of them lived on islands virtually devoid of mammals apart from a few bats. The legendary tameness of island animals is a result of long periods of time during which they have had nothing to fear; with the advent of predatory animals this has proved their downfall. Introduced birds have also made their mark. Many, such as the starling and the mynah, have evolved successfully in areas where there were large numbers of competing species; they may be considered 'tough' birds, evolved in the rough and tumble of a continent. In contrast, island birds have had a sheltered life and are often ill-adapted to withstand such successful competitors whether in their search for food or for nesting sites. In some cases also it is possible that the introduced birds have brought with them diseases to which the native birds had no immunity.

The Palm chat *Dulus dominicus* is usually placed in a family of its own and is confined to the island of Hispaniola. The birds build a large, communal nest, often incorporating large twigs. As many as four pairs may occupy the same nest structure though each pair has a separate entrance.

Most kingfishers live along lake and river banks. Two Australian species are shown here; (1) the Azure kingfisher *Alcyone azurea* and (2) the very small Little kingfisher *Alcyone pusilla*. Both species fish from twigs along the sides of rivers and streams.

Birds of rivers and lakes. These are the main habitats for storks and herons, three of which are shown here (1) the Jabiru stork *Jabiru mycteria* from Central and South America, (2) the massive-billed Shoebill stork *Balaeniceps rex* from central Africa, which catches lungfish, such as the *Protopterus* shown here, mainly in the dusk and at night and (3) the Little bittern *Ixobrychus minutus* a small species only about 1 ft (0·3 m) long which is widely distributed in Europe, eastern Asia and Africa. A number of species of terns live primarily on fresh water, this is the Black tern *Chlidonias niger* (4) a species which breeds in temperate areas of both the Old and New Worlds and spends the winter in warmer areas. In the marshes of most warmer parts of the world one may find stilts; this species (5) the Blacknecked stilt *Himantopus mexicanus*, comes from the New World.

Rivers and Lakes

Life depends on water; the sun's heat evaporates water, often from the sea, and it rises into the atmosphere, forms clouds and is subsequently precipitated once again as rain or snow. Eventually this finds its way back into the sea and so the cycle is repeated. Water that falls on land eventually flows into lakes and rivers and these provide rich habitats for birds.

Rivers start as small streams which join together to form larger and larger bodies of water, until they reach the sea. They may flow for 3,000 mi (4,800 km) as is the case with the Mississippi and the mighty Amazon. Not all rivers flow into the sea: they may flow into large inland lakes or even into areas of desert where they slowly weaken, eventually cease to flow and dry up altogether. The different stages of a river provide quite different habitats for birds. By and large the upper reaches are steep and fast-flowing; plants find these difficult to grow in and small animals are easily washed away. Hence food for birds is not always rich at these levels of the river and birds are scarce, both in species and in total numbers. Nevertheless, some species are specially adapted for living in such places. The torrent ducks of South America and the Blue duck of New Zealand inhabit fast-flowing streams where they are able to collect algae by gleaning them from the rocks. The Dipper is also a bird of fast-flowing reaches, foraging on the bottom of the streams for small insects. By walking upstream, holding on with its powerful claws and keeping its head down, it allows the pressure of the running water to keep it against the bottom of the stream; it may also beat its wings underwater, apparently to help keep itself submerged.

Further downstream the rivers run across less mountainous land and tend to flow more slowly. Plant life, and hence animal life, is richer and so the birds have more food available to them. Fish eating birds such as herons, kingfishers and mergansers become more common here. Towards the seaward end of their length,

Bitterns are relatives of the herons, usually they are well camouflaged and live secretively in reed beds. This species the European bittern *Botaurus stellaris* occurs through much of Eurasia. It is shown here preening after fishing.

Rails are most commonly found in marshes, (1) the Purple gallinule *Porphyrio porphyrio* is a large species found in a number of areas of the Old World and Australia, (2) the Moorhen *Gallinula chloropus* is even more widely distributed in the Old World, though unlike the Purple gallinule it does not reach Australia, and is also widely distributed in the New World and (3) the elusive Water rail *Rallus aquaticus* from Europe and Asia.

rivers may be very large; often they flow slowly and meander gently. They are also tidal; large mud-banks show at low tide. Here one may find an even wider variety of bird life, including cormorants, gulls and terns, and many wildfowl. Where the rivers are particularly large, they may impose a barrier to the landbirds on either side; the dangers of crossing such large bodies of water with no cover from marauding predators are so great that many small birds rarely take the risk. In extreme cases, such as the lower reaches of the Amazon, the other bank may not even be in sight! As a result, one may find that different subspecies or even species of bird inhabit the opposing banks.

In temperate areas of the world one tends to think of rivers as flowing, more or less steadily, throughout the year, but in many places this is far from the case. In some, marked seasonal fluctuations in rainfall result in widely varying levels in the river; in others, spring brings thawed snow from mountain areas with large rises in level. During the wet season or the thaw the rivers may overflow their banks and inundate wide areas of the surrounding country. The marshlands burst into growth and huge areas of reed beds and seasonal grasslands flourish. Later, during the dry part of the year, the waters fall back within their banks, shrink and even disappear completely. The birds respond to such changes according to their way of life. Birds that feed in marshes breed when the areas are most extensively flooded and the growth of vegetation is most marked. Those that feed in the river may take almost the opposite approach; for example, kingfishers and some herons need to be able to see their prey and this is not easy in turbulent, discoloured floodwaters. However, when the fish are confined within small areas of clearer, slower-flowing water, fishing is much easier; then is the time to breed. The kingfishers are also able to use their favoured nesting holes in the banks of rivers only when they are not flooded. Not only the flow of water but the vegetation tends to obscure the fish. Hence even in temperate areas one tends to find some herons breeding early in the year, before the waters warm up and become covered with a profuse growth of plant life.

The Black heron *Melanophoyx ardesiaca* of Africa raises its wings over its head while hunting. Apparently this helps the bird to catch fish either because they flee into the shade, or because the heron can see better with the glare of the bright sun removed.

The Reddish egret *Dichromanassa rufescens* of Central America and southern USA is a medium-sized heron. It is found chiefly in brackish lakes and saltmarshes. There is also a white form.

When danger threatens, bitterns stretch themselves upright and stand very still hoping that they will blend with the surrounding reeds. If discovered they may flap their wings and make themselves appear as large as possible in the hope of frightening the enemy away. This species is the European bittern *Botaurus stellaris*.

Other seasonal variations pose problems for the water bird. Although in most parts of the temperate zone the rivers do not dry up in summer, they may freeze over in winter. Fresh water freezes at a higher temperature than does salt water, so the birds of salt water areas do not suffer from this problem so acutely. In the polar areas the waters freeze every year and the birds have no option but to migrate to milder areas, and this they do. However, in areas that are further from the poles many birds try to remain for the winter. Their success is dependent upon the harshness of the winter. If the winter is unusually cold, then most inland waters freeze and the birds are in trouble; they must try to reach areas of open water either on or by the sea or to get to milder areas where the water has not frozen. Severe winter weather in Europe causes many of the wildfowl to move further west into Britain in an attempt to find areas where they can survive. However, these areas tend to become overcrowded so that it is still a struggle to get sufficient food. Birds that are dependent on getting their food from the water may starve at such times; herons and coots die in large numbers once the water freezes over and their food supply disappears beneath the ice; kingfishers are equally susceptible.

Some rivers never reach the sea but pour into lakes. These may vary in size from quite small to the size of Lake Superior, at some 31,000 sq mi (80,000 sq km) the largest body of fresh water in the world, or to as deep as Lake Baikal, almost a mile (1.6 km) from the surface to the bottom. The richness of the fauna of lakes varies in relation to their depth. The deep montane lakes—oligotrophic lakes—are too deep for light to reach the bottom and so plant life cannot flourish there and the whole fauna is poor as a result. Lakes of less than 20 ft (6 m) or so in depth—the eutrophic lakes—are much richer. Here plants can obtain sufficient light to grow freely on the bottom and a rich animal life is to be found. Such shallow waters have the highest productivity of almost any habitat. As a result they tend to fill with dead and dying vegetation and to become marshland and it is difficult to distinguish between where lakes end and swamps begin.

Such rich lake and swamp-lands abound in birds. Herons and cormorants, ducks, grebes, gulls, terns, kingfishers, rails and waders are among the groups that flourish there. Some ducks and rails may feed on the vegetation of the lake, but large numbers of the birds feed on the fish; grebes, cormorants and ducks dive for them and hunt

90

Kingfishers commonly breed in dry sandbanks along rivers. They usually breed in the summer or dry season when the banks are not liable to flooding; at the time when the rivers are low the small fish can be more easily seen and caught. This species is the Common kingfisher *Alcedo atthis* from Eurasia and Africa.

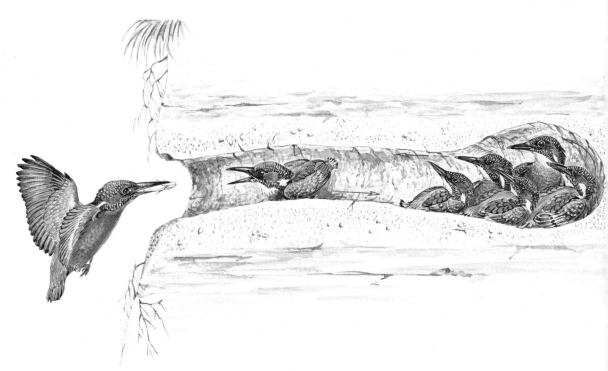

The Boat-billed heron *Cochlearius cochlearius* (1) is an inhabitant of mangroves and other dense vegetation in Central and South America. The Black-crowned night heron *Nycticorax nycticorax* (2) is a secretive, largely nocturnal species which has a very wide distribution in the warmer areas of the world.

Many of the rails have slender bodies so that they can slip quickly and quietly through the reeds or other waterside vegetation. This species is the Water rail *Rallus aquaticus*.

them underwater, terns and kingfishers dive on them from the air as do the Ospreys and fish eagles, though the latter catch them in their feet not in their beaks. Herons stalk from the bank; one species, the Shoebill, hunts for eels and lungfish in swampy ground and grabs them with its immense beak.

Not all lakes are fresh, many are either brackish or salt; some are even highly saline as are the soda lakes of East Africa. The Caspian and the Black Sea are the two largest salt lakes in the world. Again the bird faunas are rich on all but the saltiest of lakes. The species concerned are often similar to those of fresh water, except that the species that seek shelter in or feed on the vegetation may be scarcer since this thrives less well in salt conditions. Pelicans may be common on salt lakes where they breed and feed in groups, taking large quantities of fish. Sometimes they dive from a height into a shoal of fish and catch them during the ensuing confusion, but they have also learnt how to hunt in groups and may encircle shoals of fish and come in on them from every side.

The most saline lakes of all harbour another group of birds, the flamingoes. These nest on small mounds that they construct for themselves in shallow water offshore or on low islands. They live in great aggregations and nest in very dense colonies. They feed on small shrimps or tiny algae which they collect by sweeping the water through their bills; having got a mouthful of the water, they close the beak and pump the water out leaving the food collected on fine hair-like strainers along the sides of the bill, from where it is removed and eaten. Flamingoes are widely spread around the warmer areas of the world and used, in addition, to inhabit Australia during wetter times when the central lakes of the continent were full.

Many fish eating birds are white, at least on their undersides. The fish cannot see the white against the sky as easily as darker colours and hence the birds stand a better chance of getting close before they are spotted by their prey. This is particularly true of many of the diving birds, less so of those that, like the cormorant, swim after the fish on the bottom of the lake. Herons catch their fish by moving very little and very stealthily; they hope to catch them without being seen at all. At least one species, the Black heron, puts its wings up as a shade and catches the fish beneath; whether they swim into the apparent cover or whether the raised wings help the bird to see better by eliminating the glare is not clear.

91

The Herring gull *Larus argentatus* has a wide range of feeding habits, including making use of man's rubbish. Here a bird is seen dropping cockles to break them on the rocks.

The Oystercatcher *Haematopus ostralegus* has a powerful beak which it uses to hammer open shells and crabs and then chisel out the contents.

The Herring gull *Larus argentatus* may dive into the water for fish; like most gulls it does not usually dive very deep, seldom disappearing from sight.

Coastal species. (1) The Mangrove kingfisher *Halcyon chloris* is a largish kingfisher with a wide distribution in South East Asia and Australia, (2) Sanderling *Calidris alba* and (3) Kentish plover *Charadrius alexandrinus*, both species common on sandy shores. The former breeds in the Arctic but winters further south, the latter is widespread through much of the world. (4) The Greater black-backed gull *Larus marinus* a large predatory gull of the North Atlantic, (5) Crab plover *Dromas ardeola* an extraordinary wader that lives on the coast of East Africa and southwestern Asia. It nests colonially, breeding in burrows. Finally (6) the Black guillemot *Cepphus grylle* of north temperate seas. It is largely resident, nesting in loose colonies in small holes in the rocks. ⇨

Coasts

Where the land ends and the sea begins one can find a wide variety of different habitats. In some areas wind may blow sand behind the beach, build up impressive dunes and so impede the flow of rivers, forcing them to flow parallel to the sea and form extensive salt marshes. Larger rivers flow out into the sea carrying with them great quantities of silt brought down from further inland. The extensive mud-banks so formed in the mouths of estuaries are very popular feeding grounds for many species of birds, especially waders. In the warmer parts of the world the muddy edges to the rivers and the coast may carry a thick covering of mangroves. In places where the land is higher the sea eats into its edge and cliffs, rocky shores and small islets are formed. Many of the birds that inhabit these areas are specially adapted to one of these habitats.

On first inspection sandy beaches and estuarine mud flats may seem barren land for birds, but a second glance shows the holes and worm casts of the small animals that live beneath the surface; when the tide starts to wash over the flats they come to life. A myriad of small shrimps, worms and shellfish live in the waters between tide marks. Although each of the waders does not always stick to just one method of feeding but will alter it to match the conditions prevailing, each species does have a feeding habit which differs from those that the other species use.

Of the many species of waders that occupy these habitats, only a few appear to prefer sand to the mud-flats. The Sanderling is one of these; it runs at top speed along the edge of the waves using its short bill to pick food off the surface of the beach in the narrow belt where the sand is wettest. The Ringed plover also has a short beak and takes small worms from the surface of the shore while the Dunlin, with its slightly longer beak, probes a little further into the sand for its food. Many rather larger waders have much longer beaks and probe more deeply into the mud in search of larger animals, especially worms, that are lying in their burrows well below the surface. The godwits and curlews are amongst those with the longest beaks. The Bar-tailed godwit is of special interest in that the female is much larger than the male and her bill is almost twice as long; it is one of the few species of wader that one can easily sex in the field. The godwits search for food in the edge of the sea, the females slightly further out to sea, in deeper water than their smaller mates. Other waders are specialized for different diets. The Oystercatcher probes in the sand for cockles or mussels, hammers them open with its powerful bill using the sharp tip to chisel the flesh from the shell. The Avocet 'scythes' through very soft, almost liquid, mud with a sideways motion, extracting small worms that come into contact with its beak.

All these waders feed on the sandy shores or the mud of estuaries. Many need a low tide to feed so that their lives are governed by the tides rather than by whether it is night or day. Many feed by touch so that visibility, except at relatively low intensity for flying, does not matter too much. When the tide is high the birds must roost on the beach above the tide line, in meadows or fields inland or on small islands waiting for the sea to ebb so that they can start to feed again.

Not many waders feed on the shingle beaches; there are few prospects for obtaining food there unless the sea has brought up large quantities of sea-weed; there one may find the Turnstones busily turning the debris in their search for small animals that live among it. True to their name, Turnstones will also turn over stones on rocky beaches in their search for animals sheltering underneath. Shingle beaches are, however, used for nesting by some waders such as Ringed plovers, Oystercatchers and some terns. Their eggs are beautifully camouflaged on stony beaches. Nesting on beaches is not a common habit among birds and may become less common; most of the birds that do so in heavily populated areas of the world are under threat from the continued human pressures on the beach throughout the summer period; in some areas such disturbance has considerably reduced the nesting success of the birds.

Cormorant feathers can become more water-logged than those of many other diving birds. By compressing the air from the feather, buoyancy is lost and so diving is easier. However, the birds then have more trouble drying out when they leave the water and so have to sit with outstretched wings for some time. This species is the widespread Common cormorant *Phalacrocorax carbo*.

The Black Skimmer *Rynchops nigra* from the New World. This bird has the lower mandible much longer than the upper one. It skims along just above the surface of the water with just the tip of the lower mandible in the water, snapping up shrimps and small fish. It is a relative of the terns and gulls.

The dunes behind the beaches are not rich in bird life. The shifting sands and monotonous vegetation of marram grass do not provide rich feeding areas and only a few birds such as the Skylark live there. However, in isolated areas large colonies of gulls and terns may nest among the dunes. When the young are ready to fly they may gather on the beach in large parties waiting for their parents to come in to feed them.

Where the large dune systems divert the course of rivers large areas of saltmarsh may be found. Saltmarsh may also occur where low areas of land are found around the mouths of estuaries. These may be richer in plants than are the dunes and in consequence we find more birds there; again it is a good breeding ground for gulls, terns and waders, but here also we may find more small birds, larks, pipits and some of the New World sparrows.

A few birds that use the beaches also use the rocky shores, especially waders such as the Oystercatcher and the Turnstone. Some Oystercatchers specialise in eating limpets. Undisturbed, limpets are relaxed and not gripping tightly to the rock; the Oystercatcher catches its prey by stalking up to them quietly, smartly inserting its beak underneath them and knocking them from the rock before they can grip tightly. This can be dangerous since there are the odd records of Oystercatchers drowning when the limpet has tightened to the rock with the Oystercatcher's bill still caught beneath. The Rock pipit lives exclusively on rocky shores and eats large numbers of small winkles—almost its sole diet during the winter; each bird may eat as many as 14,000 per day.

Many birds use the cliffs above the shore though some of these are not in any way dependent on the sea. Peregrines and other birds of prey, the Black redstart, and the wren may spend their lives in these places oblivious of the sea beneath; they would live in just the same way on inland cliffs. Some cliff-nesting birds, however, are more intimately connected with the sea; once there, they are much safer from mammalian predators, including man, than are their cousins on the dunes. The Gannet, the fulmar, gulls, Kittiwakes and some of the tropical terns nest on cliffs, often in huge numbers. In the north Atlantic and the north Pacific many auks nest, often in countless thousands, on the cliffs. They use their wings for 'flying' underwater and as a consequence have small and stubby wings which need to be beaten fast for take-off before flight is possible. By launching themselves from cliffs and gaining speed by use of gravity, they are much less vulnerable to predators than they would be if taking off from flat ground. Some auks, among them the Puffins, live above the cliffs but they too need to get up speed before they can fly properly. They nest close to the cliff

Guillemots *Uria aalge* nest on small ledges on sheer cliffs where they are relatively safe from predation. Nevertheless, marauding gulls such as the Herring gull *Larus argentatus* still manage to snatch eggs and chicks if the parents are not on their guard.

Many terns nest on sand dunes where they make only small scrapes for their nests. These are dug out by the bird lying on its belly and kicking out the sand with its feet. This is the Common tern *Sterna hirundo*.

Kittiwakes *Rissa tridactyla* nest on very narrow ledges; the nest often overlapping the edge. The birds have a number of displays which prevent undue fighting on such limited areas.

The young of many water birds are able to swim freely soon after hatching which enables them to move long distances; exceptionally, as here with the Goosander *Mergus merganser* the young may be carried by the female.

edge and run down the grassy slope before launching themselves into the air. They are poor at taking off from flat land and so easily chased by gulls and robbed of the fish that they are bringing to their young. Those that nest on the very edge of the cliff are more successful in raising their young than those that nest a little inland. Just these few yards may be enough to cause the difference between successful and unsuccessful breeding. In North America the increase in numbers of gulls has been held to be one of the main reasons for the decline of Puffins.

In warmer parts of the world coasts may be thickly fringed with mangroves. These plants, which live part in the sea, part on the land, may stretch for hundreds of miles in a thin belt along the shores. Being tidal, the floor of the mangroves is not a suitable area for birds to live but there are a wide variety of species which spend their whole lives in the mangroves and, in addition, many sea birds build their nests in them. A wide variety of warblers, flycatchers and other small birds live in them and, as anyone who has walked amongst the mangroves knows to his cost, there is a large stock of small insects present for their food, especially mosquitoes. Large birds also inhabit mangroves such as cuckoos, butcherbirds, bitterns and other small herons; there is often a kingfisher or two. Many of the species that live in mangroves are specific to that habitat occurring almost nowhere else.

Other birds also occupy the coastal habitats; some ducks such as eiders, scoters and the Common shelduck live on the shore. When winter comes in the northern hemisphere many birds that have spent the summer in inland Arctic areas migrate southwards to milder climates for the winter, some even reaching the southern hemisphere. Amongst these migrants are many ducks, geese, terns and waders, and many of them spend the winter in coastal areas. Indeed in many coastal areas of Europe and North America the avifauna in winter is much richer than in summer. In areas of mud-flats, especially where the eel-grass *Zostera* grows, ducks and some of the geese, especially Brent, may gather in large numbers. However, it is the waders that in many places are most impressive. Leaving their breeding grounds all over the Arctic they concentrate on the coast in winter. Some species, such as the Dunlin and the Knot may gather in flocks of thousands, or even tens of thousands. They fly in close formation, performing wonderfully co-ordinated movements, almost acting like a single bird.

Sadly many of the coastal habitats are severely threatened by man's activities. Pollution, reclamation, barrages to hold fresh water, all threaten the coast, especially the estuaries on which the waders rely so heavily.

Terns, such as the Arctic tern *Sterna paradisea* bring fish to their chicks in their beaks. The young spend much of their time hiding in cover, but rush out to beg for food as soon as the parents appear. Occasionally the parents may feed the chicks while still in flight.

The male Magnificent frigate bird *Fregata magnificens* has an inflatable red pouch which he uses during his displays. The birds breed, often in large numbers, on small tropical islands.

The Gannet *Sula bassana* nests in large colonies, each nest being placed just out of pecking range of the next pair. The single egg is incubated under the webs of the feet.

The Inca tern *Larosterna inca* is found on the west coast of South America. It is the only species of tern known to nest in holes in rocks, most other species nest on the open ground.

Sea birds. Albatrosses live predominantly in the windy areas of the southern seas. This species (1) is the Wandering albatross *Diomedea exulans*, its wing span of nearly 12 ft (3·5 m) exceeds that of any other bird. Tropic birds are confined to the warm seas, the Red-tailed tropicbird *Phaethon rubricaudata* (2) inhabits the Indian and Pacific Oceans. Storm petrels are the smallest sea birds, this species (3) is Leach's petrel *Oceanodroma leucorhoa*. Phalaropes are waders which spend the winter out at sea picking up small animals from the water's surface, this example (4) is the Red-necked phalarope *Phalaropus lobatus* in winter plumage. Frigate birds live by chasing other sea birds and forcing them to regurgitate their last catch of fish. This species (5) is the Ascension Island frigate bird *Fregata aquila*. ⇨

Oceans

Oceans cover over three fifths of the surface of the world and stretch from the frozen waters of one pole to the ice packs of the other; only at one point, where the Americas stretch across the globe, are they almost completely divided. As on the land, the animal life of the seas depends on the plant life that grows there. This in turn is dependent on the light, temperatures and minerals in the water. Apart from exceptional circumstances, light does not penetrate more than the top 200–300 ft (60–90 m) of sea in sufficient strength for plants to photosynthesise at all, and in most seas the water is not clear enough for light to penetrate this far. The greatest plant growth occurs within close reach of the surface. Yet many of the minerals in the water tend to fall to the bottom of the ocean where they cannot be utilised by plants unless they are in some way brought to the surface of the sea. Hence the areas of greatest plant— and therefore animal—life tend to be where upwellings occur within the sea. Two factors produce such upwardly-directed currents. Where an onshore current meets a continental shelf the water is thrust upwards to the surface in turbulent masses. The Humboldt current off Peru brings rich waters to the surface and is famous for its anchovies and for its great sea bird colonies. Wherever such upwellings occur there are rich supplies of fish for the birds; the Benguela current off southwest Africa produces another rich area for sea birds.

Upwellings also occur where cold and warm waters meet. In the Antarctic a warm current flows southwards below the northward-flooding surface current. Because of differences in density of the water, caused by the different temperatures, the warm water rises to the surface bringing with it rich supplies of nutrients. During the summer season at the poles, the long periods of light enable the phytoplankton to grow richly and form the base for the food chain through fishes to birds. Because of these upwellings, the polar regions of the oceans tend to be much richer in animals than are the tropical waters. Large numbers of auks, gulls, penguins and shearwaters breed in and around the polar areas of the oceans; they stay only for the brief summer season, leaving as soon as they have bred and before the winter closes in. One bird, the Arctic tern, makes use of both rich seas. It breeds in the north temperate areas in the northern summer and migrates southwards to spend the northern winter in the rich seas of south temperate and Antarctic waters.

Many of the birds in the tropical seas breed in huge colonies around areas of upwelling, but others breed in places where the food supply is not so richly concentrated; they must spread out to forage for their prey, often ranging over large areas of ocean. Some species appear to be dependent on large fish such as tuna chasing their smaller prey to the surface. As soon as a shoal of tuna attacks a shoal of smaller fish, some of the latter come to the surface in an attempt to escape. Birds congregate seemingly from nowhere and grab the food while it is near the surface. These birds may search for prey for longish periods without success and then have a brief period of very successful fishing. For at least some of the species this means of fishing, although highly rewarding, may be dangerous; by landing on the surface in the vicinity of very large fish the birds themselves are in danger of becoming prey. Not infrequently sea birds can be seen to be missing pieces of foot or leg, apparently nipped off by a fish; presumably some of their number suffer more serious injuries from which they die and still others are eaten—indeed rings from sea birds have been found in the stomachs of large fish. Many of the birds that roam the open waters of tropical seas in search of food have small numbers of young, often only one, and these must wait long intervals between the times that they are fed and so grow slowly. Presumably these habits are related to the difficulties of raising young in these conditions and to the large distances that must be covered in search of food.

The staple diet of most oceanic birds is, of course, fish but others take a large number of small squid; these do not seem to be easily caught in nets of the fishery research vessels so that their movements and behaviour are not well-known.

SOCIAL BEHAVIOUR

The nest of the Sociable weaver *Philetarius socius*. This species is one of the few birds where a communal nest structure is built. A large dome is made of strong twigs and the individual nests are underneath.

Colonial species. (1) The Antarctic Emperor penguin *Aptenodytes forsteri*, (2) Magnificent frigatebird *Fregata magnificens* from warm seas of the Atlantic and eastern Pacific, (3) Common or Grey heron *Ardea cinerea*, (4) Black-headed weaver *Ploceus cucullatus* from Africa, (5) Arctic tern *Sterna paradisea* and (6) the Southern carmine bee-eater *Merops nubicoides* from South Africa.

Colonial Behaviour

Although a number of bird species nest in huge and sometimes spectacular colonies, these represent only a small proportion of the total numbers of birds. Only some 13% of birds nest in colonies; the remainder are solitary nesters. Many birds both nest and roost in colonies; such colonies may be small or very large—some of the larger colonies of the African finch, Quelea, which is a pest of seed-crops, may number many millions. A number of explanations for large gatherings have been suggested though probably none explain them all. Colonial nesting is common amongst sea birds; penguins, shearwaters, Gannets, cormorants and terns may nest together in great numbers. Their colonies are usually on small offshore islands where the birds gather near rich feeding grounds. Such feeding grounds need to be rich since a large colony of sea birds requires many tons of fish per day. However, the main reason that the birds nest on these islands is probably that they are relatively safe in such places as they are out of easy reach of mammalian predators—including man.

Another group of fish eating birds commonly found nesting in colonies are the herons. Heronries may often contain a number of different species of birds: herons, egrets, darters, spoonbills and fresh water cormorants. Other birds that nest in

The extinct Passenger pigeon *Ectopistes migratorius* used to nest in some of the largest colonies ever recorded among birds. An average colony might have covered an area of 30 sq mi (77 sq km).

Colonial nesting birds. (1) The Puffin *Fratercula arctica* nests in burrows, usually on rat-free islands, (2) Cliff swallow *Petrochelidon pyrrhonota* from the New World builds its bottle-shaped nests on cliff faces or buildings, (3) Eleonora's falcon *Falco eleonorae* breeds in the Mediterranean region and raises its young in the autumn when it can feed them on the small migrants heading south to spend the winter in Africa and (4) the Argentinian Green parakeet *Myopsitta monachus* builds large communal nests in trees.

colonies on fresh water include the pelicans and the flamingoes, and the inland gulls and terns.

Amongst the smaller birds, a number of seed eaters nest in colonies, though during the period when they are in the colony, the birds may be primarily insectivorous. The same is true of some of the American orioles; the Yellowheaded and Tri-coloured blackbirds eat insects during the nesting season, but much seed at other times of the year. Most colonial land birds are probably insectivores. The groups that nest in colonies most frequently are those that take flying insects such as swallows, swifts, bee-eaters and some of the smaller falcons. By way of contrast, almost all those birds that feed on insects such as caterpillars collected from the trees nest solitarily; such birds include the warblers and the tits.

Some of the sea birds that nest in huge colonies probably do so because the small area of land available necessitates that they crowd into it; there is no other land nearby. Others may get more positive advantage from nesting in large colonies. The Wide-awake or Sooty terns nest in such large concentrations that any individual's chance of being taken by a predator is small. This too is one of the likely explanations for the huge colonies of nesting Quelea; they arrive in an area in great numbers, breed quickly and have raised their young before any significant build up in numbers of their predators can occur.

The nesting terns—and many other species—get additional advantages from being in a colony as they can 'gang-up' to attack a predator. When danger threatens, the numbers of birds attacking a potential predator are often sufficient to drive the animal away, although the attacks of a single pair might be of no avail. In an experiment, hen's eggs scattered in a colony of Black headed gulls were taken by Carrion crows less frequently than those scattered just outside the colony. As soon as the crows penetrated the colony, the gulls rose and attacked in force, thus keeping them off the hen's scattered eggs as effectively as they kept them off their own. A few other species of birds are reported to nest within the colonies of aggressive gulls and terns in order to use these birds' ability of combined attack to protect their own nests.

Many species grow breeding plumage for the period of courtship and nesting. In some this may involve the production of new scutes on the bill. Here three species of puffins in breeding dress are compared with a winter specimen of the Atlantic species, *Fratercula arctica* (1); (2) Atlantic puffin, (3) Horned puffin *Fratercula corniculata*, (4) Tufted puffin *Lunda cirrhata*.

Cranes are noted for their wild courtship dances, often associated with powerful bugling calls. This species is the African Crowned crane, *Balearica pavonina*.

In many species pairs may feed each other during courtship. Here a pair of Hawfinches *Cocothraustes coccothraustes* are indulging in courtship feeding.

Pair Bonds

Some birds are noted for their unusual mating systems, such as the lek displays of the Black grouse or some of the birds of paradise. Nevertheless, we should not lose sight of the fact that the large majority of birds, well over 90 % of them, have normal monogamous breeding partnerships; in spite of the interesting adaptations of the few, simple pair bonds are the norm.

Complicated mating systems are more common in vegetarian birds than in those that eat animal food; large groups of birds such as sea birds, birds of prey and aerial insectivores (swifts and swallows) are all monogamous. Most of the other birds that raise their young in the nest are also monogamous; the unusual mating systems tend to be in nidifugous species where the precocious young leave the nest soon after hatching. However, such broad generalizations are not without exceptions.

Although most birds are monogamous, it is an old wives' tale that many, such as the swans, mate for life or will not remate if they lose their partner. Birds are by no means always so faithful. Partners may change between one year and the next, even between the beginning and the end of a season. With some of the longer-lived birds such as the shearwaters, a new pair may not settle down with one another very quickly; even if the pair is formed well before the start of the new season they may not breed in their first year together. In these longer-lived species, pairs are more likely to separate if they lose their eggs or young than if they nest successfully. Clearly there are advantages in staying with a partner with whom one has bred successfully. Further, well-established pairs breed earlier and more successfully than those breeding together for the first time.

Some species are polygamous, the males taking several mates: the weaver finches and some of the New World orioles are amongst these. Often the males will court a single female, mate with her and accompany her while she builds and lays, only to desert her as she starts to incubate the eggs and then go through the same procedure with the next female. In other species the males may take no interest whatever in the nesting, but merely congregate, often in the company of other males, at a display site where the females come for mating. The females then leave, build the nest, incubate and rear the young entirely on their own. Many American game birds, cotingids, manakins, birds of paradise and a few waders have these communal leks; so do some hummingbirds though the mating systems of relatively few birds from this large group are known.

A few other unusual mating systems may be mentioned. In the phalaropes and a few other waders the female lays the eggs and leaves the male to incubate and raise the young; in the phalarope the female also has the brighter plumage in the breeding season. In a few cases the female may lay two clutches, leaving the male to raise the first while she goes on to lay and raise a second; this may happen in a few waders and also has been suggested for the Red-legged partridge. In the Ostrich and the Emu the male mates with several females who all lay eggs in a single nest; the male incubates and looks after the young. In some tinamous several females lay together in a single nest and then go on to lay 'clutches' for other males to care for.

In many bird groups, especially passerines in warmer parts of the world, there are species where groups of birds, often as many as ten or more, care for the young in a single nest; these are the so-called co-operative breeders. The full details of many of these groupings are not yet fully understood, but many of the non-breeding birds are young that were raised in the territory in previous years and are not yet old enough to breed. As far as the pair bond is concerned, however, most of these groups do not appear as complicated as they were first thought to be. It seems that there is usually an older, dominant pair which mate and lay eggs and that the pair bond is therefore a simple monogamous one, except that the pair are accompanied by large numbers of additional birds which, though they may help raise the young, are not involved in the production of the clutch.

Courtship and nesting. (1) The male Winter wren, *Troglodytes troglodytes* builds the nest by himself and then displays to attract a female to it. Once the female is incubating he may go on to build another nest and find another mate. (2) Kingfishers *Alcedo atthis*, the male offering the female food. During the time that the female is forming eggs she needs considerably more food than usual and the male may help her. (3) Courtship flight of the Black-and-white warbler *Mniotilta varia*. Many small birds, especially those that nest in grassland or shrubby areas have striking aerial displays. (4) The male Redstart *Phoenicurus phoenicurus* leads his mate to a nest site by displaying his red tail; he may then enter the hole and display to her by moving his white forehead back and forth across the entrance. (5) In some species, such as the Roseate Spoonbill *Ajaja ajaja* nesting material is offered during courtship.

A pair of Black woodpeckers *Dryocopus martius*. The male attempts to assess whether the bird on its left is a female or a male intruder in its territory. The female has a smaller red cap than the male and, by turning away, a bird discloses its sex.

Territorial disputes occur in most species. In the Gannet *Sula bassana* (1) disputes are confined to keeping rivals out of beak range enabling the birds to nest very close together. (2) In the Winter wren *Troglodytes troglodytes* disputes take place on the edge of the territory. In many species actual fighting is rare and the disputes are confined to threat. (3) In the European robin *Erithacus rubecula* the male bird displays his red breast as fully as possible to his opponent while (4), in the Golden Eagle *Aquila chrysaetos* a bird may make close passes at his opponent as if about to attack. ⇨

Territorial Behaviour

A territory is an area which a bird defends against other birds. Many definitions of territory have been proposed, but there are so many types of territory that none of the definitions fit them all; the simplest and safest definition is probably 'a defended area'. Birds vary markedly in the type of territory they defend. One tends to think of birds, such as the Blackbird, which may defend an area in a garden and live and nest in that area most of their lives. However, in other birds such as some hole-nesting species, each male may defend only the area around the nest-site, leaving the woodland area between it and the next male undefended. Cliff-nesting species such as the guillemot may merely defend a tiny piece of ledge where they lay their egg and raise their youngster; all the feeding is done in the sea away from the territory. By way of contrast, the shelduck defends a feeding territory on the estuary and nests in an undefended area in the dunes away from the river. The drake stays on guard in the territory while the duck goes to the nest. Some species such as the Woodchat shrike, may hold territories while on migration; at each place they stop, they will vigorously defend an area for the few days that they are there. Other species may defend territories in winter quarters. In the European robin both sexes hold separate territories in winter, defending them equally against intruding males or females. Only as spring approaches does the female relinquish her territory and join the male in his; often, where the two territories are adjacent, they may be amalgamated into a single larger territory.

Once a bird becomes established in a territory—either as a result of driving the previous owner out or, more frequently, by taking over one vacated as a result of the death of the previous owner—it tends to retain this territory for the rest of its life. Even if the bird is a migrant, it usually returns to the same patch of country each year to breed. Once established, the right of 'ownership' seems to give the bird ascendancy over most challengers. When two neighbours quarrel on their common boundary they may be equally matched; however, if one enters the territory of the other it is likely to back down in the ensuing dispute. If chased back into its own territory by the owner of the land, the tables become turned and the fleeing bird becomes the pursuer. Hence ownership gives some sort of strength to the competitor; it is not only in humans that possession is nine tenths of the law! Once they get to know their neighbours, birds tend to abide by the agreed boundaries and so avoid energy-consuming and potentially dangerous battles. Even with the species which live in one area the whole year round, the vigor with which they defend their territories varies with the stage of the year. During moult they tend to be quiet, but when feeding young and in mid-winter, they may be much too busy searching for food to spend time defending their territories.

One of the major functions proposed for territories is that of population regulation. By spacing the birds out over the available habitat the territory holders may prevent some of their kind from obtaining territories. When all areas are 'full' the remainder have no place to go and either perish or, wandering as outcasts, do not breed. The higher the population the greater the number of outcasts there might be. There is strong evidence that some birds are forced, as a result of territorial disputes, into poorer and more marginal territories, though less evidence that there is any appreciable number of birds that fail to become established in a territory at all and so perish. Experiments have been undertaken to see whether there is a surplus of birds; these have involved the removal of established territory holders in spring in order to see whether other birds filled the vacancies made. The results have often been rather inconclusive at this time. However, earlier in the year, especially during the brief period of autumn territorial behaviour, there is some evidence that a number of birds may be excluded from holding territories. Further understanding of the functions of territory is badly needed; once again it may be wrong to expect that the same explanation will hold for all species.

Courtship display of the Magellan penguin *Spheniscus magellanicus*. When displaying, many species of penguin draw themselves up to their full height, spread their flippers and give a trumpeting call.

Many birds of prey, such as the Goshawk *Accipiter gentilis* have remarkable aerial displays, the members of the pair stooping at one and other high in the air.

Courtship activities of (1) Buzzard *Buteo buteo*, (2) Great bustard *Otis tarda*, (3) Grey or Common heron *Ardea cinerea*, (4) Red-breasted merganser *Mergus serrator*, (5) Superb lyrebird *Menura superba*, (6) Standardwing or Wallace's bird of paradise *Semioptera wallaceii*, (7) Greater prairie chicken *Tympanuchus cupido*, (8) Wandering albatross *Diomedea exulans* and (9) Yellow wagtail *Motacilla flava*. ⇨

Courtship

Courtship covers the behaviour by which birds recognize others of the same species, find a member of the opposite sex and become established members of the breeding population. Much of the behaviour depends to some extent on the type of pair bond which is formed; for example, in species where groups of males hold communal display grounds or leks, the females go to these for mating and no lasting pair bond is formed. However, in most normal, monogamous birds a lasting bond is established.

Courtship serves to ensure that each individual bird successfully pairs with a mate from the correct species. Elaborate displays or songs are characteristic of each species enabling the females to select a correct partner more easily; the more prolonged the courtship the more likely that one or other bird will recognize its mistake if it is courting with a member of another species. It is said that hybrids are more common in species where the female only briefly visits the male at a display ground for mating, such as with some of the birds of paradise. Since mistakes might be more likely where there are a greater number of closely related species it is not surprising that one finds bright, distinctive plumages or songs in males where several species are gathered together and less distinctive ones where species are not so intermixed. The ducks provide a good example of this. In several areas of the northern hemisphere many species of ducks gather in the same areas and the plumages of the drakes are very distinct. In contrast, the drakes of isolated oceanic islands, where there is only one species in each area, have plumages which tend to be dull and female-like; problems of correct identification do not exist. As one would expect, birds tend to emphasize those patterns which distinguish them from other species by using them as central parts of their displays. The mechanism may be visual or auditory. Commonly where one finds closely related birds in very similar plumage, one finds that their songs are very different. A good example is the Willow warbler, Wood warbler and Chiffchaff where the songs are easily distinguished though the birds themselves are not.

Courtship performs a second important function. Apart from the cases where the species are promiscuous and only come together for mating, the continual presence and display of one bird to the other enables them to increase their confidence in one another so as to behave as a pair and, eventually, to breed. Close 'understanding' of one another is sometimes important, since in some species the female helps her mate in territorial conflicts with rival pairs. Further, the male's presence and display may induce the female to start nest-building and, in some species, also to start ovulation.

Normally a pair come together gradually through courtship. This may be so where new pairs are formed and also in others such as the European robin where the pairs split up between seasons; indeed in this species individuals of both sexes maintain an exclusive territory against all others of their species. However, as spring approaches, the two sexes must reduce their aggression towards one another if they are to pair successfully. In the case of the European robin, the female is attracted by the male's song and leaves her own territory to approach him. He, seeing an intruder in his territory, attacks. If the intruder were a rival male he would either contest this challenge or flee. The approaching female however, does neither; although she will flee if persistently attacked, initially she stands her ground and crouches—in a submissive as opposed to a threatening posture. This has the effect of inhibiting the male's aggressiveness and although he may still threaten he does not usually push home his attack. By persisting in approaching in a submissive manner the female becomes gradually accepted by the male, his aggression wanes and he turns to courtship; slowly the pair is formed. Full acceptance of each bird by the other may take days or even weeks. Under these conditions the female is normally submissive to the male for most of the period that she shares the territory formerly occupied by him alone. However in some species she may come to be the dominant member of the pair during the height of the nesting period, particularly near the nest.

The Great skua *Stercorarius skua* is a relative of the gulls. Both members of the pair take an active part in the courtship displays. Here they are bowing to each other.

Courtship pairs of grebes have a 'dance' in which both members of the pair rise up on the water and swim very rapidly along side-by-side. These are Red-necked grebes *Podiceps griseigena*.

The Common tern *Sterna hirundo* in one of its display postures. Note the raised head and wings and the drooped tail.

The plumage and displays of the birds of paradise have long been known as being some of the most dramatic among birds. The display involves the erection of bizarre plumages and is often accompanied by loud whip-like or cracking calls; frequently the bird's posture is upside down on a branch. The species shown here are (1) Magnificent rifle-bird *Craspedophora magnifica*, (2) Magnificent bird of paradise *Diphyllodes magnificus*, (3) White-plumed bird of paradise *Paradisea guilielmi*, (4) Prince rudolph's blue bird of paradise *Paradisea rudolphi*, (5) Red-plumed (or Count Raggi's) bird of paradise *Paradisea raggiana* and (6) Twelve-wired bird of paradise *Seleucides ignotus*. ⇨

The first stages in the prelude to courtship involve the recognition of the sex of the other bird; in many cases this is by no means easy from the appearance of the plumage. In birds such as the European robin it is done initially through the female's recognition of the the male as a singing bird; thereafter behavioural differences separate the sexes. However, in many species the plumages of the two birds are clearly distinct. The ducks are a good example; in many of these the drakes are clearly different from the duller females and separation is easy. In many other species the individuals need to get close to one another to identify the sex; even then behavioural clues may be essential.

There is an almost infinite variety of ways in which courtship leads to pair formation, but the above description for the European robin probably covers the most common way in which it comes about. The male occupies a territory, advertizes his presence and the fact that he is without a mate; the female approaches and there follows a prolonged period during which the female's appeasement gradually reduces the male's aggression until the pair can co-exist. This happens in many species whether the territory be a large area of woodland or a small part of a colony as in the case of a gull.

Many birds appear at their breeding site already paired and, in cases where they are known not to have been paired the year before, they must have paired either in winter quarters or in their winter flocks; ducks and tits are examples of these two. The males are not isolated as in the case of the European robin, but are often in flocks so that the details of courtship must be slightly different. Most birds in flocks maintain small individual distances from one another; again this must be broken down for pair formation. In some such cases the courting male may accompany the female closely and defend a small area around her.

In most of the species covered by the description given above, the male displays and the female comes to him, but takes a small or negligible part in the displays. In many species however, both members of the pair undertake equal shares of often very elaborate displays; Gannets, swans and some herons may be cited as examples, while the elaborate bill-scissoring displays of some of the albatrosses show them to be on even terms. In the grebes, the courtship is also mutual and may occur at any time of the day or night. Courtship displays often involve highly vocal aspects as well as the upright 'penguin' dances, often accompanied by the birds rushing side-by-side across the surface of the water in an almost vertical position.

In many of those species where the female takes little part in the courtship display, the males are much more strikingly coloured than their mates. The species where the male holds a lek are good examples; the highly coloured or ornamented males (some of the American game birds, the Ruff, cotingids, manakins and birds of paradise) use striking displays to court the females who stay only briefly at the leks for mating and do not take part in the display. In a very few species, such as the phalaropes, the female is the larger and more brightly coloured; she arrives first at the breeding ground, takes and defends a territory against the other females and displays to attract the attentions of the male. Having paired and mated, she lays the eggs and leaves the male to incubate them and to care for the young. Apart from the laying of the eggs, the female takes over almost every aspect of breeding which, in most species, would be the responsibility of the male.

The female lays eggs and in many species she does all the incubation. Both these activities place a strain upon her; she requires more food than usual in order to form the eggs and in addition, when she is incubating, she has little time to collect food since she must spend much of the day keeping the eggs warm. At this time in many species the male provides what is known as 'courtship-feeding'. The female starts to behave like a small fledgling, gaping and quivering her wings and the male begins to bring her food. This behaviour often commences around the same time as copulation occurs. The male's contributions to the female's diet may be considerable—in some species up to 40% of her daily requirements are supplied by the male at this

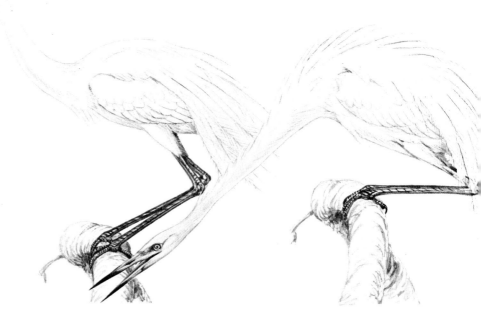

The Blue-footed booby *Sula nebouxi* is a relative of the gannets. Although they have dull brown plumage, they have very bright blue feet which they display to full effect during courtship, walking with a high-stepping action to draw attention to them.

Sarus crane *Grus antigone* displaying. The bird stands erect with wings drooped and uttering a loud call. In many species of crane, at the peak of their display, the pair indulge in a wild dance.

time. The male continues so-called courtship feeding during the incubation period, either calling the hen off the nest when he has brought her food or, while she is off, by foraging with her and so enabling her to get twice as much food in the time. In some game birds where the male does not feed the female he may scratch up the ground in order to make it easier for the hen to search for food.

In certain species courtship feeding is a prelude to copulation, the male bringing his mate an item of food and, in some passerines, accompanying the feeding with a special pre-copulation song. In other species the feeding has become ritualized in that the actual food is replaced in the courtship ceremony by other items such as nesting material.

Courtship feeding may have another function besides helping the female with her material needs at this time; it may help her to gauge how good a parent the male will be and thus how much help she will get from him when the young are in the nest. It has been shown in the USA that female Common terns lay more eggs if the male brings the female more food during the laying period; if he is of very little assistance she may leave him and look for another mate. It is unlikely that the number of eggs laid is solely dependent on the amount of food that the male brings, but more likely that the female can estimate the assistance that she will receive with the hungry broods and modify her clutch accordingly.

In those species where a proper pair bond is formed, the pair may remain together all the year or they may re-pair each spring. Geese and swans tend to remain paired the whole time even on migration. Other species such as some of the tits and many of the small tropical birds tend to remain within their territories all their lives and hence stay paired. Others re-pair each spring. In order to find each other again, they must come back to the same place. It seems likely that the birds that do re-mate remember one another. Courtship and acceptance seem to be faster amongst previously mated pairs than among those that are pairing for the first time. Indeed in the Kittiwake, pairs which have bred together in a previous year not only lay earlier than pairs breeding together for the first time, but also raise more young.

Since part of the function of courtship is to ensure that birds obtain a mate of the correct species, even the patterns of display between closely related species may be quite different. In many species the initial contact between a pair is made through

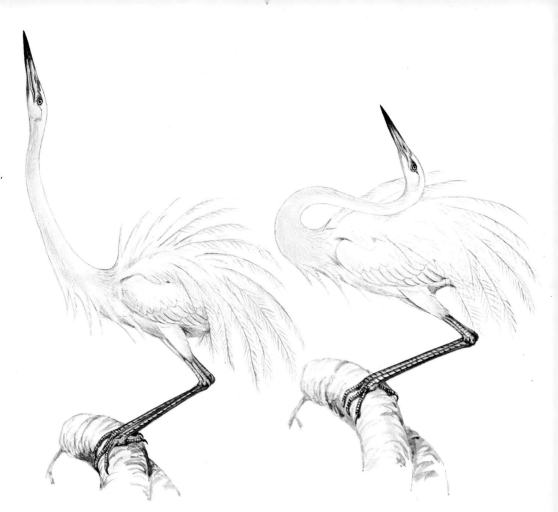

The American Common egret *Casmerodius albus* in a variety of the display postures it uses during courtship. In some species of herons, the beak colour can change at the peak of excitement during courtship, apparently as a result of a flush of blood. Note also how the plumes on the back are raised. It was these feathers that caused the rush of collectors to kill so many herons for the plume trade earlier during this century.

Bustards display on the ground. They enlarge their necks and frequently move their tails forward and puff up the back feathers. The species shown here is the Kori bustard *Choriotis kori*.

Many herons grow plumes with which they display in the nesting season. During courtship they may also expand the neck by raising the neck feathers. This species is the Night heron *Nycticorax nycticorax*.

the female being attracted to the male's song. These are usually very distinct between related species, especially in cases where the plumage is only slightly different. Under circumstances such as these the female's initial discrimination for a mate of the correct species may be made from afar. Once close, the male is able to make use of visual displays. The male may undertake a wide variety of displays, including aerial acrobatics and song flights in order to further attract his mate. During these displays the male shows off the most striking parts of his plumage. One can think of an almost endless variety of such adornments all of which are usually spread, fanned or enlarged in order to make them more striking. An obvious example is the peacock's train, which is erected into a fan and rustled vigorously in front of his prospective mate. The birds of paradise are also brilliantly coloured and display—often in groups at communal display grounds—in most eye-catching ways; some even hang upside down and fluff out their feathers at the height of their displays. A closely related group of birds, the bowerbirds, are much less strikingly coloured and build bowers or arenas where they display to the visiting females. The bower of each species is of different design or decorated with stones and fruits of different colours. Although basically not brightly coloured, the males of some species possess bright crests of coloured feathers which are normally concealed beneath the other plumage. A wide variety of birds keep their brightest colours concealed beneath their normal plumage, presumably for reasons of camouflage and safety; only at the peak of their displays are these flags of bright colours unfurled. It is not only the plumage that may be brightly coloured. The male frigate bird has an inflatable throat pouch of bright red. He sits on his nest and throws his head back so as to display the bright red balloon to females passing overhead; he utters a loud call while doing this display. The male Blue-footed booby is a dull brown bird except for his brightly coloured feet. These he displays to his mate by continually 'goose-stepping' before her or by taking off, and circling around; on coming into land he throws his blue feet up and waves them prominently before touching down.

Although pair formation is not always smooth at first, gradually through courtship the two birds get to know one another better and settle down to a more regular routine. The territory is often chosen by the male, but the pair spend more and more time in each others company and begin to prospect for a suitable nest site.

109

During copulation, the female usually closes her tail and moves it to one side allowing the mounting male to bend his body over to bring the two cloacae into contact. These are Common terns *Sterna hirundo*.

Perhaps surprisingly, most water birds normally copulate on land. The ducks, however, are an exception; the male mounts the female on the water, often almost submerging her. Ducks have a penis-like structure, possibly to aid the transfer of sperm when copulation occurs on water. These are Shoveler ducks *Anas clypeata*.

Black Redstarts *Phoenicurus ochruros* copulating. The male positions himself on the back of the female and is very dependent on her remaining still if mating is to be successful.

Copulation. (1) Common swift *Apus apus* sometimes copulates on the wing, (2) Kingfisher *Alcedo atthis*, (3) Black-winged stilt *Himantopus himantopus*, (4) Little ringed plover *Charadrius dubius* and (5) Bewick's swan *Cygnus bewickii*. ⇨

Copulation

Normally even birds who are not strikingly territorial maintain some form of 'individual distance'; they keep at least a little way away from one another. Even within flocks, an individual distance is kept and birds do not normally come close together. Courtship functions not only in order to get a pair of birds used to one another so that their behaviour may be synchronized for breeding, but also to break down the maintenance of these individual distances. Until birds are sufficiently well acquainted with one another for individual distances to be dispensed with, the close approach necessary for copulation cannot be achieved. In certain birds, such as those where the males maintain leks, the prelude to copulation is very short; the females only come to the lek for brief visits when they are ready to be fertilized. Nonetheless, even in such cases, the pair may be more familiar with each other than one might think from such brief encounters; it is quite possible that each female visits the same male for the successive matings required for her clutch.

Unlike mammals, most birds do not possess a penis; sperm must be transferred by contact of the cloaca of the male with that of the female. In order for this to be achieved the male must mount the female and she must move her tail to one side so that he can bend the back of his body over so that the two cloacae can meet. The positioning of the two birds is such that the male is rather finely balanced and in order to complete copulation he requires the full co-operation of the female; she must remain still. Hence by his previous displays the male must have fully prepared his mate. When the two birds have their cloacae in contact, that of the female is usually somewhat everted so that the male can more easily reach over and make contact with it. When she withdraws the cloaca to the normal position, she draws the sperm into her and hence aids them in their journey up the oviduct towards the unfertilized egg.

Because of the close co-operation required by the two birds, many attempts at copulation appear to be unsuccessful, the male failing to get into the right position. Because there are no external differences in the sex organs of the two sexes 'reverse mountings'—where the female tries to copulate with the male—are frequently recorded in birds. These are said to be particularly frequent in species where there is little difference in the appearance of the plumage of the two sexes. Also homosexual pairings are relatively frequent; 'matings' within such 'pairs' of birds are commonly observed.

In the prelude to copulation, the male bird displays and sings to the female and, in some species, brings her presents of food; this is the basis for the phrase 'courtship-feeding', though the act is also important to the female in that it helps her to get sufficient food to form the eggs. In certain species, a particular song has been associated with the final prelude to copulation. Sexual chases are frequent in some species prior to the final display which leads to copulation.

Matings take place primarily during the period in which unfertilized eggs are present in the female; at this time she is most responsive to the male. The period is normally about two days before the egg is laid, but its length will depend greatly on how many eggs are to be laid in the clutch; the ten eggs of a tit or game bird may require several fertilizations over a period as opposed to one mating needed to fertilize the single egg of other species. As far as is known the females of most species do not store sperm for long periods of time so that a series of successful copulations may result in better fertilization of large clutches. However, there are exceptions, for in some of the ducks one successful copulation may be all that is necessary for the fertilization of the whole clutch. In addition, hornbills must be able to store sperm. The females are walled into the nesting chamber by the male some time before the first egg is laid. Thereafter, although copulation is impossible, the female lays five or more eggs; it seems that sperm from earlier copulations must remain viable for two or even three weeks in order for such eggs to be successfully fertilized.

1

2

3

4

5

BREEDING

The nest of the Lesser noddy *Anous tenuirostris* a tern from the Indian Ocean. The nest is of seaweed, cemented together and to a branch by the birds' excreta. Only one egg is laid.

The Lesser crested swift, or Tree swift, *Hemiprocne comata* at its nest. In this species the nest is tiny, a very small patch of material being cemented to the side of the branch with the bird's saliva. The nest barely holds the single egg, the incubating adult, and later the growing young, have to support themselves on the branch.

Nests in a variety of species. (1) Long-tailed tit *Aegithalos caudatus,* (2) Goldcrest *Regulus regulus,* (3) Ruby-throated hummingbird *Archilochus colubris,* (4) Common or Barn swallow *Hirundo rustica,* (5) Wagler's oropendola *Zarhynchus wagleri,* (6) Osprey *Pandion haliaetus,* (7) Baya weaver *Ploceus philippinus,* (8) African palm swift *Cypsiurus parvus,* (9) Kentish or Snowy plover *Charadrius alexandrinus* and (10) Fairy tern *Gygis alba.* ⟹

Nests and Nest Building

Birds build nests in order to raise young and hence it is most important that the nest should be safe from disturbance. However, as man well knows, both eggs and young birds are highly edible; in nature a wide variety of predators share this view and search diligently for the nests of birds; often the predators themselves are breeding at the same time as the birds and so they have a greater need of food than at any other time of year. Many mammals such as squirrels, racoons, stoats, weasels, monkeys, pigs, foxes and many members of the cat family make short work of any nests and adults which they can find. While some of these predators are confined to the ground, others are good climbers and many can reach nests in trees. Birds also are serious raiders of the nests of other species; gulls, birds of prey and many members of the crow family are among the worst offenders, but herons, toucans, woodpeckers and other birds may also take their toll. In the tropics snakes are responsible for the loss of many a nest; there are even egg-eating snakes, especially adapted with 'teeth' far back in the throat so that they can puncture the eggs and eat the contents only when the egg has been completely swallowed; the snake can then close its mouth so as not to risk spilling and losing any of the contents. Ants may often take a nest and kill the occupants. Sometimes one wonders how, in the face of so many enemies, birds manage to raise their young at all!

There are, perhaps, two main ways in which birds seek to protect their nests. The most widely used one of these—especially amongst small birds—is concealment. By hiding the nest in an out-of-the-way place, covering it with camouflaging materials and taking great care to visit it cautiously so as not to draw attention to it, the birds hope to protect their young. A second method of protection is to put the nests in inaccessible places; here the value of secrecy is less since the birds rely on their enemies being unable to reach the site at all. Rooks and herons in tall trees, swallows in sand cliffs or building mud-nests on a wall and sea birds on islands are all examples; often many members of the family may group together, possibly because safe sites are hard to find. This method is also used by large birds which are relatively well able to defend themselves. These, such as some eagles and the swans, build large and sometimes more easily accessible nests. Here, too the nests are reasonably well protected from mammals, but are readily found by birds though they easily can be defended by the large owners. Concealment is by far the widest method practised: it is better to avoid conflict with a potential predator than to look for trouble. Small predators pose a threat even to large birds since they may sneak up to the nest in unguarded moments and take the eggs or small chicks.

Small birds have almost no chance of defence once they have been found, though many may use both concealment and inaccessibility to try and prevent this. In the tropics in particular many small birds suspend their nests from thin vines or the tips of twiggy branches; these nests may be roofed, making it particularly hard for potential predators to establish whether or not there is anything worthwhile there anyway and, by using stealthy approaches, the birds may get through the nesting stage untouched. Nevertheless, the life of small birds in the breeding season is diffi-

The Rufous ovenbird *Furnarius rufus* from South America builds a strong mud nest with two chambers. The nests are often built on fence posts or in close proximity to man.

Owls use a wide range of nest-sites; often taken over from other birds that have finished with them. (1) The New World Elf owl *Micrathene whitneyi* often nests in a saguaro cactus using old woodpecker holes, (2) another New World species, the Burrowing owl *Speotyto cunicularia* uses abandoned lairs of the prairie dog, (3) the Short-eared owl *Asio flammeus* nests on the ground, sometimes under the edge of a bush, (4) the Great grey owl *Strix nebulosa* of the northern forests uses old nests of birds of prey, (5) the Snowy owl *Nyctea scandiaca* nests on hummocks in the arctic and (6) the Eagle owl *Bubo bubo* nests in crevices and small caves, hollow trees and old nests of other birds.

cult. In a study of Blackbirds in English woodland only some 14% of the nests produced fledged young, while in Trinidad Black-and-white manakins raised young from only 19% of their nests. Such low figures do not mean that the birds are quite as unsuccessful as they might at first appear. Persistence is the other quality necessary for such birds; each time they lose their nest they start again and perhaps eventually each female may lay three, four or even five clutches. Hence she may have about a 50:50 chance of raising a brood within the season. The nesting success of larger birds is usually higher than this and one group of small birds, the hole-nesters, also have a high success. Small birds which nest in holes in trees cannot be reached by the large ground-dwelling predators and most bird predators also cannot reach them. Not surprisingly therefore, their nesting success is much higher, only some 15–30% of the nests being lost to predators. One wonders why more species do not nest in this way. Two factors probably contribute to this. Firstly, such sites may be in great demand, so great in fact that some birds may be unable to find a suitable nesting site, a situation that almost never occurs in birds that choose a bush to nest in. Some birds of course, such as the woodpeckers, make their own holes, but these are hard work to construct and may take several weeks; even then another bird may come along and evict the rightful owner. Secondly, there are dangers associated with nesting in holes. If a predator finds the nest while the female is incubating, she cannot easily escape. In a study of tits in England some 20% of the females were taken when the predators took the eggs; in a more conventional open nest, the female must have a much higher chance of escape. Hence the advantages of holes as nesting sites may be in part offset by the difficulties of finding one and by the dangers to the female of being caught in it.

A few species make large holes smaller so as to reduce the chances of larger stronger

The Penduline tit *Remiz pendulinus* builds a finely woven nest of a felt-like material. This is usually suspended from a thin twig at the tip of a branch, often over water.

Unusual nests. (1) The Sun-bittern *Eurypyga helias* builds a precarious nest of vegetation and mud on a thin horizontal branch. (2) The Shelduck *Tadorna tadorna* is unusual for a duck in that it nests in burrows in sand-dunes. (3) The Common tailorbird stitches two sides of a leaf together as a support for its nest. The edges are held together by knotted fibres passed through holes made in the leaf edge. (4) The Horned coot *Fulica cornuta* builds a foundation for its nest by dropping stones into shallow water offshore. The platforms may grow to a considerable size over a period of years.

birds trying to take them over. The nuthatches plaster the entrance of a hole with mud until they themselves can only just squeeze through. In most hornbills, the female enters the nest chamber and then the male walls her in with mud until only a tiny opening is left. He feeds the female through this hole and she is wholly dependent on him throughout egg-laying, incubation and the earlier part of the nesting stage. After this she breaks out, and the young then help wall themselves in again until they are full-grown, but get fed by both parents.

Many species nest in even more inaccessible sites and suffer much less predation as a result. Sea birds are the most obvious examples of this. Their nests are often on cliffs or on small offshore islands. Mammalian predators cannot easily reach the nests on cliffs and even if they could reach the offshore islands they could not survive there at times when the sea birds were not breeding. There would be no food during the 'off-season'. Moreover these islands are often without fresh water, so that drinking would also pose a problem. Certain other species such as divers nest on small islands in lakes in temperate areas; again mammalian predators cannot easily reach them. Some Arctic species such as eider ducks, gulls and terns that nest on small islands just offshore are said to delay their nesting until after the ice has thawed and the Arctic fox can no longer reach the islands; the birds are then safe from their main predator.

Nesting on islands does not confer total protection; some birds are serious enemies of other nesting species. The larger gulls, for example, are predators of auks, shearwaters and storm petrels. Most of the latter species protect themselves by either nesting on tiny cliff ledges where the gulls cannot easily land, or by nesting underground—in burrows or under fallen rocks. Even then the marauding gulls may attack the parents, either to eat the birds themselves or to get the food that was being

Weavers of the family Ploceidae build some of the most intricately woven nests found in birds, some having long funnel-like entrances. They are built of grass strands or strips of palm leaf. Usually the male alone builds the nest; being polygamous, he may build a succession of nests for different females.

The male Mallee fowl *Leipoa ocellata* builds a large mound in which the female lays her eggs. The male opens the nest daily to check the temperature. Initially the mound is kept warm by heat generated from decomposing vegetation placed inside the mound (1), but as this begins to lose effect later in the season the bird may spread the sand from the top of the mound over a large area so that it is heated by the sun and then pile the warm sand back into the mound (2).

brought to their chicks. To reduce this danger the Puffin nests close to the edge of the island in places where it can quickly land and get down its burrow and equally quickly take off again. The shearwaters and the storm petrels are even more defenceless than the Puffin and the only way that they can safely come to their nests is to do so in the dead of night when the gulls are asleep; one small auk, the Cassin's auklet, has also become completely nocturnal. In tropical seas frigate birds are a constant threat to nesting terns on many islands.

A small number of species build their own 'islands' and some of the marsh-dwelling terns build floating nests of vegetation, anchored to sticks or reeds protruding from the water. These too deter many of the mammalian predators which would have to swim to reach them. In South America the Horned coot builds its nest by dropping stones in shallow water until the tip of the small island emerges above the level of the lake; there, safe from mammalian predators, it builds its nest.

The nest itself varies markedly in complexity in different groups of birds. Some birds such as the waders or shore birds do little in the way of building a nest: their eggs are laid in mere scrapes on the ground. The same is true of some of the penguins, though the Adelie penguin builds a small mound of stones on which it lays its eggs; by raising them just this much above the ground it keeps them out of the melting ice on their nesting grounds. The Emperor penguin, which lays its egg and incubates it through the long winter nights period (so that it hatches early in the Antarctic spring) has no nest at all. The single egg is kept on top of the feet and warmed by a flap of skin that hangs over it. During its vigil, the incubating bird is free to shuffle around and huddle against other birds in periods of blizzard.

Many other birds, such as auks, build little or no nest though sometimes they may put small amounts of material around the egg. Others, such as the shearwaters and petrels, do not produce much in the way of a nest lining though they may have to dig a burrow in which to nest. Many gulls and terns put only little or no material into the nest though others may build more elaborate structures, especially those mentioned above which make floating nests. Some birds that nest in holes in trees, such as some owls and parrots, also put little material into the nest. Yet others 'steal' nests that were constructed by other birds; some owls may take old nests of other species in which to place their own young and one of the cowbirds of North America is said to specialize in nesting in old nests of other species.

The simplest type of nest is probably that of a pile of sticks in a tree where a flimsy platform is formed on which to put the eggs; pigeons, birds of prey, herons and cormorants for example build nests of this type, those of cormorants often being built on ledges on cliffs. The nests of some members of the crow family are similar though better constructed and often lined with small rootlets well woven into the structure. A wide range of other species build nests of increasing complexity, though nearly all the most elaborate forms of nests are built by passerines. Only a few non-passerines go beyond the level of nesting on the ground, in holes in trees or in a nest of twigs in the branches of a tree. The latter type of nest may be large, in some of the eagles it is immense, but the structure remains simple. The Hammerkop, an aberrant stork, is an exception, building a completely domed nest of sticks with one, or sometimes two, entrances to the nest chamber. Amongst other non-passerines, the hummingbirds build neatly woven nests held together with spiders web and some of the

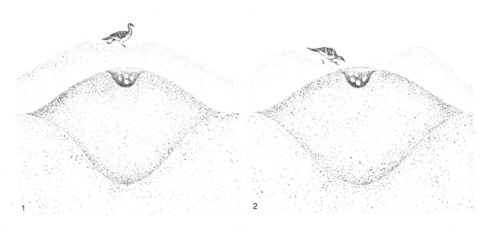

1   2

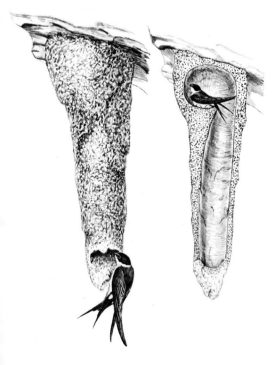

The Scissor-tailed swift *Panyrila sancti-hieronymi* builds a long tubelike nest, using its saliva to hold the structure together. The nest chamber is at the top of the tube. In nature, the nests are usually built on rock faces, but they are sometimes placed on buildings.

The Golden oriole *Oriolus oriolus* builds a flimsy nest towards the end of the branch. Usually the nest material is composed of thin strips of grass or bark.

Stages in the building of the nest of the Edible-nest swiftlet *Collocalia fuciphaga*. The nest, built virtually entirely from the bird's saliva, is cemented to a rocky surface, usually in a cave. These are the nests which form the basis of birds' nest soup.

swifts, whose edible nests we use for soup, build nests projecting from a cliff face.

The basic passerine nest is also built of twigs on a branch of a tree, or in the undergrowth in birds such as the Blackbird or American robin. The nests tend to be better constructed than is the case with the non-passerines and most of them are lined with grass or rootlets; some birds, such as the Song thrush, neatly surface the interior of the nest with mud, making a smooth lining. The methods of construction used in nest building are about as varied as the sites chosen. A great many nests are domed: all the birds in the wren family for example build domed nests and, as mentioned previously, a great many of the nests built by tropical species are also domed.

Some of the smaller species using lichens, mosses and similar materials build nests held together with cobwebs. These nests are extremely warm and well-insulated enabling the incubating birds to snuggle down inside with a minimum of heat loss. The extremes of design of this type of nest are reached in the long-tailed tits of the Palearctic, the penduline tits of Africa and the bush-tits of America. The nests are purse-like structures of great intricacy, made of moss and lichens bound together with spiders web and often richly lined with feathers; in the case of the European Long-tailed tit more than 2,000 feathers may be used to line the nest and a considerable variety of complex building behaviours are needed during the course of construction. So pliable are these nests that they seem to expand to hold the growing brood; in Africa the nests of penduline tits are used by natives as purses. The European Long-tailed tits start to roost in the nest as soon as it is roofed and weather-proofed even though the birds may not lay eggs for some weeks.

The sunbirds also often build intricate domed nests, though these are not usually as neatly built as those of the tits; they may be suspended from the very tip of a branch so as to be very difficult to reach. A small group of warblers, the tailorbirds, from southeast Asia build their nests between two large leaves which they have sewn together—hence their name. These birds take a pair of more or less opposing leaves and make small holes in their borders through which they pass their 'thread'—either plant material or spiders web. Each stitch is made separately and the ends of the threads are bent over or knotted to prevent them slipping through. Not only is the nest difficult to reach, it is also very difficult to see.

Pride of place among the avian architects is usually given either to the Old World weavers or to the New World orioles. Some of both groups make magnificently woven nests of grass or other strips of vegetation. These are hung from trees, often in small colonies. Many are long pendulous structures. Apart from size—the orioles are larger than the weavers and their nests may be as much as 6 ft (1.8 m) long—the main difference is that the entrance and nest chambers are in different places in the two groups. In the weavers, the bird enters the nest at the bottom and climbs up through a long tube to the nest chamber at the top; in the orioles the entrance is at the top and the nest chamber at the bottom. The passage down the long tube presumably deters any predators that may reach the nest, though some of the orioles are heavily parasitized by other orioles—the cowbirds. The Social weaver of southwest Africa builds a nest of an entirely different kind; the woven nest is similar to that of other weavers though simpler in design, its main difference being that it is interwoven with many nests of adjacent pairs, forming a single gigantic mass, one of the very few truly communal structures built by birds.

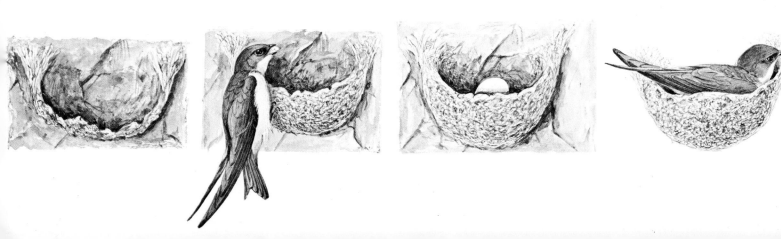

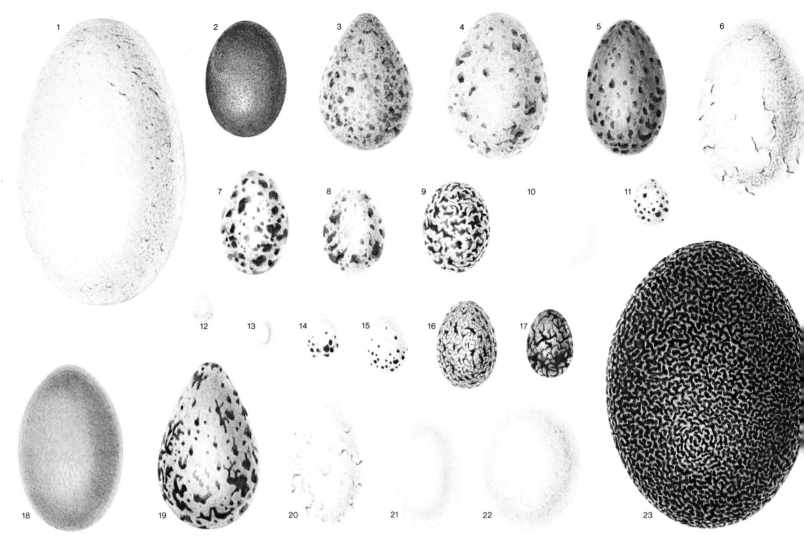

Eggs

Eggs of (1) Kiwi *Apteryx australis*, (2) Crested Tinamou *Eudromia elegans*, (3) Curlew *Numenius arquata*, (4) Herring Gull *Larus argentatus*, (5) Black-throated diver *Gavia arctica*, (6) American White pelican *Pelecanus erythrorhynchos*, (7) Black skimmer *Rynchops nigra*, (8) Common tern *Sterna hirundo*, (9) Guira cuckoo *Guira guira*, (10) Snowy egret *Egretta thula*, (11) Hawfinch *Coccothraustes coccothraustes*, (12) Goldcrest *Regulus regulus*, (13) Broad-billed humming bird *Cynanthus latirostris*, (14) Scissor-tailed flycatcher *Muscivora forficata*, (15) Song thrush *Turdus philomelos*, (16) American Crow *Corvus brachyrhynchos*, (17) American Jacana *Jacana spinosa*, (18) Scrub fowl *Megapodius freycinet*, (19) Guillemot *Uria aalge*, (20) European cormorant *Phalacrocorax carbo*, (21) Great crested grebe *Podiceps cristatus*, (22) Eagle owl *Bubo bubo* and (23) Emu *Dromiceius novaehollandiae*.

The egg of the Guillemot *Uria aalge* is very pointed. When pushed, it rolls around in a small circle and it is thought that this shape may reduce the chance of the egg being knocked off cliff ledges.

The hard shelled, often distinctively shaped, eggs of birds are well known. They are composed of three main parts—yolk, albumen and shell. The yolk is the most nutritive part, being relatively rich in fats and proteins. On the surface of the yolk there is a small patch, the germinal spot or blastodisc, which houses the tiny unfertilized ovum. After fertilization this develops into the embryo and, eventually, into the young bird. The growing embryo 'floats' on the surface of the yolk throughout its development. The egg white or albumen surrounds the embryo and, although relatively low in nutrients compared with the yolk, holds much of the water essential to the growing chick's survival. Two cords, the chalazae, attach the yolk to the shell keeping it central to the albumen and enabling it to turn as the incubating bird turns the egg; when small, the embryo stays uppermost on the yolk all the time. The albumen is surrounded by two layers of shell membranes just internal to the shell itself. The egg shell is a porous structure composed mainly of calcium carbonate; an average-sized hen's egg weighs about 2 oz (60 gm) and of the 0.2 oz (6 gm) of shell some 0.08 oz (2.25 gm) are calcium.

The developing chick must obtain all its nutrients from within the egg shell. The chick draws on these as it develops and also obtains the calcium it needs for its bones by withdrawing calcium from the shell. In most small birds the yolk is almost completely used up at hatching, but what remains is drawn into the body as a yolk sac just prior to hatching; this store helps the baby bird to survive if, for example, it hatches in the night when the parents cannot feed it. In a few species a considerable amount of the yolk remains at hatching. Young swans may hatch with 25% of the yolk still unused in the yolk sac; they are able to survive for a week or more on this food store. The largest yolk stores at hatching are found in penguins where some species hatch with as much as 50% of the yolk unused.

In order to metabolize its food the developing chick must be able to breathe and for this oxygen must be absorbed into the egg and carbon dioxide expired; a series

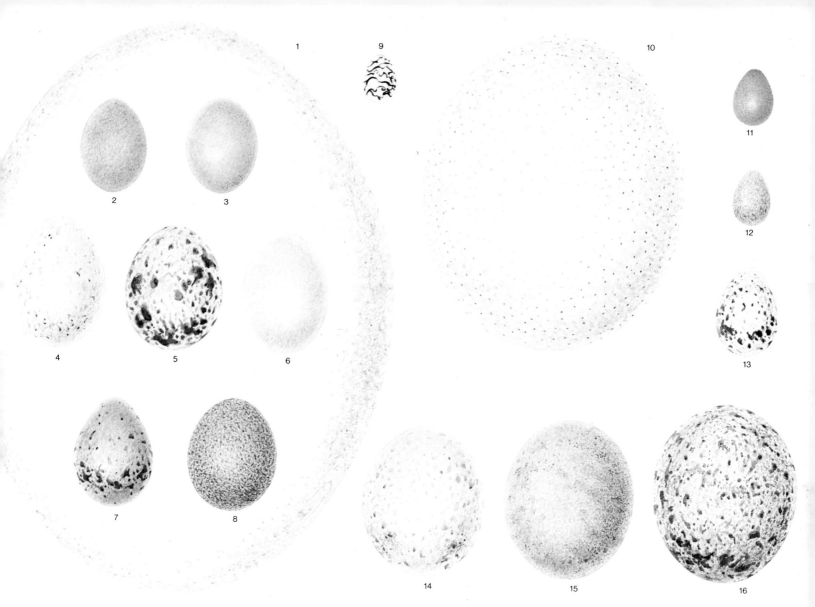

Eggs. (1) Extinct Elephant-bird *Aepyornis maximus*, (2) Glossy ibis *Plegadis falcinellus*, (3) Common bittern *Botaurus stellaris*, (4) European spoonbill *Platalea leucorodia*, (5) Osprey *Pandion haliaetus*, (6) Steller's eider *Polysticta stelleri*, (7) Long-tailed skua *Stercorarius longicaudus*, (8) Gyrfalcon *Falco rusticolus*, (9) Baltimore oriole *Icterus galbula*, (10) Ostrich *Struthio camelus* the largest egg laid by any living bird, (11) American robin *Turdus migratorius*, (12) Redwing *Turdus iliacus*, (13) Roseate tern *Sterna dougallii*, (14) Golden eagle *Aquila chrysaetos*, (15) Lammergeier *Gypaetus barbatus* and (16) Black vulture *Aegypius monachus*.

Some birds have a single large incubation or brood patch that covers all the eggs, others such as the Black-headed gull *Larus ridibundus* may have discrete patches for each egg, three in this species. The Emperor penguin *Aptenodytes forsteri* keeps its single egg on the top of its feet and incubates it with a fold of skin which hangs down and covers the egg.

of blood vessels throughout the egg, outside the chick, enable such respiration to occur. The egg shell is surprisingly porous to these gases and, during the latter stages of incubation as much as 30 ml of oxygen and a similar amount of carbon dioxide may pass through the shell of a gull's egg each hour, a considerable amount for a seemingly solid object. The difficulty for the embryo is that the egg also loses water through the shell during incubation; this is why a fresh egg sinks if placed in water whereas a well-incubated one floats: the loss of water has reduced its density. If too much water is lost the embryo may dry out and die. In many species, the loss of water produces an air space within the egg; this space forms between the two shell membranes and is called the air sac. Just before hatching the young bird forces its beak into this space and starts to breathe air through its nostrils in addition to that still being 'breathed in' through the embryonic blood system still visible in the egg. In this way the change-over to air breathing on hatching is facilitated. The growing embryo also produces waste products which are excreted into a bag within the egg—the allantois—where they are kept separate from still unused food resources. The small packet of waste materials is left in the egg on hatching.

The laying bird must find extra amounts of food in order to form eggs. It is estimated that this may increase her food demands by as much as 40% during the laying period; in addition she may have to search for particular foods at this time. For example the female Quelea finch takes more insects than her mate just prior to laying, apparently needing the high protein content of the insects. Other birds have to collect the calcium required for the egg shell: they may take calcareous grit, snail shell, egg shell or other materials at this time. Laying Dunlin in the Arctic eat the bones of dead lemmings in order to get calcium. Fish eating birds probably get sufficient calcium from the bones or their prey; one insect eating marsh tern is known to switch to a diet of fish during the laying period.

The size of eggs varies markedly. The smallest eggs are laid by the smallest hum-

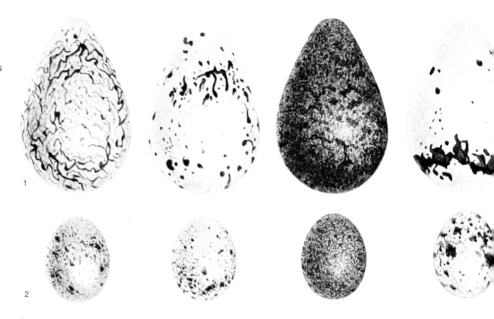

Variation in egg colour in the Guillemot *Uria aalge* (1) and the Kestrel *Falco tinnunculus* (2). In certain species the variation in the egg colour may be considerable. In the case of the Guillemot, which nests very densely on cliff ledges, the variation may help a bird to recognize its own egg. Individual birds tend to lay eggs similar in colour throughout their life times.

Depicted here are a range of egg shapes that are found in different species, varying from elliptical to conical in shape. (1) Steppe buzzard *Buteo vulpinus*, (2) Red-necked grebe, *Podiceps grisegena*, (3) Crowned sandgrouse *Pterocles coronatus*, (4) Barbary falcon *Falco pelegrinoides*, (5) Moorhen *Gallinula chloropus*, (6) Pygmy cormorant *Phalacrocorax pygmaeus*, (7) Tufted guineafowl *Numida meleagris*, (8) Sabine's gull *Xema sabini*, (9) Golden plover *Pluvialis apricaria*, (10) Lapwing *Vanellus vanellus*, (11) Spotted redshank *Tringa erythropus* and (12) Greenshank *Tringa nebularia*. Owls and Kingfishers lay some of the most spherical eggs while swifts and woodpeckers lay some of the most slender elliptical ones. The most conical eggs (such as 8–12) are often laid by waders and gulls; in the waders these are commonly kept in a tight cluster, pointed ends inwards to minimise the surface area occupied.

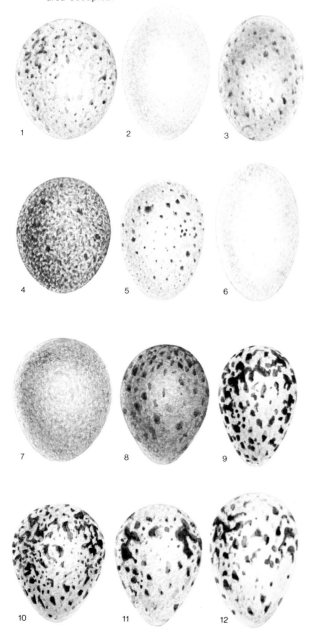

mingbirds and weigh about 0.02 oz (0.5 gm), while the largest, those of the Ostrich, weigh about 3.3 lb (1.5 kg); the eggs of the extinct Elephant-bird were much larger and, it is estimated, would have weighed about 20 lb (9 kg). Larger birds tend to have larger eggs, but there is considerable variation for other reasons as well; for example the Razorbill and the Carrion crow weigh about 28 lb (800 gm) and 17.6 lb (500 gm) respectively, but the former species lays an egg weighing about 3 oz (90 gm), the latter one of about 0.6 oz (18 gm), one fifth the size. If the clutch is large, eggs tend to be small, but perhaps the greatest factor is whether or not the young are precocial or altricial, the former hatching relatively larger than the latter.

The shape of the eggs also varies greatly, being almost spherical in some birds such as kingfishers and owls and long and pointed in some such as the woodpeckers, swifts and the guillemots; in the last species the egg, when knocked, spins round in a small circle; it is said that the egg is this shape to reduce the chance of its being knocked off a narrow ledge into the sea. The quality of the egg surface may be very chalky as in some of the cormorants, or smooth or even highly polished as in the tinamous and some babblers. Eggs of some babblers are so glossy that one can see reflections in them.

The most striking aspect of the appearance of eggs is their colour; this to some extent has been their downfall since their attractive colours and patterns have encouraged egg collectors. The reasons why there is a wide variety of egg colours have not been well explained except that in the waders and certain other ground nesting species such as some terns and the nightjars, they are beautifully camouflaged against their background. In the Indian Yellow-wattled plover, the ground colour of the eggs differs in different areas, but matches the general colour of the soil within that area. Eggs in dark sites such as nests in burrows tend to be either white, white with faint reddish spots or light blue. While eggs of these colours can be found in nests in other situations, the predominance of these colours in such sites— laid by birds from many different and often only distantly related groups—strongly suggests that there must be some good reason for having such colours. In more open places many eggs are beautifully marked with spots, blotches and streaks. The highly patterned eggs of the Common guillemot are said to enable the birds to recognize their own eggs from those of others—certainly the individuals tend to lay eggs of similar patterns in successive years.

There is some evidence that the eggs of a few species may not be highly palatable; in these cases they are often quite conspicuous; possibly since the risk of predation is lower, the predators may learn that the eggs are unpalatable and leave them alone.

Young and their Care

Young birds hatch from the eggs at the end of the incubation period; this may be as short as 11 or 12 days in some small birds or as long as 11 to 12 weeks in some of the larger albatrosses. The young weigh around 70% of the weight of the freshly laid egg and this amount is relatively constant in different species. Hence the size of the hatching chick is closely related to the size of the egg. On average, smaller birds produce relatively larger eggs and therefore relatively larger chicks than larger birds.

Young birds are normally divided into two sorts, precocial and altricial. Precocial young, such as those of the domestic hen, can run around within a few hours of hatching whereas altricial young such as those of the Blackbird or American robin are relatively smaller and incapable of looking after themselves. Not only is there a difference in relative size between the two groups, but also different parts of the body have developed to a different level at the time of hatching. Comparing a wader with a crow the former has a brain 6% of its total weight, compared with the latter's 3% and the wader's eyes are 10% of its total weight compared with 5% in the crow. By way of contrast, the digestive tract of the crow is some 13% of the total compared with the wader's 6%. Those parts of the body needed for activity—sight and brain—are well developed in young precocial birds while the young altricial birds are little more than a food processing machine. These differences are lost by the time the young birds are fully grown as a result of differential growth rates in different parts of the body. In the altricial young the legs grow relatively earlier than the wings; legs are needed to help the young birds reach up above its brothers in order to gain the food brought in by the parents while wings are not needed until the young birds fly at the end of the nestling period.

Altricial young hatch from the egg with little or no down and are usually blind. They are entirely dependent on their parents, not only to bring them all their food, but also to brood them and to keep them warm. In most cases if they did not get this warmth from the parents at least intermittently throughout the day and especially overnight, they would die of cold. Such young are also usually nidicolous—nest-dwelling—and remain in the nest for more or less the whole of the nestling period. Almost all the passerines are altricial.

Precocial birds hatch from the egg as well-developed chicks, covered with down and with open eyes; they are nidifugous—nest-fleeing—leaving the nest within a few hours of hatching. Almost all precocial young are still dependent on their parents for care, though the megapodes are not. Megapode eggs are laid in areas where the sand or rotting vegetation is warm enough to provide the heat for incubation and the young may not even see a parent bird when they hatch and emerge from the sand; even if they do, they do not recognize them and run away into the bush. They are well-

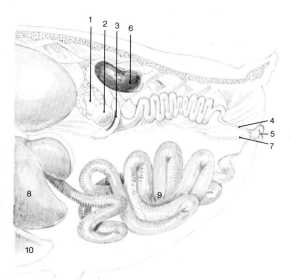

Section of an egg showing (1) shell, (2) shell membranes, (3) albumen, (4) air space, (5) chalaza, (6) and (7) vitelline membranes, (8) white layers of yolk, (9) yellow layers of yolk and (10) germinal disc.

The reproductive system of a female bird, showing (1) ovary, (2) ovum (egg) passing into the top of the oviduct (3), (4) vagina and (5) cloaca. The reproductive system lies close to the kidney (6) and the ureter (7) which runs from the kidney into the cloaca. Also shown in the lower part of the diagram are the stomach (8) and intestines (9); the lower tip of the breast bone (10) is also just visible.

The shape of eggs may be related to the shape of the ▷ pelvic girdle. Birds with a deep pelvis lay rounder eggs than those with narrower, more flattened ones. Shown here are the eggs and pelvic girdles of (1) Buzzard *Buteo buteo*, (2) Barnacle Goose *Branta bernicla*, (3) Great crested grebe *Podiceps cristatus* and (4) Eagle owl *Bubo bubo*.

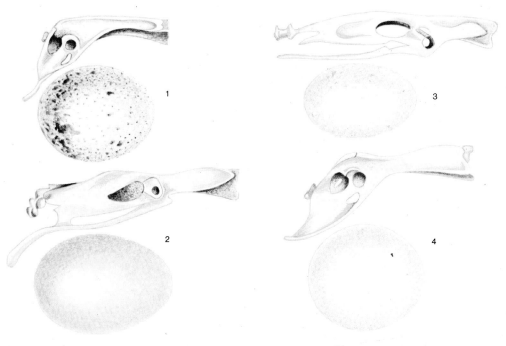

Most small birds keep their nests very clean. During the nestling period this usually involves the removal of faeces, wrapped in gelatinous faecal sacs. These sacs may be eaten or carried from the nest and dropped some distance away. This bird is a Sedge warbler *Acrocephalus schoenobaenus*.

Parent birds search the nest lining for foreign material, perhaps looking for parasites. They may also shake the lining vigorously, possibly they are then 'making the bed' by fluffing up the lining and improving the insulation.

Care of the young. (1) a Black vulture *Aegypius monachus* carries water in its bill to its young, (2) an adult European swallow *Hirundo rustica* (left) feeds its newly fledged young, (3) a young Herring gull *Larus argentatus* pecks at the red spot on its parent's beak so stimulating the adult bird to regurgitate food, (4) a Water rail *Rallus aquaticus* removes egg-shell from hatching young and (5) young Hoatzins *Opisthocomus hoatzin* which apparently may be cared for by a number of older birds. ⟹

feathered and look after themselves entirely from the moment of hatching. Uniquely among birds they are able to fly within a very few hours of hatching. The amount of care and attention given to other young precocial birds varies markedly though most will remain in contact with their mother during the day and will run to her for warmth and shelter during rainstorms and at night. Some, such as many of the ducks and shore birds, gain little more than this since they search for food for themselves and are self-sufficient in this sense. However, they still gain great advantage by remaining in the presence of their mother so as to benefit from her warning cries and general watch-fulness. Others such as some of the game birds are shown where to feed by their mother, indeed as in the domestic hen the mother may scratch up food for them. Yet others may actually be fed by the parents bringing them food: some rails, the Oystercatcher and the Magpie goose do this; gradually the young birds take over feeding for themselves. Parent grebes also bring food to their young in the early nestling period though they may well carry the young on their back to good feeding areas.

So many groups contain exceptions to the above rules that generalizations are unwise. The auks provide a good example of variation in the nestlings though all would be classified as precocial; they hatch well-feathered and with open eyes. Some such as those in the genus *Synthliborhamphus* leave the nesting ledge within a day or two and swim out to sea in the company of their parents, completing their de-velopment at sea. The Common guillemot and Razorbill fall into the next category, the young departing from the nesting ledges when they are about one third grown. They leave in the fading light of the evening, bouncing or tumbling down into the sea in ways that one would think were almost certain to injure them and yet they arrive safely. Although the main flight feathers have not grown at this stage, some covert feathers provide them with little wings that help them to break their fall. The apparent purpose of departure at this time is that it is then too dark for marauding gulls to see them and so they can be safely away to sea before dawn. At the other extreme from those that leave soon after hatching, birds such as the Atlantic Puffin and the Black and Pigeon guillemots stay in the nest until they are fully grown, about six weeks in the case of the Puffin. Well able to fly, it sets off to fend for itself without the help of its parents; the Puffin leaves its burrow nest in the dark, again presumably since it is safer from predators at this time.

Like some of the auks, other birds fall between the definitions of altricial and precocial. Herons and birds of prey usually hatch with their eyes open and with a good covering of down, but they nevertheless remain in their nests for the whole of the nestling period. Owls are similar except that in their case they are born blind. Gulls and terns hatch with their eyes open and with a good covering of down, usually well camouflaged in this case. These birds stay near the nest though often they move a little distance away to hide under cover of grass or bracken; when necessary they can run well. Young nightjars are beautifully camouflaged against their backgrounds and though able to move away from the nest (the barest scrape on the ground) they do so only to a very slight extent.

Parental duties are many; if the young are vulnerable to predation the parents must take great care to conceal their nest from predators and make sure that they do not give the location away by careless visits. They must also ensure that the nest area is kept clean of tell-tale marks or droppings. Most small birds produce their droppings neatly packaged in small gelatinous bags—faecal sacs. The parents eat these when they are small but as the young grow and the sacs get comparatively larger, they carry them away to drop them at some distance from the nest. In birds such as the waders where the nest is in an exposed site, the parents also remove the egg-shells to some distance; their white inside is conspicuous to crows or other marauders passing overhead and could endanger the brood.

Many parent birds try to deter a predator that approaches the nest by 'dive-bombing' it and mobbing it in order to distract its attention. Others may press home

1

2

3

4

5

A few waders that live in very hot areas bring back water to dampen and cool both eggs and young. This bird is the Egyptian plover *Pluvianus aegyptius*.

Most species of birds will vigorously defend their young against any predator which they can physically hope to defeat. Here an Adelie penguin *Pygoscelis adeliae* attacks an Antarctic skua *Catharacta skua* which is trying to take its chick. Penguin chicks which wander any distance from the parent are at risk since the skua moves so much faster than the penguin.

their attack; even a Blackbird can deal quite a hard blow with its feet or beak as it passes overhead. Others—especially ground nesting species—may feign injury, dropping to the ground and pretending that they are unable to fly; the predator, thinking that it has found an easy meal, runs after it only to find that the bird is always just out of reach; only once it has lured the predator to what it believes to be a safe distance from the nest does the bird fly off again.

The parents must also keep the young warm and, particularly with small and naked young, the female must brood them in order that they get sufficient warmth. As soon as the young are sufficiently warm she will go in search of food for them, intermittently staying to brood them on her return if they are getting chilled. The amount of brooding that she has to do will therefore depend upon the weather: the colder it is the more that she will have to brood the young and the less time she will have to collect food for them. In really bad weather the female may have to spend almost all her time brooding the young and leave the feeding solely to the male. Hence the young only get about half as much food as they would otherwise have done and many perish.

The food and the rate at which it is brought into the brood varies markedly in different species. Some, such as the small woodland insectivores, may bring in caterpillars almost every minute of the day; their trips to collect food may be very short and if food is relatively easily found there will be few delays. Most of the small insectivores bring food back to the nest at frequent intervals; in the Blue tit the pair may make as much as 1,000 visits to the nest each day in order to feed the rapidly growing young. No other bird is known to make so many visits, but many birds may return every three or four minutes during a sixteen or eighteen hour day, a rate of over 200 visits per day. Birds such as swifts tend to feed their young on great bolusses of food that they bring back from their long aerial foraging flights; they carry these masses of small insects in their throats and many visit their young only a few times during the day with these large meals. Similarly finches which bring seeds back to their young may bring cropfuls of seeds at infrequent intervals. Many of the larger birds such as gulls, herons and storks make irregular visits with large quantities of fish

Care of the young by carrying. The Nightjar *Caprimulgus europaeus* was first observed to carry its eggs (1) and young (2) from danger by Audubon, a habit questioned ever since by naturalists. However, there are better authenticated sightings of the Woodcock *Scolopax rusticola* (3) carrying its young in flight.

Although thrushes *Turdus* use stones as anvils on which to break the shells of snails when feeding themselves, the habit almost certainly ensures that their young receive food that is easy to digest.

or other food which they regurgitate to their young from their crops. Owls and other birds of prey also visit their young relatively infrequently but with large amounts of food. In these cases the prey may have to be broken up for the young before they can swallow it. At one extreme some of the most oceanic sea birds search for food over wide areas of sea; these birds may come to feed their young only every four or five days, sometimes at even longer intervals. Even with both parents feeding, the young may not get more than two or three meals per week. The birds such as the shearwaters and petrels which fly great distances to collect food for their young must expend great amounts of energy flying back to their nest with food; in order to economize in energy consumption and to fly back to the nest with as much food as possible, they have gone one stage further than other species of birds, they predigest the food to some extent so as to reduce the water content. Fish, like most animal matter contains a very high proportion of water—up to 70%. The thick soup that the birds feed to their young is therefore much richer than plain, raw fish.

The pigeons have an unusual method of feeding their young. During the nestling period the inner crop lining swells and the cells in this tissue break off forming a whitish liquid, the so-called crop milk. The young birds are fed on this; they obtain it by putting their heads into the parents' mouths and drinking it from the crop. This habit is unique among birds. Most species feed their young on food similar to that which they normally take for themselves, though it may vary slightly in size. Some of the finches are an exception to this rule since they may feed their young on an insect, instead of a seed, diet. Probably the need for a rich supply of protein for the rapidly growing young dictates this move though it is also possible that the water content of seeds is too low to enable the young birds to grow since they would not get enough water to drink. A few birds such as the American Wood-ibis bring their young water in their beaks. Sandgrouse have special absorptive feathers on the breasts. They soak these in water and carry this back to their young who then sip it from the tips of the feathers.

Large prey may have to be broken up for the young, as in the case of that brought back by birds of prey. The parents may have to take steps to ensure that the young are not injured by the prey. Bee-eaters remove the stings of wasps and the Secretary bird

125

The Royal albatross *Diomedea epemophora* feeding its chick. Albatrosses raise a single chick, some of the largest species take over a year to care for the one young and so only breed every alternate year. They bring their young a regurgitated mush of fish and squid.

When disturbed, young terns and gulls may swim out to sea in order to try to escape from their enemies. This is a dangerous habit since they might easily get lost, but the risk may be worth it if the danger of remaining behind is great. At times some adults may accompany them. These are Lesser crested terns *Sterna bengalensis*.

Fledgelings. (1) Song thrush *Turdus ericeforum,* (2) Lapwing, Green plover or Pewit *Vanellus vanellus,* (3) Dotterel *Eudromias morinellus,* (4) Crab plover *Dromas ardeola,* (5) Red-breasted merganser *Mergus serrator,* (6) Great black-backed gull *Larus marinus,* (7) Gannet *Sula bassana,* (8) Golden eagle *Aquila chrysaetos* and (9) Greater or Roseate Flamingo *Phoenicopterus ruber.* Numbers (1), (7) and (8) are nidicolous and remain in the nest until they can fly. The gull (6) only wanders a short way to find cover. Numbers (2), (3), (4), (5) and (9) are nidifugous and are able to follow the parents from the nest within a few days of hatching. However, the Crab plover (4) does not usually do so until it is older; unique among waders, its parents bring food to the young bird. ⇨

pulls off the heads of snakes before feeding them to its young. Even birds bringing in large caterpillars to their young beat in the head or remove it so that the strong jaws cannot injure the young bird while it is being swallowed.

There may be subtle changes in the diet during the course of the nestling period. In the tits small young are fed only small caterpillars, possibly because these are the only ones that can easily be swallowed then. When the young get larger, they are fed larger prey. As yet unexplained is the increase in the proportion of spiders brought in around the middle part of the nestling period, just before the young birds start to get their feathers. It is not known why this happens, but it has been recorded in several different habitats in different countries and at different times of the season. Presumably spiders provide some essential substances that are not found in sufficient quantity in caterpillars.

The young bird communicates its needs for food to the parent birds by begging: the hungrier it is the more incessantly it begs. Begging has the effect on the parents of making them go out to search for more food. When the young beg incessantly the parents, wherever possible, step up their feeding rates. A noisy brood is in danger of attracting predators; more large than small broods of tits are taken by predators because they are hungrier and noisier. Hence the parents endeavour to keep their young satisfied. If a predator is in the vicinity the parents' warning cries will immediately silence the calling young, but by then it may already be too late.

The number of young in a brood varies widely from species to species. In the case of many species the number of young can be related to the maximum that the pair can successfully raise. The larger the brood the more mouths there are to feed and so the parents have to speed up their efforts. However, the possible increase in feeding frequency is not proportional to the increase in the number of young so that in larger broods the individual young get less food than those in smaller broods. As a result of this lack of nourishment, the young in larger broods leave the nest at a lower weight than those in smaller broods and they stand less chance of surviving.

Apart from the availability of food, other factors affect whether the young birds will get sufficient for their needs. As mentioned, the temperature while they are in the nest will affect how much food they need. As with man, young birds need more food in cold than in warm weather in order to maintain their body temperature since the colder it is the greater the heat loss from their body. Although in terms of feeding young birds suffer if too many brothers and sisters are present, in one way they gain from their presence also. The larger the number of young the more easily they can huddle together and keep each other warm. At times in cold weather this is a considerable advantage since the young can keep each other warm for longer periods in the larger broods, so freeing the hen bird from the need to brood and allowing her to go and get more food.

Each species of bird has a fairly characteristic number of young in its brood. Many nidifugous species such as rails, ducks and game birds have large numbers of young in a brood—say 6 to 15, though waders have a smaller number—2 to 4. Small birds tend to have larger broods than large ones (though hummingbirds have only 1 or 2) and many of the very large birds of prey, albatrosses and penguins have only one young at a time. Once again there are many exceptions to these rules, but some other general trends are also apparent. Species breeding in the tropics tend to have smaller clutches than those breeding in temperate areas; this has been explained in terms of a greater upsurge in spring food supplies in temperate areas making the feeding of a larger brood more practicable there than in the tropics. Sea birds that feed far out in the ocean and visit their young infrequently tend to have smaller clutches than those that feed inshore. Hole-nesting species tend to have larger broods than birds in more exposed sites; in this case the birds are in relatively safe nest sites and spend longer in the nest, growing more slowly than is the case with young in open nests.

Where the food supply is very sparse the brood size may be adjusted during the

Woodpeckers nest in holes in trees, usually ones that they have excavated for themselves. Large young may race to the entrance when they hear the parents arriving with food and so the parent does not have to enter to feed them. These are Green woodpeckers *Picus viridis*.

nestling period through starvation. In many species the bird does not start incubating until all the eggs have been laid, with the result that the young all hatch at more or less the same time. However, if the bird starts to incubate before all the eggs are laid then a number of the young will hatch after the others. Where such asynchronous hatching occurs the young are staggered in size and, if food is scarce, the larger young can easily get what food is necessary; the smaller young cannot compete and so may die. Only when the larger young have been satisfied will the smaller receive food. Hence in times of food shortage the smallest quickly starve without taking much of the food that could have been fed to the larger young. If the young did not hatch asynchronously all would compete on equal terms and, even if any survived, all would be weakened and light in weight. Nature's way is to give some the maximum chance of surviving even if others quickly starve. Asynchronous hatching is found in many groups of birds that hunt live prey such as herons, birds of prey, owls and swifts. In other groups it is not uncommon for the last one or two young to hatch a little behind the others and so stand slightly less chance of surviving.

If well-fed, the young may reach almost adult weight before they leave the nest. In a few cases they may greatly exceed it. Some shearwaters leave the nest weighing about $1\frac{1}{2}$ times the weight of their parents. They apparently use this surplus fat for their first migration, before they seriously start to feed for themselves. In these and a few other species the young are not cared for after they have left the nest; as soon as they have fledged they are on their own. A young Common swift left its nest in Oxford, England and was killed in Madrid, Spain, four days later when its parents were still roosting in the nest. Relatively few birds are like this, most need intensive parental care in the dangerous period when they enter the wide world and start to learn to fend for themselves.

The parents of most species look after their young during this period. In some small passerines, this may be only for a week or so and even then the care may be somewhat desultory on the part of the female if she is preparing to start another brood. Others may remain with their parents for many months or even years getting some limited care from them; many of the birds that hold group territories fall into this category. Others such as some of the northern geese may remain as family parties throughout the southward migration and the ensuing winter; during this time the young birds can learn the traditional routes and feeding areas of their parents. Others such as frigate birds, other large sea birds and the large birds of prey may look after their fledged young for many months after they have left the nest, so long in some species that the adults do not breed the following year, continuing to care for the young of the previous season. Even the European Tawny owl which leaves the nest in May or early June may be cared for by its parents until at least September.

After this the young birds are on their own. Learning to fend for themselves, finding a territory and breeding are hazardous occupations for young birds and many perish before they themselves can attempt to raise their own young.

Many ground-nesting species can recover eggs that are accidentally knocked out of the nest. Here a Grey-lag goose *Anser anser* retrieves an egg by rolling it with the underside of the bill.

A young Black-throated honeyguide *Indicator indicator*, a species which parasitizes other birds such as barbets and woodpeckers. The newly-hatched honeyguide kills the young of the host species with sharp hooks on its bill tip; hooks that later fall off. Note the large protective pads on the ankles; the bird spends much of its nestling period sitting on these.

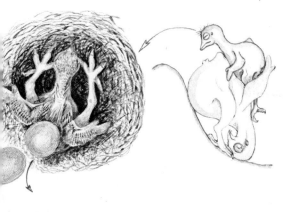

A newly hatched European cuckoo *Cuculus canorus* can evict eggs or young of the host species, here a Hedge sparrow *Prunella modularis*. The young cuckoo has a dip in its back into which it can manoeuvre the eggs. After leaving the nest, the young cuckoo continues to be fed by its foster parents, even though it may be many times larger than they are. Here a Winter wren *Troglodytes troglodytes* a rather unusual host, feeds the young cuckoo.

Brood Parasites

A small number of birds have specialized in laying their eggs in the nests of other species so that the young are raised by foster parents; in this way the birds themselves may go on to lay more eggs in other nests. Although rather few species have developed this method of breeding, this habit has been evolved at least five and probably six times in birds. To a varying extent it is found in ducks, honeyguides, cuckoos, New World orioles and amongst the weavers where it has probably evolved independently on two occasions, in the Parasitic weaver and in the Viduinae, a group of estrildine finches.

Although some of the parasitic birds are extremely specialized, one can see a possible way in which the habit may have evolved by looking at the different species, since they show a whole range of different degrees of specialization. An American cowbird looks after its own young in the normal way, except that it lays its eggs in old nests of other species. The Black-headed duck lays its eggs in a wide variety of nests of other species and leaves the owners of those nests to incubate and hatch its eggs. Since this species is nidifugous and most ducks can feed themselves after hatching, possibly the young Black-headed ducks need little after-care from the foster parent. In the Common cowbird of North America the female lays eggs fairly indiscriminately in a wide variety of species nests of small birds; the eggs are not at all well-camouflaged and may be rejected by the host species. At the other extreme, some cuckoos lay eggs which often closely match the colour of the eggs of the host and in some cases the plumage of the young is also a close match with that of the foster parent. In the viduine finches the patterns of the mouthparts of the young parasite, together with its calls, are remarkably similar to those of the host.

The degree of perfection of these adaptations is, of course, the result of the behaviour of the hosts. It is a major disadvantage for the host to raise the young parasite; by so doing it decreases the number of its own offspring which it raises. In species such as those parasitized by the European cuckoo, which ejects the eggs or young of the host, the host raises no young of its own. Even where the young parasite is raised alongside the young of the host, there is often some mortality and so the host would raise more of its own young if it avoided being parasitized. The host can do this in a variety of ways; it may chase the female cuckoo away before she can parasitize the nest or if it finds a strange egg in its nest it can desert and nest again, thus being more certain of only raising its own young. Possibly also it could learn to recognize its own young and not feed young that differ from these. As a result of any of these actions on the part of the host, the parasite would die. Hence there has been strong selection for the parasite to evolve better and better camouflage in order that its young may be successfully raised and also strong selection for the host to learn to discriminate between its own young and those of the parasite. Such evolution of two species that are closely associated with one another frequently produces quite remarkable specializations, and it is not surprising to find many among parasitic birds.

The cuckoos, Cuculiformes, are probably the most highly adapted brood parasites; although by no means all the species of cuckoos are parasitic, many raise their own young. The European cuckoo has been the most studied; it lays its eggs in the nests of small passerines such as the European robin, Meadow pipit or Reed warbler. Each young cuckoo weighs about as much as the whole brood of the host. Presumably this is one of the reasons why only a single egg is laid in each nest: the host birds could not raise more than one cuckoo. In addition to being a close match in pattern, the egg is unusually small for a bird the size of a cuckoo, being only some 2.5% of the weight of the female. In contrast, the related Great spotted cuckoo lays its eggs in the nests of birds such as the Magpie which are about the same size as itself. In this case the cuckoo's egg is about 7% of the female's weight, a much more usual size. The young cuckoos are raised alongside the young Magpies and more than one cuckoo egg may be laid in a single nest. Not only can the female European cuckoo lay her egg

The Cuckoo *Cuculus canorus* (1) is one of the most highly specialized brood parasites. Here it is seen removing an egg of the Meadow pipit *Anthus pratensis* prior to laying one of its own. The Giant cowbird *Scaphidura oryzivora* (2) is a New World Oriole which specializes in parasitizing nests of other members of its own family, here a Montezuma oropendola *Gymnostinops montezuma*. The Black-headed duck *Heteronetta atricapilla* (3) lays its eggs in the nests of a variety of other species of waterfowl and leaves the other birds to incubate the eggs.

remarkably quickly, but she has a protrusible cloaca enabling her to place the egg more nearly into the nest than she would otherwise be able to do. Nevertheless, the egg often has to be dropped into some nests. Not surprisingly the egg has an unusually thick shell in order to reduce the chance of its being broken by the fall.

Parasites have evolved a wide range of adaptations to enable them to carry out their strategies successfully. In honeyguides, the male attacks the barbet hosts and draws them away from their nest while the female slips in to lay the egg. In some other species the female may lay the egg elsewhere and fly to the nest carrying it in her beak. In a few species such as the European cuckoo the eggs may bear a remarkable resemblance to those of their host; each female lays only one pattern of egg and specializes on a particular host species. The close match is believed to have been brought about as follows: young hatch only if their eggs are not recognized by the host; the females that are successfully raised carry with them an image of the nest site or of the parent which raised them so that when they return as adults they specialize in parasitizing that particular type of nest.

The eggs of many parasites hatch very quickly, before those of the host. Hence the young can grow faster than the host young and, being larger, can dominate them in their demands for food. In the European cuckoo, which lays eggs only every other day, it is possible that 'incubation' starts while the egg is in the female's oviduct, so giving it the ability to hatch a day or two before the normally incubated eggs of the host. The European cuckoo is raised alone in the nest, being roughly equivalent in weight and food demands to the whole of a brood of the host. This cuckoo evicts the eggs or small young of the host by manoeuvring them into the small of its back and then standing up, so tipping them out of the nest. Young honeyguides kill the host young with a specially adapted egg-tooth which enables them to stab the young to death. This sharp point drops off after a week or so.

Young of some parasites show a remarkable series of adaptations that enable them to pass for young of the host. The Indian Koel (a cuckoo) parasitizes crows. The young of both sexes are black like the crows, but when the young have fledged the females moult into a brown plumage which they wear for the rest of their lives, though the males remain black. The young parasitic weaver and the young of the host warblers are identical in appearance—on the back; if one turns them upside down the belly feather colour is quite different—the host parents cannot see this in the nest so the parasite has not needed to evolve matching plumage here. The young of the whydah finches are raised by the parents of closely related estrildine finches. The latter have a remarkable series of protuberances and coloured marks around the gape which are different in each species; apparently these have been evolved to enable the parents to distinguish between their own young and the young whydahs. However, the latter have evolved identical marks to combat this. They have even evolved almost identical calls and so are exceedingly difficult to distinguish from the young of the host while they are in the nest.

Parasitic birds. (1) The viduine finches parasitize the nests of other small finches. The males of the Paradise wydah *Steganura paradisea* hold leks to which the females come for mating; the females then go and lay their eggs in the nests of the host species, here a Green-winged Pytilia *Pytilia melba*. (2) Each female European cuckoo lays eggs of a characteristic pattern which resembles that of one of the host species. Here Cuckoo eggs (the left of each pair) are compared with eggs of the following host species; (3) Reed Warbler *Acrocephalus scirpaceus*, (4) Great Reed Warbler *Acrocephalus arundinaceus*, (5) Dunnock (or Hedge sparrow) *Prunella modularis* and (6) Siberian Meadow Bunting, *Emberiza cioides*. (7) A pair of Black-collared barbets *Lybius torquatus* chase away a parasitic Lesser honeyguide *Indicator minor* from their nest.

1   2   3   4   5   6   7

MIGRATION

Winter wrens *Troglodytes troglodytes* may conserve energy in cold weather by huddling together in a communal roost. As many as 30 to 40 birds have been found together in a single hole. Here they are seen (viewed from behind) in the nest of a House martin *Delichon urbica*.

Ptarmigan *Lagopus mutus* live in very cold areas. They conserve energy overnight by making tunnels into the snow and roosting in these. The temperatures down such holes is higher than on the surface and the birds are also sheltered from bitter winds. They may have to dig their way in and out of their burrows in snowy weather. Here a Ptarmigan is seen leaving its burrow.

Wintering

When autumn comes, birds that spend the summer in temperate areas must make a 'decision' as to whether or not they should remain. Migration involves long flights over often inhospitable or dangerous areas where there is little on which to feed, into areas which the young birds have never experienced before. On the other hand, to remain means that the birds must face the rigours of the winter in the hope that it will not be too severe. This 'choice' is not, of course, made every year but, as a result of natural selection, each species has evolved the habit which has proved to be safest. For some the 'choice' has been clear; birds that breed in the high Arctic or are wholly dependent on insects for their diet must leave. Others may go southwards only if their food supply fails. We call such birds irruptive species; many of the seed eaters such as the tits and finches are included in this category as are some predatory birds such as the Snowy owl and the Rough-legged buzzard.

Another group of birds, known as partial migrants, face a slightly different dilemma. In species such as the Chaffinch, Blackbird and European robin, some individuals migrate and others winter near to their birthplace or their breeding place. It has been said of the Chaffinch that one can see the even balance of the two alternatives; over the course of a series of mild winters more and more birds spend the winter in the breeding area while after a severe one almost all the birds are migrants. If the weather is mild in winter those that remain survive better than those that risk the dangers of migration, but if a hard winter prevails then migration proves less dangerous than wintering. Presumably the offspring of each type of bird inherit the same tendency as their parents and the relative number of each type depends on the hardness of recent winters. Over a period of time the advantages of each habit are fairly evenly balanced and so both habits persist.

In species where partial migration is observed more young birds than old ones migrate and more females migrate than males. Both young birds and females are less successful than old birds and males in competition for food; if fighting occurs for food, the latter groups tend to be the ones that are successful. Hence the young birds and the females are the groups which are less likely to be able to survive the winter on the breeding ground and so it is not, perhaps, surprising that larger proportions of these birds migrate.

Most birds that winter in temperate areas must search hard for sufficient food; the insects and fruit are gone so that the birds that eat these in the summer must change their diet. Many of the birds that remain are waterfowl and waders. In fact the large majority of these spend the summer in the higher latitudes and migrate some way southwards, but still spend their winter in temperate regions; marshlands and shore may be occupied by more birds in the winter than in the summer. Since these birds need water that does not freeze and make their food disappear, many of them move not north and south but from the centres of land masses to the edges where, with the warming influences of the oceans, the weather tends to be milder. In Western Europe many of the waterfowl, lapwings, starlings and blackbirds have come from as far east as Poland and Russia.

Species that spend the winter in cold climates. At least some populations of all these species spend the winter in areas where there is thick snow on the ground. (1) Pine grosbeak *Pinicola enucleator*, (2) Steller's jay *Cyanocitta stelleri*, (3) Crested tit *Parus cristatus* and (4) Snowy owl *Nyctea scandiaca*. Jays and tits store food in the autumn which they use to help them survive the cold, short winter days. Some, such as the Snowy owl and some of the crossbills, may move south in winter when their food supplies fail in the north.

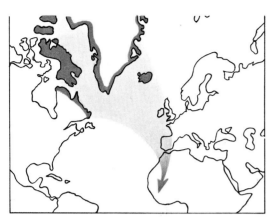

Wheatears *Oenathe oenathe* breed over much of the north temperate area of the world. Those that breed around the Atlantic may have to make long sea crossings to their wintering grounds in Africa. Birds leaving the southern tip of Greenland may not make landfall until they reach northern Spain, a flight of 1,850mi (3,000km) over sea, taking perhaps three days.

A range of migrants. (1) European cuckoo *Cuculus canorus*, (2) Lazuli bunting *Passerina amoena*, (3) Long-tailed skua *Stercorarius longicaudus*, (4) Yellow-throated vireo *Vireo flavifrons*, (5) Red-headed woodpecker *Melanerpes erythrocephalus*, (6) European crane *Grus grus*, (7) Nutcracker *Nucifraga caryocatactes*, (8) Sooty shearwater *Puffinus griseus*, (9) Grey-headed albatross *Diomedea chrysostoma*, (10) Barn swallow *Hirundo rustica* (American race), (11) Storm petrel *Hydrobates pelagicus*, (12) American avocet *Recurvirostra americana*, (13) Common swift *Apus apus*, (14) Rufous hummingbird *Selasphorus rufus*, (15) Blue-winged teal *Anas discors*, (16) Sandwich tern *Sterna sandvicensis*, (17) Pomarine skua *Stercorarius pomarinus* and (18) Short-eared owl *Asio flammeus*. ⇨

Eleonora's falcon *Falco eleonorae* breeds in the winter in the Mediterranean region. Its own range is not well known, but some of the birds from the eastern Mediterranean spend the northern winter in Malagasy, some 3,700mi (6,000km) away.

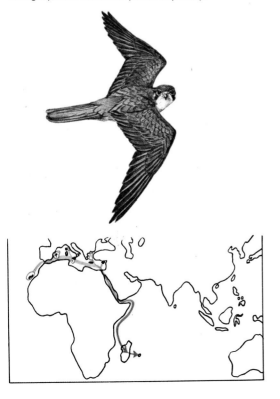

Migration

At the end of each Ice Age, as the sheet of ice covering the land retreated, progressively more birdless land appeared. In the height of summer these areas provided rich breeding grounds and any bird living further to the south that moved up into the empty areas would have found food in plenty, though they would have had to move back south again for the winter. Gradually, as the ice receded further, the birds that could make use of the empty lands in the north found that they had to fly progressively further and further to reach them. This, we believe, is how the migration routes of birds evolved. At the present time we see the outcome of migratory routes that have evolved gradually over many thousands of years of changing climate.

One may consider true migration to involve a major shift of the majority of a population from a reasonably well-defined breeding area to a reasonably well-defined non-breeding area and back again, each movement taking place once a year. Under such a definition, cold weather movements and the altitudinal movements of birds on mountains are excluded. Practically no species is known which breeds in both the areas where it spends part of the year.

Birds usually migrate because the area in which they spend the non-breeding season is not as good an area to breed on as their summer grounds and because they cannot survive on their breeding grounds during winter. In the latter case they must feed up and get ready to migrate before the bad weather comes; it is no good waiting until conditions are already poor before leaving since by that time it will be difficult to lay down the fat needed for migration and the whole journey may be put in jeopardy. Normally, long-distance migrants lay down considerable stores of fat to provide the fuel for the long journey. Small warblers such as the Blackpoll or Sedge warbler, which normally weigh about 0.4 oz (12 gm) at most times of year, may set off on migration weighing twice as much as this. The Sanderling, a wader, may double its weight from 2 oz (60 gm) to 4 oz (120 gm) just prior to departure. Larger birds such as geese put on rather less fat, but even they may weigh as much as 50% more than normal just before they set off on their long flights to the north. These fat stores are laid down shortly before departure and plainly highly rich supplies of food must be available if the birds are to be able to fatten up to this extent.

Some migration routes cover considerable distances. Even birds as small as a Willow warbler, weighing about 0.3 oz (8 gm) may undertake very lengthy migrations. A small population of this species breeds as far east as Alaska and, like their more easterly colleagues, they apparently fly to Africa for the winter—a flight of some 8,000 mi (13,000 km) or more. The Arctic tern which spends the northern winter in the Antarctic waters and so gets two summers in each year, flies about 9,000 mi (14,500 km) each way. Some journeys involve a long non-stop flight. When small land birds make long sea-crossings one can be certain that they have found no place to rest en route. Wheatears from Greenland make land-fall on the north coast of Spain, a distance of 2,000 mi (3,200 km), and Golden plovers from Alaska reach the Hawaiian islands some 2,500 mi (4,000 km) away.

A few small birds get lost on the eastern seaboard of North America each autumn and arrive in Europe; such flights are even further than the figures quoted. However, many of those that successfully make the journey undoubtedly owe their survival to having been able to rest on a ship. Others probably only arrive if they have had strong tail-winds that decrease the amount of flying time involved.

Sea-crossings are not the only ones where the birds find landing unrewarding. In the autumn, many of the small birds leaving Europe may have to cross as much as 600 mi (960 km) of the Mediterranean, yet cannot expect to find anything worth stopping for in North Africa. At its driest in the autumn, the Sahara is almost as daunting as the sea. For small birds the total distance of inhospitable surface may be at least 1,500 mi (2,400 km) and possibly more. The recent droughts on the south side of the Sahara coupled with man's clearance of the vegetation to feed goats and cattle

Although birds making long journeys may have to fly both during the day and night, most can be classified as primarily day or night migrants. Day migrants. (1) Brambling *Fringilla montifringilla*, (2) Redwing *Turdus iliacus*, (3) European swallow *Hirundo rustica*, (4) Red-winged blackbird *Agelaius phoeniceus* and (5) Chimney swift *Chaetura pelagica*. Night migrants. (6) Blue grosbeak *Guiraca caerulea*, (7) Rose-breasted grosbeak *Pheuticus ludovicianus*, (8) Black-and-white warbler *Mniotilta varia*, (9) Bluethroat *Cyanosylvia svecica* and (10) female Blackcap *Sylvia atricapilla*.

The Bristle-thighed curlew *Numenius tahitiensis* breeds around the Bering Straits and winters in remote Pacific Islands. Its nearest landfall is the Hawaiian islands, a non-stop flight of some 2,500mi (4,000km).

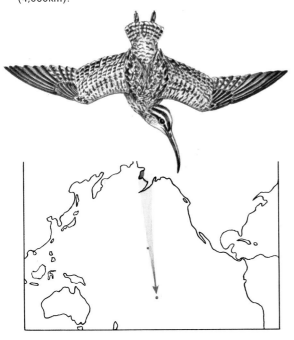

may well be making life much more difficult for some species by increasing the distance that they have to cover in order to reach good feeding areas. Some species which migrate to this general area, such as the Whitethroat, seem to have become scarcer.

Small wonder then that the migrants put on so much fat as fuel for the journey. Warblers fly at barely 30 mph (48 kph) though the larger waders fly a little faster. In order to cover 1,500 mi (2,400 km) some of these small birds must face non-stop flights of at least 48 hours; flying time will be longer for more extensive journeys or when they are slowed down by unfavourable head-winds. Normally they set out with enough fat to have some reserves in case this happens.

Warblers are night migrants at least in the sense that they take off at dusk. However, on these long journeys they must fly both day and night. Other species, in particular the finches, usually fly by day but these birds make, on average, much shorter journeys. In the Caribbean, the warblers tend to fly across the sea from the USA whereas the finches and buntings fly around the edge; they do not go so far south in any case.

Birds of prey, storks and cranes also usually fly by day, but they do so for a different reason. These large, relatively heavy birds try to save energy by soaring rather than using flapping flight. In order to do this they have to make use of thermals—which occur only in the day—and the upcurrents off mountainsides. Both these manoeuvres require careful positioning and accurate vision. Soaring species not only migrate by day, but they also stick to relatively narrow routes—along mountainsides for example; their course is largely plotted for them by the geography. In Europe, where many soaring birds leave to spend the northern winter in Africa, the birds avoid possible long sea-crossings by crossing the Mediterranean either at the Straits of Gibraltar or from Greece to Turkey over the Bosphorus. Other diurnal migrants fly on relatively narrow routes. In North America the waterfowl use 'flyways' that

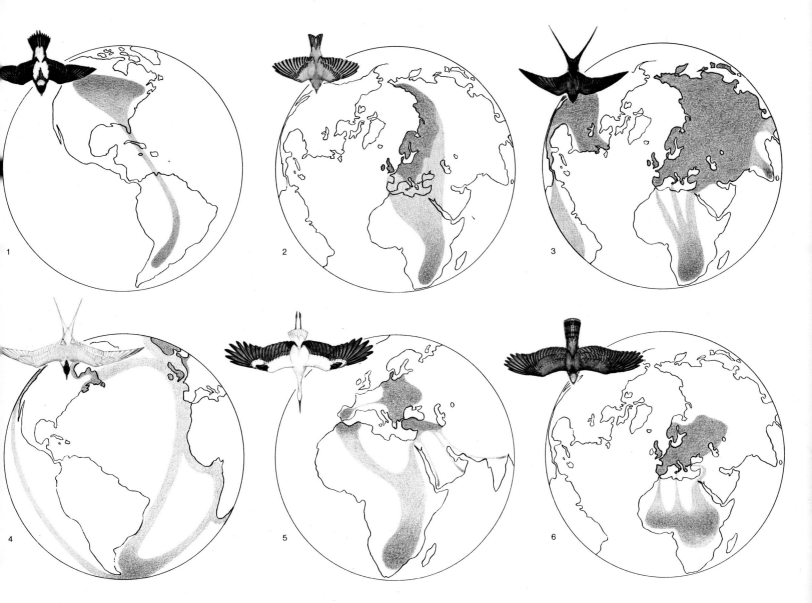

Long-distance migrations of (1) Bobolink *Dolichonyx oryzivorus* one of the longest migrations of a New World passerine; (2) Willow warbler *Phylloscopus trochilus*; (3) Swallow and Barn swallow *Hirundo rustica*; (4) Arctic tern *Sterna paradisea* has the longest journey of any species; and (5) White stork *Ciconia ciconia* and (6) Honey buzzard *Pernis apivorus,* which both cross the Mediterranean by the shortest routes so as to avoid long sea crossings.

The Mutton-bird *Puffinus tenuirostris* breeds in southeastern Australia; during the non-breeding season at least some of the birds make a long journey in a figure-of-eight around the Pacific.

largely follow the course of some of the major rivers; in this way they can stop wherever they want to and are never out of sight of their favourite habitat. Many diurnal land birds such as the finches and the crows follow the coast, not straying out to sea if they can avoid it. The Chaffinches that visit Britain for the winter from northern Europe do not make the crossing of the North Sea direct, but fly down the coasts of Holland and Belgium and cross into Britain from Cap Gris Nez, the shortest route.

Nocturnal migrants again contrast with diurnal ones in that they usually fly on a broad front; also they tend to fly singly, perhaps in order to avoid collisions. Vast numbers of these small birds cross the coast of North Africa on their southwards migration in the autumn. Over 200 species of birds leave Europe for the winter and there must be at least 1,000 million individuals involved, possibly as many as 3,000 millions. Since the north coast of North Africa is about 2,500 miles (4,000 km) long, this is equivalent to something of the order of 0.5 million birds (possibly 1.5 million) crossing each mile of coast or some 4,000–12,000 birds per day for each day of a two month migration period.

The figures given here are obviously only crude estimates based on calculations of the numbers of breeding birds in Europe and the numbers of young they raise. Yet they must be roughly correct and similar huge numbers of birds must move southwards from USA and Asia seeking warmer climates for the winter. There is no equivalent migration on this scale for land birds from south temperate regions, there being insufficient land masses at that latitude. Nevertheless a few birds migrate to warmer climates for the winter; the Swift parrot leaves Tasmania and flies northwards into other parts of Australia for the southern winter. Within the tropics also, many birds migrate, avoiding areas when these are dry. In Africa a number of species cross back and forth across the equator to take advantage of two rainy seasons.

Navigation and Orientation

From early times it has been known that birds could find their way rapidly over long distances, hence the use of pigeons, and occasionally other species, for carrying messages. The Egyptians certainly used pigeons for carrying messages and the Romans are reputed to have tied coloured cottons to the legs of swallows so as to give early information to those at home about the results of chariot races. In more recent times the technique of ringing birds has demonstrated that individuals can find their way accurately over very long distances. The European swallow nesting in a barn in the northern hemisphere migrates to South Africa for the northern winter and returns, each summer of its life, to nest in the same place. In recent years it has also become apparent that most migrant birds also spend the winter within a relatively confined space, rather than wandering at large over wide areas. In addition there are now a few records of small migrants which, on their way between Europe and North Africa, stop in the same place each year. Hence an individual may acquire not only two 'homes' but also known 'ports of call'. Obviously if this is possible, it confers upon the bird the benefits of stopping at places that were safe the year before and where the bird can gain advantage of previous knowledge. Nevertheless in order to do this the birds must be able to navigate accurately and each individual bird must have a relatively restricted flight path.

A number of experiments have been performed with birds taken from their breeding grounds and released some distance away. Often these birds have returned to their nest in a remarkably short time. A Manx shearwater from Skokholm Island, Wales was released in Boston U.S.A. and returned to its nest within $12\frac{1}{2}$ days, and a Laysan albatross made a journey of a similar length back to Laysan in 10 days. These times imply that the birds must have headed more or less directly back to home from their release point; they had no time for wandering around while searching.

In order to find one's way from one place to another, one requires two sets of information, a map and a compass. A map is useless unless one knows how to find the direction between one place and another. Similarly a compass is no use if one does not know in which direction one wants to go. Migrating birds plainly possess both a map and a compass inasmuch as they know where they are going and, in addition, can take up a compass bearing. However, although the bird may be born with certain parts of this information, other parts may have to be learned. For example, Common starlings migrating southwestwards through Holland spend the winter in north-western France. Some were caught and moved to Switzerland. When released the young and old birds behaved differently. The old birds adjusted to being moved off course and, flying northwestwards, returned to northern France (where they had been before). The young birds, on the other hand, flew in a southwestward direction from Switzerland, along a route parallel to their original course, and spent the winter in the vicinity of the Pyrenees. Hence the old birds had a map-sense in that they could somehow appreciate that they had been displaced and could rectify the situation. The young birds did not possess this map knowledge; they had no experience of the place where they were going to spend the winter. They could however fly in what was the correct direction, and perhaps also had some means of gauging the correct distance they had to fly to reach their winter quarters, since the area where they stopped in southern France was about the same distance from the place of release in Switzerland as was their normal wintering place from their place of capture in Holland. These young birds later returned successfully to the area in which they had been raised and after that some continued to migrate to the area in which they had, 'wrongly', spent the winter. Hence although they had a 'compass sense' they were not able to fly to an area unless they had previously visited it.

Many birds obtain their direction by use of the sun. Common starlings, kept in chambers from which they can see no land-marks but from which they can see the sun, will take up a direction relative to the sun. By altering the direction from which the sun

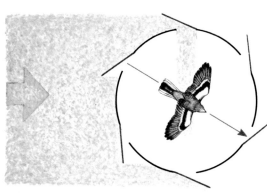

Orientation. Birds primarily establish their direction by use of the sun or stars. In order to be able to do this, they must know the time of day; it has been shown that they have an accurate internal clock. Here a Chaffinch *Fringilla coelebs* is in an orientation cage; it can see the sun through a series of windows (upper picture). If the windows are covered by mirrors (lower picture), the sun's rays cannot be seen directly, but only indirectly where they are reflected in off the mirrors. Under such experimental conditions the Chaffinch changes its orientation so as to maintain the same position relative to where it believes the sun to be.

Almost unique amongst birds, oilbirds of the genus *Collocalia* are able to navigate within dark caves by means of echo-location. They emit a series of clicks and use their echoes to determine whether there are rock surfaces nearby.

appears to come, the experimenter can cause a bird to alter its orientation thus showing that the bird is really using the sun and not some other celestial clue. If the weather is cloudy, the bird does not take up a fixed direction in the cage. The sun's position changes during the day, so that in order to maintain a constant compass direction, the bird must adjust its bearing to the sun in relation to the time of day. In other words, it must know the time; in addition to its map and compass senses it must also have a clock. Curiously, it is more difficult to train a Common starling to maintain a constant bearing to the sun throughout the day, than it is to train it to keep a fixed compass direction. In many ways the former is, at first sight, easier since it does not require information about the time.

Man can pin-point his position accurately with a good clock and sextant. These tell him the height of the sun at midday, and the time at which it reaches that highest point, and are sufficient to enable him to calculate both the latitude and longitude of his position. It seems clear that a bird can do something of this kind and, in addition, do it at times other than midday. It has been suggested that in order to do this the bird needs to be able to observe the movement of the sun along a tiny section of its arc and extrapolate the rest of the arc. There has been much controversy as to whether or not a bird is capable of taking such measurements. However, there is growing evidence that the discriminatory powers of many animals are far sharper·than those of man and that therefore birds may be able to do such things. Further, it is a weak argument to say that such-and-such a measurement could not be taken accurately enough. Birds make many very striking journeys and arrive safely. Whatever means they use seem to be beyond our abilities; small wonder then that we find the explanations that have been proposed hard to believe.

In addition to being able to use the sun, birds can navigate by the stars. A great many migrant birds normally fly at night and experiments similar to the ones testing birds' abilities to use the sun have been made by putting birds in orientation cages at night under starry skies. Hand-raised warblers that have never seen the sky can take up an orientation under the star patterns in a planetarium, hence at least certain aspects of the direction-finding techniques of birds are inherited from their parents. It appears that the birds use only certain portions of the star patterns in order to enable them to find their way. Indeed one of the greatest dangers to a migrating bird, especially a nocturnal migrant, is that it will fly into a change of weather. Not only may this obscure the stars but it may also bring a change of wind direction. The birds, bereft of navigational clues, cannot then maintain their direction and are in danger of getting swept off course into inhospitable areas, perhaps blown out over the sea. It is under such conditions that bird-watchers have a 'good' day at a bird observatory, many rare birds having arrived in the area. However, such a day is a bad one for the birds, many of which have become lost, may never find their way back on course, and so will perish. However, at least some of the older, more experienced birds may be able to re-orientate themselves and get back on course if only they can find sufficient food to survive until the weather improves. As with birds migrating during the day, thick cloud reduces the ability of night migrants to maintain a fixed flight path.

Under normal circumstances it seems likely that birds usually find their way either by use of the sun or the stars. However, recent research suggests that there may be occasions when birds can use some form of magnetic clue to find their way. How they do this is not known, but it may be only a subsidiary method to the normal use of sun and stars. Nevertheless, although at times discredited, it seems that magnetic, and possibly other clues, may be used by birds in addition to the more usually accepted methods. We still do not know how birds get home so quickly. However, in many of the release experiments (often made with homing pigeons) the birds determine which is the home direction within a few moments of being released from their light-proof carrying cases. Long before the birds have flown out of sight of the release point, most of them have turned in the direction of home. Indeed, a great many of them are flying in roughly the right direction within 30 seconds of release.

BIRD POPULATIONS

The Royal albatross *Diomedia epomophora* is an example of a very long-lived seabird. A study of this species showed that only some 3% of the breeding adults died each year. This means that the average age of the breeding adults is about 38 years.

The European robin *Erithacus rubecula* is fairly typical of a small temperate passerine in that around 50–60% of the adults die between one year and the next. Hence only a tiny fraction of the birds will survive to reach 10 years of age.

Longevity

Many studies, usually involving ringed birds, have been made of the age to which birds live and of the numbers that die each year. Small birds of the temperate regions are among the best studied, and it is known that many have short life-spans. In birds such as tits and the European robin, only about 50 % of the individuals that breed in one year survive to breed again in the following year. In a few other, larger, species such as the Common starling or Blackbird, the adult survival rate may be as much as 66 %. Although there are some exceptions, large birds tend to live longer than small ones, and the greatest ages known are found amongst sea birds and large birds of prey which may reach an age of 30 years. Some bird species are known to have adult survival rates of 95 % which means that the average age of individuals is 20 years. It is thus likely that some members of the population live to an age considerably older than 30 years.

The generalizations above appear to hold true for many birds in temperate regions but few intensive studies have been made elsewhere. In particular, survival rates in the tropics appear to be quite different from those quoted above. There are now several studies of small forest species suggesting that the birds may live much longer there than do those in temperate areas. The Black-and-White manakin, a tit-sized bird of Trinidad, has an annual survival rate of about 90 %.

The death-rates of birds follow a rather different pattern from those in mammals (including man). In mammals after initial, often high, juvenile mortality there follows a period of 'middle-age' when relatively few animals die. After that the death rate increases again; we say the animals have reached old age. In birds, once the initial period of high mortality has been passed, the death rate remains fairly steady throughout the rest of the bird's life-span; there is no plateau in middle-age followed by an increasing death rate in old age. Hence, for birds it is more meaningful in most cases to say that the annual mortality is, say, 10 % than to give an age to which birds of that species usually survive. It does not follow from this that birds never die of old age, but only that most studies have been unable to show that they do. One can say, however, that very few birds normally die of old age and that ages, such as those recorded occasionally in captivity, are very rare indeed. Hence the information on longevity of individual birds in zoos has little, if any, relevance to what happens in natural populations in the wild.

Bird-ringing has produced a number of records where wild birds have attained quite high ages. It must be emphasized however, that only a tiny proportion of wild birds live for very long periods. For example, if 50 % of Robins die each year (the average figure) then only 1 out of every 1,000 Robins will survive 10 years. Ringing records show that a few gulls, Manx shearwaters and a Curlew have reached ages of 30 years or more, while a number of other gulls, terns, and birds of prey have survived between 20 and 30 years. For the smaller passerines in temperate areas, 10 years is a very good age, though there is a record of a 15-year-old swallow.

The Black-headed gull *Larus ridibundus* has an adult mortality of around 25% per year, meaning that once they reach breeding age these birds may expect to live about 3½ more years on average. As with other species, the survival rate of the young birds is lower than that of the adults.

In many species of small birds living in temperate areas mortality during the summer is surprisingly high, almost equalling that in a normal winter. The effort required for breeding, together with the dangers of being caught by predators, either at the nest or while searching for food for the young, offset the milder weather and the longer hours for feeding. Often females live slightly less long than their mates since they are more closely associated with the nest and so more likely to be taken by predators.

The survival and mortality rates discussed above are for adult birds. Juvenile birds suffer much heavier mortality than their parents. Since numbers of birds remain stable in the long-term, it follows that the numbers of young birds reaching breeding age must balance the numbers of adults dying. For example if, as is roughly the case, 50 % of adult Blue tits die between one year and the next, one adult per pair dies and so one young bird per pair is needed to replace it. Hence, on average, one chick must be produced by each pair and survive in order to maintain the numbers. Since Blue tits lay, and often raise, ten or more eggs, it follows that only one of these eggs can produce a young bird which survives long enough to become a breeding adult. Ringing studies support such theoretical calculations. In the Great tit where about 50 % of the adults die each year, the birds fledge about 5 or 6 young per pair, on average, and about 17 % of the resulting population survive to breed.

In larger birds, losses may be slightly lower, but there is still a very high loss of young before they reach breeding age. Many of the larger species have an immature age of several years during which they do not breed. Most of the mortality usually occurs in the first year of life, but throughout the immature stage the young birds have a higher mortality than do the adults.

Deaths of young birds are high throughout the nestling stage, but in many species it is thought that there is a very high loss during the period just after the young have left their parents and when they are learning to fend for themselves. This high loss of young birds has important implications in population studies.

The Mute Swan *Cygnus olor* (1) lays a clutch of about six eggs. Some 40% of these hatch, but only about half reach the flying stage. Less than a quarter of the young that fly survive to breed at four years of age. Once adult, the birds may expect to live about five years; about 18% die each year. The equivalent figures have not all been worked out for the Trumpeter swan, *Cygnus buccinator* (2), but are likely to be similar.

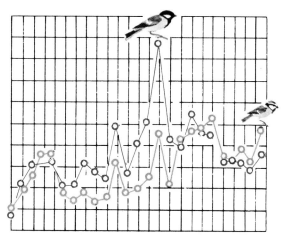

The number of pairs of Great tits *Parus major* (red graph) and Blue tits *Parus caeruleus* (green graph) breeding in a small wood in central England. In spite of their large broods, the numbers remain remarkably stable. Large increases in numbers usually follow a winter in which beech seed was in plentiful supply.

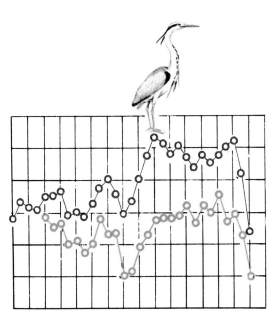

The numbers of European or Grey herons *Ardea cinerea* in two regions of Britain. The synchronous declines result from high mortality of herons in severe winters when their fishing grounds freeze over. If the succeeding winters are mild, the populations quickly recover to their previous levels.

Population Changes

Perhaps one of the most surprising features of bird populations is how little their numbers vary from year to year. We say that they are stable. Each spring a householder will notice that his garden contains perhaps a pair or two of Blackbirds, a pair of European robins and one or two pairs of tits. Numbers remain similar each summer; there are never five or six pairs of Blackbirds or none at all. When one considers the hazards that birds face and the numbers of young that they can sometimes raise this stability is rather surprising.

Such casual observations are borne out by accurate counts of the numbers of breeding birds in different areas. Although, of course, the numbers vary from time to time, the size of the fluctuations is surprisingly small in relation to the amount that they could theoretically change. Consider, for example, a pair of small passerines such as the Blackbird or the American robin; they may have two or three broods each year and may raise eight young in the season. If all these birds survived, then there would be ten birds (or five pairs) the following season. If all the parents and young lived, this single pair would increase to 25, 125 and 625 pairs in the third, fourth and fifth years.

One does not need accurate counts to know that this does not happen, but what prevents it? The numbers of birds in an area are dependent on the numbers of births and the numbers of deaths. If there are more births than deaths then the numbers will increase, if there are more deaths than births the numbers will decrease. When the population is stable, the numbers of births will equal the numbers of deaths. Hence in our example of the garden birds, the number of birds that die each year must be the same as the number of eggs laid. This may not happen in each garden but on average this must be the case.

One factor which could affect such calculations is the movement of individuals into and out of the area of study. This undoubtedly happens, with the populations in some areas over-producing and birds subsequently moving into other poorer areas where the population has been unable to maintain itself.

Ornithologists tend to conduct surveys of breeding birds during the summer. At this stage the birds are resident and, often, more easily counted than at any other time of year. However, one should always remember that all these counts of numbers hide one important facet of bird populations, namely that there are large changes in numbers within a year. At the start of the breeding season the number of birds is at its lowest. Once the young birds have hatched, a mere two to three weeks later with small birds, the numbers rise rapidly reaching a peak at the end of the nestling period. Thereafter when the young birds leave the nest there is a sharp decline in numbers since many of them perish. The large majority of the young birds have probably perished by the autumn and thereafter there is a slower decline in numbers until, once again, low numbers are reached just prior to the following breeding season.

Although taken as a whole populations are relatively stable, there are of course changes. Most populations show changes in numbers from year to year and at times these may be quite large. However, in most cases such fluctuations are of a temporary nature and the population soon reverts to its previous level. The reasons for these year to year changes are many and varied. Often, as in the case of the Grey heron, Common kingfisher and other birds dependent on open water for their livelihood, severe winter weather may bring about large numbers of deaths. Once the water has frozen over, these birds can no longer reach their food and so perish in large numbers. Similarly, severe cold affects many of the birds that feed on the ground, such as the thrushes and waders. Unless they can move elsewhere, they suffer the same fate as the water birds. It is not the cold weather in itself that brings about the birds' deaths. Even small birds are remarkably resistant to severe cold, provided that they can get their food. In the early part of 1963, southern England suffered its coldest winter for about 200 years and there was thick snow on the ground for 2–3 months. Nevertheless some species survived well because their food supply was plentiful. Bullfinches were

The Puffin *Fratercula arctica* is a relatively long-lived species; about 6% of the adults die each year, and the average age of the breeding population is about 20 years. However, each pair only produces a single chick each year, many of which do not survive. Hence if there are heavy losses for some reason, the numbers of breeding pairs will not recover nearly so quickly as is the case with the heron which may raise three young each year.

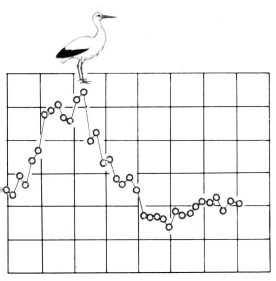

The numbers of White storks *Ciconia ciconia* in part of Germany. Here a long-term decline seems to have been taking place, possibly as a result of drainage of the wet meadows where the storks like to feed. The birds spend the winter in Africa and may also be suffering increased mortality there.

able to take seeds from the ash trees and this seed was unusually plentiful that winter. As a result, in spite of the weather, many Bullfinches survived the winter. In contrast Chaffinches, which feed largely on the ground, perished in considerable numbers.

Unfavourable weather in winter may not be the only cause of reduction in numbers. Heavy rain during the chick stage can cause large numbers of deaths amongst young gulls and terns. Even prolonged dry and sunny weather may not be good for certain birds. Blackbirds are dependent on soft, wet soil if they are to collect worms for their young. When the ground dries out and hardens, they may not be able to feed their brood properly and they may starve. During unusually dry summers they may have fewer nesting attempts than in wet moist summers.

Sharp increases in numbers of birds can often be related to unusually favourable conditions, especially to occasions when the food supply is unusually abundant. Many birds depend on seed crops during the winter and when these are plentiful, the birds will feed on them in large numbers. In Europe, seeds are an important source of

Sharp increases in numbers of birds can often be related to particularly favourable food for Common pheasants, Wood pigeons, Chaffinches, Bramblings and several of the tits. When the beech mast is plentiful, the tits tend to feed on it throughout the winter and large numbers survive to breed the following summer.

As has been mentioned already, most populations show year to year changes, but these are still relatively small compared with the changes that are theoretically possible. The potential power of increase described earlier for a pair of Blackbirds practically never occurs. Normally the doubling or halving of the breeding numbers of small birds between one year and the next is rather exceptional, though drastic reductions in numbers of some small birds were noted after the very severe winter of 1963 referred to above. In Europe, the Long-tailed tits, the Winter wren, the Green woodpecker, the Barn owl and several water birds suffered marked reductions in their numbers. However, these species recovered their numbers during the years following the hard winter.

Figures approaching those theoretically possible have, however, occurred under certain conditions, especially when a bird has been introduced to an area of the world where it had not previously lived. Often such changes have been brought about by man's introductions. A classic example is that of the introduction of the Common pheasant to Protection Island in the state of Washington, USA. Two cocks and six hens were released early in 1937. The area was obviously highly favourable for this species since within only six years there were almost 2,000 birds. Even this rapid increase was not so fast as is theoretically possible since there was always a lower number in spring than in the previous autumn; in other words, considerable numbers of birds must have died each winter.

Increases such as this do not occur within a small area, but only when a bird arrives in a new area which it can successfully exploit. The introductions of both the Common starling and the House sparrow to the USA have been well documented. About 150 Common starlings were introduced into New York State in 1890. Within a mere 60 years the birds were estimated to have increased by at least a millionfold and had spread throughout most of the country. Some of the birds reached Ontario in 1919 and within 15 years Common starlings were estimated to be the commonest bird in southern areas of the state. Similarly, the House sparrow, introduced in 1850, has reached all the states within about 50 years and must have increased by about the same amount. Elsewhere in the world these two birds and other species have shown dramatic increases in numbers after arrival in a new area. For example the Indian mynah is now widespread in many of the warmer areas of the world. In all these cases birds showed some of their potential for rapid increase in numbers.

We have seen that birds, introduced into a new area, can increase rapidly—at least for a number of years. However, most bird populations do not achieve these vast increases in numbers although, theoretically, we know that they could. What prevents them doing so? We get some insight into the problem by looking at the numbers

The Fulmar *Fulmarus glacialis* used to nest in Britain only on St Kilda. In 1878 the first nests were found elsewhere. Since that time the species has steadily expanded until it now breeds throughout the coasts of the British Isles. In 1970 it was estimated that there were more than 300,000 nests. This expansion has been achieved even though the Fulmar only lays one egg each year and does not normally breed until it is seven or eight years old.

of Grey herons, which have been recorded in Britain for many years. The numbers remain relatively stable for many years then, when a severe winter occurs, the numbers drop as birds starve to death. Breeding numbers are low the following year, but rapidly build up to around their previous numbers when they then level off once more. There seems to be a ceiling to their numbers which the birds cannot easily exceed.

We see this phenomenon in many species; birds are reduced in numbers after some natural disaster, but rapidly recover until they are around the previous level. Only during the few years after a marked reduction in numbers do the birds increase in numbers rapidly. Nature puts a ceiling to the numbers because there is a limit to the resources available. As a result of competition between individuals for these resources an upper limit is set. When a resource is scarce fewer birds (in relation to the number of birds present) can obtain sufficient to survive and breed. When the resource is plentiful in relation to the numbers of birds, more birds find sufficient and so a higher proportion survive and the population increases. We call such a response 'density dependent' since the survival of the birds is dependent on their own density. Many different resources have been held to limit the numbers of different species. Food is an obvious example. Nest sites may be in short supply, especially where a special type of site is needed such as a hole in a tree or a cliff site on a safe island. In some cases there may not be enough for all the birds to obtain a territory suitable for breeding.

We can now see what happens in the case of the Grey heron and a hard winter. After the winter, numbers are reduced and so each bird finds it easier to obtain food. However, as numbers increase again it becomes more difficult for each individual to find sufficient food and so the mortality increases until there is no more room for additional herons and the numbers level off once more.

This interaction between the individuals in a population has another important facet. It is that since there is an upper limit to the numbers which can survive, the death of one bird may mean that another—which would have otherwise perished—may be able to survive in its place. The relatively high reproductive rate of birds ensures that the population will be high at the end of the breeding season. Density dependent mortality reduces the numbers to a point where the resources can support the numbers remaining.

The interplay of these two factors—high production followed by high numbers of deaths—has important consequences for those concerned with the conservation of rare birds, the wildfowler and those concerned with the control of pest species. In a natural state, birds will produce far more young than will survive to breed. Hence, after a natural disaster, when numbers are low and survival rates high, the birds will rapidly recover to a higher population level. The protectionist, therefore, need have no fear for birds following such a disaster. After the very cold weather of the 1963 winter, Long-tailed tits disappeared from many areas and were rare for a year or two. However, their natural productivity enabled them to spread back into almost all their normal habitats within a few years.

The wildfowler shoots some of the doomed surplus. Provided he does not kill more than would have died anyway he can crop the population without danger. Properly controlled, such 'cropping' can provide not only food, but sport for man without in any way endangering the species concerned. Indeed, in a way, it may be beneficial since in many parts of the world, political pressure from huntsmen is an important factor persuading governments to preserve marshlands and forests. The farmer wishing to control a pest such as a pigeon faces a harder task. To reduce numbers he must kill more than the doomed surplus or the breeding level will remain the same. Further, even if he does reduce the number, keeping it at a lower level is extremely difficult. Again the high reproductive rates coupled with the high survival rates of the birds when living at low density enable the pest species to quickly recover its numbers. Temporary reduction in numbers is of little use and permanent reduction very difficult.

144

Rapid colonization. The Common starling *Sturnus vulgaris* was introduced to New York in 1890. It spread extremely rapidly and within a little over 50 years was widespread throughout the whole of the United States. This probably reflects an increase of about a millionfold.

Although most species of birds were found and named many years ago, there is still a steady trickle of new discoveries. (1) *Conioptilon mcilhennyi*, a cotingid from Peru (1965); (2) *Amytornis barbatus*, a grass-wren from Australia (1968); (3) *Pseudochelidon sirintarae*, an aberrant swallow from Thailand (1968); (4) *Grallaria eludens*, an antpitta from Peru (1967); (5) *Monarcha sacerdotum*, a flycatcher from Flores (Indonesia) (1973); and (6) *Hemispingus parodii*, a tanager from Peru (1968).

Long-term Changes

While populations tend to be stable from year to year, changes take place over long periods. The history of the evolution of the avifauna has been one of change, with one species taking over from another. Such changes happened very slowly, often over millions of years. As one habitat declined, so another increased and the species adapted to those earlier habitats either had to adapt to the changes or suffer the same fate.

Not all such changes happened over millions of years. The habitats in most areas of the world have changed considerably even in the last 10,000–20,000 years. Some 12,000 years ago the temperate regions, in the grips of the last Ice Age, were dominated by ice and snow. Gradually as the ice receded new areas became more habitable to birds, but areas of central Europe did not become richly forested with deciduous woodland for several thousand years after the ice started to recede. It should be stressed that the woodlands which we know today still existed, probably in very similar form, during the Ice Age, but much farther to the south. As the successive Ice Ages have come and gone so the habitats have ebbed and flowed across the world. Thus the birds that have evolved to live in particular habitats have usually been able to find that type of habitat somewhere else; the habitats did not disappear, but merely shifted.

Still more recently many other changes have been brought about by man. These are usually different from those described above. Often they have involved the reduction of habitats without equivalent replacements elsewhere. Only those species which have been able to adapt to the new artificial man-made habitats have benefitted. The long-term changes brought about by man differ from the natural ones in that they have occurred more rapidly and hence the birds have had less chance of adapting to them. It is perhaps worth pointing out that man-made changes are occurring ever more swiftly as man becomes progressively more mechanised. In Mediterranean regions man has been changing the habitats for more than 5,000 years. In many other areas the small numbers of natives clearing tiny patches of trees caused

Rapid natural increases. (1) The Collared dove *Streptopelia decaocto* has spread rapidly across Europe during the last 50 years. It first bred in Britain in 1955 and within 10 years it was thought that there were probably at least 20,000 birds in the country. It is likely that the original colonists were further augmented by other birds. (2) The Cattle egret *Bubulcus ibis* is an Old World species that was found breeding in Guyana, South America, in 1930. Since then it has spread round the Caribbean into the United States where the increase continues. During the last 15 years there has been about a 20-fold increase. Unlike the Collared dove in Britain, further waves of colonists from Europe are likely to have been negligible, so that all the increase must have sprung from the original colonists.

Extinct birds. For birds which have become extinct in recent times, dates are given. For those known only or virtually only from fossils (1–5, 10 and 11) the colours are hypothetical. (1) *Ichthyornis*, (2) *Hesperornis*, (3) *Archaeopteryx*, (4) *Diatryma*, (5) *Teratornis*, (6) Great auk *Alca impennis* (extinct by 1844), (7) Reunion starling *Fregilupus varius* (1832), (8) Passenger pigeon *Ectopistes migratorius* (1914), (9) Huia *Heterolocha acutirostris* (1907), (10) Moa *Dinornis maximus* (the last species of moa to become extinct, perhaps as late as the eighteenth century), (11) Elephant-bird *Aepyornis titan* or *A. maximus* (possibly one species survived until the seventeenth century), (12) Dodo *Raphus cucullatus* (1681) and (13) Madagascar coua *Coua delandei* (1930). ⟹

almost no effect on the habitats which remained unchanged until the last 50 years or so when western man arrived with powerful tools. Hence the chances of birds being able to adapt to the changes brought about by man may have been different in different parts of the world.

We have, of course, very little quantitative data on the effect such changes have had on birds. We can usually only guess which species would have been in a certain area by working out what the habitats were. However, within the last 100 and more especially the last 50 years, there are better data and we know what has happened to some species. Many of these changes, such as the introduction of the Common starling and the House sparrow to the USA have been brought about by man. Changes in other species also may be a result of man's alteration of the habitats in ways which we have not recognized. The Cattle egret, however, certainly reached South America by its own efforts. It was first recorded breeding in Guyana about 1930 and then spread rapidly up the coast, reaching Florida within eleven years. In 1956, fifteen years later, there were estimated to be 1,100 nests in Florida and the bird is still spreading north today.

In Europe there have also been some large expansions in numbers of certain species during recent years. In Britain the Fulmar formerly only bred on the islands of St. Kilda. In 1878 this species was recorded breeding in the Shetlands and since then has spread throughout large areas of Britain, breeding in all the coastal counties. In 1959 there were estimated to be some 100,000 nests in the country. Even this figure is thought to be an underestimate and 305,000 sites were located in Britain and Ireland in 1969. This species has achieved its remarkable spread although each pair lays only one egg each year and the young birds do not normally start breeding until they are about 7 or 8 years old.

The Collared dove spread rapidly across Europe from the Middle East, first breeding in England in 1955. By 1964 there were estimated to be 20,000 birds in Britain. In this case, and perhaps in the case of the Fulmar, the increase may have been speeded up through further immigration after the first arrivals started to breed.

The Indian Myna *Acridotheres tristis* is a relative of starlings and has been successful at colonizing many areas where it has been introduced. It is now widespread in parts of southern Africa, Australia and many oceanic islands.

Endangered species. (1) The Everglades kite *Rostrhamus sociabilis* is primarily a South American species which occurs in very small numbers in Florida. It is highly specialized for feeding on snails in marshes. Drainage of this habitat throughout its range represents a great hazard. (2) The American bald eagle *Haliaeetus leucocephalus* has been greatly reduced in numbers in recent years, primarily as a result of toxic chemicals polluting the rivers and the fish on which it feeds.

Effects of Man

Man has had a profound effect on the landscape and has often markedly affected the habitats which birds use. Basically man has altered the natural habitats in two ways, either by changing the landscape physically or by poisoning it with toxic substances.

In many areas of the world man has made a few simple, but often drastic, changes. He has drained the marshlands and cut down the forests replacing them by farmland and later, often, by cities. In the early days man was a wandering hunter who made no more impact on his surroundings than any other animal, perhaps less than some. As he began to settle down, especially when he started to use fire and tools and to grow crops, he altered the landscape in more significant ways. First he cleared the light hill woodland for farmland, then, as his tools improved, he started to clear the larger trees from the fertile lowlands. Forest clearance has often been on an enormous scale. In Britain and other parts of Europe and in Australia the clearance was often done for sheep-farming. It is difficult nowadays to realize the scale on which this was done since so much has re-grown or been re-planted. In the United States almost all the lowland hardwoods of the eastern states were cleared for farming; again the forests we seen now are those that have re-generated. In the wetter areas of the tropics clearance is often short-sighted; crops can be grown on such ground for only a few years before the heavy rainfall washes away the nutrients and the area must be abandoned. Even where forests have not been cleared, the selective use of certain trees (such as oaks for building ships) resulted in a change of the composition of the forests,

The Starling *Sturnus vulgaris* has been one of the most successful birds in coming to terms with the changes brought about by man. It likes open country and has made good use of farmland and cities. As a result it must now be more numerous than it was before man altered the landscape.

The House sparrow *Passer domesticus* has probably been even more successful than the Starling in adapting to the changes brought about by man. Both species have successfully used man's transport to colonize new areas and both have used his buildings for nesting and obtained their food from gardens and farms. The House sparrow was probably even more numerous in the centres of cities at the beginning of the century. At this time, the sparrows obtained much of their food from the grain supplied for horses. The advent of the car has probably led to a decrease in their numbers.

at times to the detriment of birds which depended on particular tree species for their livelihood.

As man's abilities increased he dug ditches to improve the drainage and straightened and widened rivers to increase the flow and to provide reliable transport routes. These changes had, and still have, profound effects on the birds. Marshland birds seem to have suffered more than woodland ones. Many of the latter seem to have been able to exist in small areas of woodland whereas the marshland species could no longer find suitable habitats.

By no means all birds have found man's changes deleterious, the species which live in open land have benefitted considerably. In some temperate areas it is not clear how, or where, these species existed when the land was completely covered with woodland. Birds such as the Common starling and the House sparrow have found the arable lands greatly to their liking. Other species such as some of the swallows and swifts nest nowadays almost exclusively on man's buildings, so much so that it is difficult to imagine where they nested previously, at least in such large numbers as they do now.

In recent times man has made yet other changes to the habitats, often including the planting of new forests. In many cases these are of different trees from the original ones such as, for example, the new coniferous plantations and eucalypt forests which have been extensively planted all over the world in suitable localities. Some of these are not easily colonized by local birds, perhaps because conifer and eucalypt forests have poor insect faunas for the birds to feed on. Other such forests may attract bird species that are different from those that occurred in the natural forests. In many parts of Europe, conifers are planted where broad-leaved deciduous woodlands would be the natural forests. However, there are coniferous woodlands in such areas, at higher altitudes or latitudes, and the birds that specialize in living in such places have spread into the extensions of their natural habitat. In particular, the Coal tit and the Crossbill have benefitted from these plantations in many parts of Europe. Modern forest management involves the removal of dead and dying wood, often to the disadvantage of birds, such as woodpeckers, that depend on such wood for their food.

Even the use of the term natural becomes difficult. For example the loss of the Great bustard from the downland areas of Britain occurred when the huge areas of sheep grazing lands were dissected by new plantations; doubtless more modern firearms were also a contributory factor. The loss of this species was regretted by many. However, this bird could only have become established in Britain after man had cleared the woodland, and so it was a temporary resident, staying for only a few centuries before disappearing.

Man has also built large reservoirs which have provided living quarters for many species of waterfowl. As with the new coniferous forests, the reservoirs provide a livelihood for many species of birds, but not the ones that lived in the habitat that was there previously. Marshland species are adapted to reed beds and shallow water, the birds on reservoirs are predominantly those that are adapted to diving in deep water for their food.

The changes brought about by man's pollution of the environment are a different matter altogether. These do not merely change the landscape so that different species can occupy a new area, their changes make it difficult for any species to survive there. Birds may not be able to raise enough young under these conditions to replace the adults that die, especially if the adult death rate also rises. Chemical poisoning of the land, and even more seriously, of the seas and rivers, is continuing at an alarming rate. Persistent poisons such as DDT have been implicated in the decline of the Peregrine and the American Bald eagle. These two species have declined because poisons have accumulated in these birds to levels which have affected their breeding success. Similarly, poisoning of the seas may be having a drastic effect on the life there. The birds die because the areas become either devoid of prey or because the prey are full of poisonous substances.

The Japanese Ibis *Nipponia nippon* is probably now extinct in China and is very scarce in Japan where some 12 birds remain.

Although it has a very extensive range, the Peregrine falcon *Falco peregrinus* has become much reduced in numbers in the last 20 years.

Endangered species. (1) The Imperial eagle *Aquila heliaca d'alberti*. This race, from Spain and North Africa, is probably reduced to fewer than 100 birds. They perhaps no longer breed in North Africa. This bird, like many eagles has been much persecuted by man. (2) Mauritius Kestrel *Falco punctatus*. Never a large population, this species has been frequently shot. There may only be one remaining pair living in the wild. (3) Seychelles owl *Otus insularis*. Very few individuals remain. Its habitat has been destroyed and it may have suffered in competition with the introduced Barn owl, *Tyto alba*.

Endangered species. The numbers given relate to the most recent estimates made in the last 10–15 years and may well be now inaccurate. (1) Monkey-eating eagle *Pithecophaga jefferyi* from the Phillippines (less than 100 birds), (2) Californian condor *Gymnogyps californianus* California (about 40 birds), (3) Takahe *Notornis mantelli* New Zealand (perhaps 200 individuals), (4) Ivory-billed woodpecker *Campephilus principalis* (the races of this species that occur in Cuba and USA are reduced to very small numbers indeed), (5) Kakapo *Strigops habroptilus* (perhaps only about 20) and (6) Cahow *Pterodroma cahow* Bermuda (some 30 pairs, possibly increasing slightly with protection). ⇨

Endangered Species

In the last 200 years or so some 70 to 80 species of birds have become extinct. Many of these, perhaps almost all of them, have disappeared as a result of man's activities. In addition, a number of other species are known to have disappeared in the few centuries prior to recorded history; most of the moas of New Zealand and the Elephant-birds of Malagasy survived until their homelands were occupied by man. In all probability man was responsible for their demise.

One can make a few generalizations about the species which have become extinct and from these and other evidence deduce which living species are likely to be most endangered. A large proportion of the species which have become extinct lived on small islands; over two thirds of the extinct species lived on islands of less than 1,000 sq mi (2,600 sq km), only nine on large continents. A number of them were flightless (Elephant-birds, moas, Dodo, Great auk and several rails).

The reasons why each of these birds became extinct are not always known, but four, possibly five, causes probably explain most of them. Some (Great auk, Dodo) were hunted by man, others were exterminated by his introduced animals such as dogs, cats and rats, others could not survive in the face of the loss of their habitats; the Passenger pigeon may fall into this category. Yet others may well have been unable to survive in the face of competition with other, introduced, species of birds which competed with them for food or nesting sites; in general, species which have evolved on a large land mass appear to win in competition with species evolved in the more sheltered environment of small islands. For example, several of the Hawaiian honeycreepers disappeared shortly after introduced species spread throughout certain habitats. The fifth possible cause of extinction is that the introduced species did not compete directly with the resident species, but brought with them diseases to which they were reasonably resistant, but to which the native birds had no such immunity. Western man almost eliminated certain native populations on islands by carrying diseases such as measles to which he was largely immune (in the sense that

During the last century, perhaps a million Steller's Albatrosses *Diomedea albatrus* nested on several small islands south of Japan. It was heavily preyed upon by Japanese plume traders, and was later believed to be extinct. However, a small colony has formed on one island, Torishima and, with rigorous protection, the birds seem to be increasing in numbers.

Endangered species. (1) Audouin's Gull *Larus audouinii* a scarce species from the Mediterranean, breeding in a number of places, but in only small numbers. There may be some 1,000 pairs left. (2) Kagu *Rhynochetos jubatus* is an aberrant relative of the cranes. It is very rare, being found only on New Caledonia. It is virtually flightless and the forests in which it lives have been severely reduced and many injurious mammals such as pigs, cats, rats and dogs have been introduced. (3) The Night parrot *Geopsittacus occidentalis* is a ground-dwelling parrot of open country in Australia; it has only occasionally been reported during the present century and has at times been thought to be extinct.

The Whooping crane *Grus americana* breeds in freshwater bogs in northwestern Canada and spends the winter on the coastline of Texas. Only some 50 individuals remain. In spite of protection, the birds do not seem to be increasing, possibly because there are so little suitable habitat remaining in their winter quarters.

he did not usually die) but to which the natives had no resistance. It could have been the same with birds. A number of New Zealand species disappeared very swiftly after western man colonized the islands, bringing with him many species of birds. These may well have carried diseases to which the native birds had no resistance.

The species which are most endangered at the present time are roughly in the same categories as those listed above. Many island species, never represented by large numbers of individuals, are threatened in part by habitat destruction and in part by man's introduced mammals. Rats, cats, mongeese, pigs, monkeys and other animals have all done damage. Several flightless species are extremely rare and threatened including the Kakapo and Takahe, both from New Zealand. At least 100 species of living birds are represented by fewer than 2,000 individuals. Although man is now aware of the threat he poses to such species and may be able to prevent hunting of these species (in contrast to the situation in the early part of this century when collectors were rushing to get the last few remaining specimens) the outlook for such species is not bright.

On mainland areas very large birds such as eagles, and birds that nest colonially such as herons and egrets, are at times severely threatened by man. The former group are not only large and therefore easy to shoot, but also they reproduce slowly, making it easier to reduce their numbers. Some egrets were brought to the verge of extinction by the plume trade earlier this century. They nested in a few large colonies and these continued to be worth a visit by the hunters even when the birds were becoming relatively scarce.

Hopefully, in many parts of the world such intentional slaughter is now being reduced, but this is not the case everywhere. Even if man can reduce his own direct threats to such species, further unintentional changes brought about by man's carelessness may always spoil the habitats in which they live. If the species concerned is rare and confined to a local area it may be exterminated. The greatest threat of this sort for the future lies in pollution which may result not only in the extermination of birds but of many men as well.

Domestic Birds

Only about a dozen birds can be thought of as successfully domesticated. However, four of these, the hen, duck, goose and turkey are important economic foods for man. All the species that are domesticated on any scale have two features in common; they eat grain and live, at least at times, in flocks. As a result, they are easily fed by man and will survive when kept in crowded conditions, a thing that many highly territorial species would not do.

The hen, a derivative of the Jungle fowl *Gallus gallus*, is by far the most important species of domestic bird, and is kept almost everywhere in the world. Presumably it was domesticated by primitive peoples who, when they could capture food animals alive, kept them until they were needed for a meal. The hen proved easy to keep alive in captivity and its additional advantage, that it laid edible eggs, led to its being kept for increasingly long periods. There is evidence that the species was domesticated in China about 1500 BC and may have been kept in India as much as 1,500 years before that. Early Neolithic men in Europe kept chickens so the habit obviously spread westwards at an early state. Most of the birds were kept for meat and eggs and little care was given to them. However, selective breeding (and therefore the necessary segregation of stocks) must have started relatively early since there were a number of distinct breeds by Roman times. Nowadays there are well over 200 breeds. Excluding the forms which could be said to be more ornamental, selective breeding has in recent years been along two main lines. First there has been selection for rapid growth rates since this produces more meat per kilogram of food than does a slow growth rate. Second there has been selection for high egg production; the natural clutch of about 6–8 eggs has given way to almost continual egg production. At their peak, birds of the best strains will lay at virtually the rate of an egg per day for the whole year.

The turkey is also a very important domestic bird. Although the history of its

All the birds on this plate have been commonly kept by man, sometimes as pets. Some, through selective breeding, have been modified by man. Others have escaped in new areas and may have become a nuisance. (1) Budgerigar *Melopsittacus undulatus* from Australia where the wild form is green, (2) Zebra finch *Taeniopygia guttata* from Australia, (3) Hill myna *Gracula reliogiosa* introduced into many of the warmer areas of the world, (4) domestic pigeon derived from the Rock dove *Columba livia* as is the racing pigeon; birds often show the white rump of the ancestral stock, (5) African Grey parrot *Psittacus erithacus* and (6) Java sparrow *Padda oryzivora,* both introduced to many new areas.

Birds that have been kept by man, mainly for food. (1) Domestic hen derived from the Jungle fowl *Gallus gallus*, (2) Turkey *Meleagris gallopavo* from the New World, not Turkey, and (3) Peacock *Pavo cristatus*.

domestication is less well known than is that of the hen, it may have been kept in Mexico for almost as long as the hen was kept in the East. In this species breeding has been for heavy birds with high growth rates more than for egg production. The largest marketable birds are currently running at about 70 lbs (31 kg) which is roughly twice the weight of any flying bird and a good deal more than that of the ancestral turkey stocks.

Ducks and geese are the other important food species. Most ducks, except the Muscovy which is derived from the wild Muscovy duck *Cairina moschata* from South America, are derived from the Mallard *Anas platyrhynchos*. Most geese are descended from the Greylag *Anser anser* though the Chinese goose is descended from the Swan goose *Anser cygnoides*. Other important commercial species include the Japanese Quail *Coturnix coturnix* and the Ostrich, though the latter species is kept for its plumes as much as for its food value.

A number of other birds are raised in large quantities. These are the game birds such as the Pheasant which are released, often in very large numbers, for shooting at a later date. Such species can barely be considered truly domesticated, but a number of the more ornamental pheasants are kept and bred under conditions of domestication. The Peafowl is a good example.

One species of pigeon, the Rock dove *Columba livia*, has been domesticated and a large number of fancy breeds are kept. However the most important form of this species is the homing pigeon which has been used for carrying messages since at least Roman times, has played a significant role in two World Wars and is now kept in huge numbers for racing as a hobby. It is also widely used in scientific research into the homing abilities of birds. Egyptian paintings suggest that this bird has been kept in captivity, if not used for homing, since about 2500 BC.

BIRD STUDY

Not only do the tits frequent houses and gardens during winter, but they will willingly accept nest-boxes that are provided for them. In the absence of these, the birds will use almost any kind of hole. Here (below) a Great tit, *Parus major* leaves its nest in a hollow fence post.

Bird Observation

Man has probably always watched birds. Early observations were usually closely related to man's need for survival. Vultures gathering were an indication that an animal had recently died and that meat might be available. Many explorers have watched the flight lines of birds for signs of the nearest source of water. Mariners used the flights of sea birds to lead them to the nearest land. Even today many of the more primitive tribes know a considerable amount about their birds—often having names for each of the more common or conspicuous species. Knowledge of the habits of these birds may be useful in a variety of ways. The birds may be used as food, the feathers for decoration or their call for indicating the presence of other animals (or men) in the vicinity. Often, in the more civilized industrial societies, we have lost this knowledge; only the wildfowler or gamekeeper knows many of these things. He learns them from others and from his own observations.

Modern industrialized societies, with more time for leisure, have started to observe birds for different reasons, often for pleasure rather than survival. In such societies one may find many people making observations and these may range from the purely casual enjoyment of bird-watching to the detailed studies of the research scientist. The latter may be organized to discover information about any aspects of birds and their lives including how we can reduce the damage caused by certain species to our crops. Hence, though a far cry from the interest in birds as food shown by primitive societies, some of man's most sophsticated observations of birds may be related to the interests in our food and hence, ultimately to our survival.

Historically, observations on birds have followed a similar sequence in many areas of the world. Early explorers made casual observations and brought back a few specimens. They were followed by more experienced naturalists who made more detailed collections, bringing back large numbers of specimens for museums where they could be compared with other specimens, described and named. After reasonably complete collections and check-lists were made available, people started recording the abundance of these species, the habitats in which they lived and their ranges in greater detail. Only where there is detailed information of this sort, where one knows the bird that one is watching, can more detailed studies of individual species easily be made. It may be difficult for people living in Europe or North America, surrounded by a plethora of bird-books and an overwhelming selection of field guides, to appreciate that in many areas of the world this basic information is not available. Most species have been identified, but new ones are still being discovered at the rate of one or two a year and the ranges and movements of many of these species are very inadequately known. Yet more detailed knowledge, such as details of the eggs and nests, the breeding behaviour and survival rates are known for very few species. As might be expected, most detailed studies have been made of birds in North America and Europe. That these may not be typical of all birds is only now becoming clear. For example, we tend to think of birds as living in pairs and defending territories. However, many tropical species have community structures which are different from this. Many live in groups: often up to a dozen or so birds live together during the

155

Many people have first become interested in birds through keeping them in captivity. For many centuries birds have been kept for their singing abilities. Finches have proved particularly amenable to such treatment, being easy to feed and maintain in small cages and having pleasing songs. This species is the Goldfinch *Carduelis carduelis*.

The Herring gull *Larus argentatus* has been one of the most studied species of birds. It is a common colonial species which has proved relatively easy to observe and was the basis of Professor Niko Tinbergen's *A Herring Gull's World*, one of the classic ornithological studies.

entire year, and help raise the young produced by a single pair. In some of these and other species territorial defence appears to be poorly developed. Hence, some of the aspects of the biology of temperate birds may well not be applicable to others.

As the background knowledge has increased, so more sophisticated and detailed studies have become possible. Although distributional studies established where birds were to be found at all times of the year, early observers were not able to discover where different populations of migrants went at the different times of year. Detailed studies of this sort have only been possible with the advent of ringing, the practice of putting small numbered rings on the legs of birds. Normally these rings have the address of the organization in the country where the ringing was undertaken and the hope is that the finder of a dead bird will return the ring. For most species, however, the chance of a small dead bird being found, especially in some of the larger forest areas of the tropics, is almost infinitesimally small. Nevertheless, by ringing very large numbers of the common species it is often possible to describe not only the breeding and wintering areas of migrants but also the routes by which they reach these places. Detailed information is, of course, only known for a relatively small number of the common species. Rarer species are still very poorly known.

It is a common misconception that ornithologists ring birds just to get information about their movements. One even meets people who think that so much is known that there can be no need for further ringing. Even if this were true, it would hold for only a tiny proportion of species. There are in fact many reasons for ringing birds and from almost no species have enough birds been ringed for us to be able to understand their movements completely. There is some evidence that movements of the Blackbird may have changed somewhat in the last 30 years. Hence, these studies may need continual reassessment. In some species there may be different movements in different winters. The Redwings from northern Europe migrate to different parts of southern Europe in different years. Another important reason for studying birds by use of ringing is that it enables one to measure the longevity and the mortality of birds at different stages in their lives. Here again we have too few data for almost every species. We need to have studies of population structure over long periods of time. In particular, where we have a landscape that is changing as rapidly as it is at present, we need to know whether the birds are continuing to face the challenge of man's changes, if only because changes in the numbers, or survival rates, of birds might stem from changes which may also affect man. Again, we need continuing measurements of these facets of the life of birds.

The studies mentioned above involve the use of small numbered rings with addresses. Many detailed studies of ecology, migration or behaviour require the research worker to be able to identify individual birds without having to catch them frequently and so disturb their everyday lives. For this reason many ornithologists use different types of marks, often coloured rings or sometimes wing-tags. These can be put on the birds in such a way, or in such a combination of colours, that each bird is individually recognizable by the research worker without its having to be caught.

Such detailed studies require a great amount of observation and therefore take time. Hence many, but by no means all, of the most detailed studies are undertaken by professionals working in universities or other large organizations. In the twenties and thirties, there were very few posts for professionals to undertake field studies of birds. The earlier pioneer studies such as Eliot Howard's *Territory in Bird Life*, David Lack's *Life of the Robin* and Mrs. Nice's *Studies in the Life History of the Song Sparrow* were all done by busy people in their spare time. However, as more became known, and as ornithological field work became possible for professional biologists, more and more of the very detailed studies, especially those requiring a number of people and the use of sophisticated equipment not available to amateurs, were undertaken by professionals. It should not be thought, however, that this means that the role of the amateur in bird observation is over. Only the professional can make

Barn swallows *Hirundo rustica* are particularly well-known to man, in both the Old and the New World. They have nested on man's buildings for at least 2,000 years and are now rarely seen nesting elsewhere. Here birds are collecting mud to build their nests.

The Yellowhammer *Emberiza citrinella* and the Winter wren *Troglodytes troglodytes* are two other species well-known to Europeans. Both are widespread in Europe and both have distinctive and far-carrying songs. The Yellowhammer has been introduced to New Zealand and some of the nearby islands.

(1) The Swift *Apus apus* is well-known to city dwellers. It nests under the eaves of houses and tall buildings. It forages, often some distance away for aerial insects. (2) The Blackbird *Turdus merula* is another well-known urban bird which has been much studied. It nests more densely in urban areas than in woodland. (3) The Reed bunting *Emberiza schoeniclus* is a bird of marshes. It was the subject of Eliot Howard's classic study, *Territory in Bird Life*.

very long-term, detailed or expensive studies necessary to learn more about certain aspects of the ways that birds live, but the amateur can make the wide-scale studies of distribution or surveys that need perhaps hundreds of people to count birds throughout a country simultaneously. For example, professionals could not undertake the detailed counts of waterfowl made in many parts of Europe once a month. Nor could they provide the stock of ringed birds all over the country for certain mortality studies. Only a small army of dedicated amateurs can do this. Many of the individuals concerned will never publish any of their material. Nevertheless, they spend their holidays making surveys in out-of-the-way parts of the world, contributing invaluable information and, at the same time, getting a great deal of enjoyment from their hobby.

As with ringing, the need for surveys does not end when they have been made. The changing face of the countryside requires that surveys of birds be made at relatively frequent intervals if we are to observe the changes that are doubtless taking place. Even in the most intensively-watched countries, such as Britain, with a small area and many watchers, there are areas that are not at all well-known, and the changing ranges of bird species go unrecorded. While some of these may well be due to changes brought about by man we are by no means certain that they all are, and further documentation is essential. In many parts of the world simple basic distributional data do not exist at all and are badly needed.

In all aspects of bird biology there is much to be learned as well as the continuous changes which need to be monitored. Not only the smaller detailed studies of individual species, but also the larger problems all need further study. To give but one example, we do not really understand the way that migrating birds find their way from one end of the world to the other. Migration may not be quite as much of a mystery as it was in Gilbert White's day 200 years ago, but much remains to be found out. The amateur who rings large numbers of birds and the professional who watches birds on migration with the help of radar and radio transmitters and investigates in detail the homing ability of pigeons, may well expect together to provide further insight into these subjects. The same is true of many aspects of the study of birds; often different approaches may combine to help provide us with a fuller picture. Bird observation remains as challenging, and enjoyable, as it has ever been.

INDEX

Italics are used for generic and specific names. Numbers in italics refer to pages on which illustrations occur.